Romantics, Rebels and Reactionaries

Marilyn Butler

Romantics, Rebels and Reactionaries

English Literature and its Background
1760–1830

Oxford   New York
OXFORD UNIVERSITY PRESS

Oxford University Press, Walton Street, Oxford OX2 6DP

Oxford New York Toronto
Delhi Bombay Calcutta Madras Karachi
Kuala Lumpur Singapore Hong Kong Tokyo
Nairobi Dar es Salaam Cape Town
Melbourne Auckland Madrid

and associated companies in
Berlin Ibadan

Oxford is a trade mark of Oxford University Press

First published as an Oxford University Press paperback 1981
and simultaneously in a hardback edition

British Library Cataloguing in Publication Data

Data available

Library of Congress Cataloging in Publication Data
Butler, Marilyn
Romantics, rebels and reactionaries.
1. English literature—18th century—
History and criticism
2. English literature—19th century—
History and criticism
3. Romanticism
I. Title
820'.9'006 PR146 80–42404
ISBN 0–19–289132–4

7 9 10 8

Printed in Great Britain by
Biddles Ltd
Guildford and King's Lynn

Contents

Poets, not otherwise than philosophers, painters, sculptors and musicians, are, in one sense, the creators, and, in another, the creations of their age. From this subjection the loftiest do not escape.

SHELLEY

Introduction

The age we call Romantic is immensely rich in English literature. Other periods produced individual writers – Shakespeare, Milton – who are equally great, or greater. But no other period has yielded so many poets, novelists, essayists and critics of true importance and individuality, writers who are not followers of greater names nor part of a school, but themselves distinctive voices. But why do they coincide? If they do not follow one another, what common factors caused them to develop so richly and variously at the same time? By what historical logic did Coleridge breathe the same air and read the same newspapers as Jane Austen? Does it affect our reading of the literature, if we find its relations to its age frankly puzzling?

Thought is the prisoner of language, and twentieth-century thinking about early nineteenth-century literature is cramped by a single formidable word: Romantic. We have come to think of most of the great writers who flourished around 1800 as the Romantics, but the term is anachronistic and the poets concerned would not have used it of themselves. Not until the 1860s did 'the Romantics' become an accepted collective name for Blake, Wordsworth, Coleridge, Scott, Byron, Shelley and Keats, and an agreement begin to emerge about what an English Romantic Poet was like. There seems to have been little inkling until the later nineteenth century that such a historical phenomenon as an English Romantic *movement* had occurred. It was not until the twentieth century that there was analytical discussion of the abstraction 'Romanticism', as a recognized term for theories of art, of the imagination and of language.

The application of the word 'romantic' has undergone great changes over two centuries. In the eighteenth century it was directly associated with 'romance'; it was a literary term denoting the archaic and remote culture of the Middle Ages and Renaissance, and applied to art-forms which included the ballad, the lay and the Ariostan and Spenserian epic. In modern popular usage, the 'romantic novel' is a sub-literary genre, a love story, probably in an unreal setting, in which the reader is invited to indulge his (or generally her) fantasies. The modern academic meaning ought to be stricter and less emotive than the vulgar 'romantic', but even academics are not as exact over the term as they like to think. It may be significant that far more twentieth-century writers have been willing to call themselves late or post-Romantics than there were early nineteenth-century writers prepared to recognize Romanticism as a current phenomenon.

Romanticism, in the full rich sense in which we now know it, is a posthumous movement; something different was experienced at the time. Yet it is clear that even if the word 'romantic' was not in general use in England, some of its more exciting and flattering connotations were already attaching themselves to the most appropriate leading writers during their own lifetimes and immediately after. The first three decades of the nineteenth century saw the emergence of a heightened interest in the personality of the artist, evidenced in the phenomenal spate of biography. The rage for these literary *Lives*, copiously illustrated by letters, was part of a passion for documenting the natural world, including the human and social world; it was a manifestation of a scientific curiosity that extended equally to the animal kingdom, to plants and to fossils. But where the poet was the subject, something more than curiosity was conveyed: a taste was beginning to emerge to see the artist *as a hero*, and this perhaps is the symptom of a special need.

Thinkers of the eighteenth-century Enlightenment had been much given to studying man in his social context, which was not necessarily a reassuring perspective. Whatever might have been the case for primitive man – the Noble Savage, the Greek or early Roman hero, the clansman or the feudal knight – in a complex advanced society the scope for the individual to make a mark in the world of action seemed to have dwindled; only in thought could he remain unfettered. The writers who achieved the greatest popular success in the late eighteenth and early nineteenth century were those who created simpler, more colourful imaginative worlds, dominated by heroes of superhuman effectiveness. Schiller's Karl Moor and Goethe's Faust fired the imagination of Europe. Scott rose to fame with *Marmion*, which again features a villain-hero, compellingly free from law and from conventional ethics. Byron, who with Scott was the most popular writer of the age in English, established himself through characters such as Childe Harold, the Giaour, the Corsair and Manfred, all moody outcasts with the mark of Cain upon them, mad, bad and dangerous to know. Byron went one better than Scott because his heroes appeared to be at least in part spectacular self-projections. His retreat from England in 1816, pursued by rumours of his sexual mistreatment of his wife and even of his incest with his half-sister, identified him for all time in the popular mind with his Satanic, guilt-ridden creations. Byron played a larger part than any other single artist in shaping the stereotype soon recognized throughout Europe, the passionate, rebellious Romantic Poet.

The myth in the making was softened and sentimentalized as Byron's portrait blended with those of his two contemporaries who died even younger, Keats and Shelley. Already, in immediate response to their deaths in 1821 and 1822, a visual iconography was supplied to go with the new cults. Keats was painted by his friend Joseph Severn as a delicate adolescent obviously destined for another world. Shelley's drowning made for a spectacular series of visual images: the slight figure in his equally frail craft, battered by the tempest; the funeral pyre on the lonely Italian beach, with Byron a bystander. (The fact that Byron and Leigh Hunt actually retired to their carriage to get drunk was an ugly intrusion of real life that attracted more pained criticism, in the early press accounts, than any other circumstances – more even than Shelley's marital misconduct and his atheism.) Shelley has not been the same man in our century since posterity in his own transformed him into Ariel: beautiful, ethereal, with the waves washing or the wind blowing through his hair.

From the start, the notion of the poet as rebel was a generous one. Along with the flamboyant Byronic model it could accommodate something more manageable, the sensitive individual who rejected worldliness, and even, literally, this vulgar material world for a better. It is interesting to see how very soon Shelley's death was being interpreted as willed. Readers who were religious idealists – and there were many of these in the 1830s and 1840s – soon found it possible to forget the inconvenient Shelleyan atheism in this congenial otherworldliness. Political idealists, of the Left especially, also managed to claim Shelley and his type by equating the world they rejected with the one defaced by the industrial revolution or capitalism. Though early notions of Byron's personality now seem naïve, and of Shelley's both false and damaging, they have not been successfully discarded because the needs which created them are still current. The idea of the 'Romantic Poet' or bohemian intellectual opposing society was as attractive following the demonstrations and barricades of the 1960s as it was after 1830 and 1848. As early as 1820, the French writer Charles Nodier summed up the artist's plight with a loaded irony which retains its topicality and (to many minds) its appeal: 'Romantic poetry springs from our agony and our despair. This is not a fault in our art, but a necessary consequence of the advances made in our progressive society.'

Nodier believed that he was living through times of social crisis, and he saw the Romantic manner as a negative, defensive response by individuals to that crisis. This is one theory of the relationship between literature and its background in the early nineteenth century, and in some form or other most of us probably still subscribe to it. However little we normally bring history into our thinking about literature, we are aware of the late eighteenth century as an age of revolution. In this respect, the popular cliché is no lie. All Europe felt the shock-wave of the chain of events in France which was symbolized by the Fall of the Bastille in 1789 and the execution of Louis XVI in 1793. Most of Europe was directly involved in the revolutionary wars in which republican France confronted the older monarchies between 1793 and 1815. But, although the political revolution and the subsequent war are the most obvious symptoms of upheaval, they are not the only ones. The same period saw a growth in the population of Western Europe, an expansion of trade and industry, and a quickening pace of social change, so that the idea conveyed by the phrase 'industrial revolution' is as important as the political change. Since culture is a way of expressing experience, we should expect to find these tensions, conflicts and signs of transition reflected in the arts.

And so of course they undoubtedly are. The arts, including literature, also by general consent underwent a profound transformation, beginning perhaps as early as the mid-eighteenth century, with Rousseau in France and afterwards with Goethe's generation in Germany, and sufficiently advanced by the 1820s for artists all over Europe to begin to theorize about it much as Nodier did. Nodier's word for the innovatory style in poetry – 'romantic' – was first used in this sense a few years after the proclamation of a French republic. Between 1797 and 1800, a handful of German writers in the Prussian town of Jena formed a group around the scholar and critic Friedrich Schlegel, who drew up a manifesto which explained how the characteristic modern style, which he called 'romantic', differed from the classic manner which preceded it. Gradually Schlegel's word has come into use for writers who display some of the modern characteristics he describes, and indeed for innovatory modern writing generally. It has also become usual, by a natural association of ideas, to link these changes in the arts of the 1790s with change in politics. While the political shackles of the *anciens régimes* were being thrown off – or so the argument runs – the artist staged his own revolution against inherited authority and rules. Literary textbooks deploy all kinds of shorthand phrases which imply a similarity between political and cultural events: 'the Romantic Rebellion' or 'the Romantic Revolution' or 'the earthquake that was Romanticism'.

Unfortunately this equation of one kind of revolution with another is much too simple. The German writers who first called themselves Romantics were not supporters of the French Revolution at all. They were, on the whole, German patriots, who increasingly came to approve of the involvement of the various German states in the war against republican France. Their opposition to eighteenth-century classicism might even be read as opposition to a style they associated with France, the home of a revolution that had turned expansive and aggressive. For the first two decades of the nineteenth century, German Romanticism remained Catholic and counter-revolutionary. In both France and England during these decades, it was the classical or antique style that was commonly linked with republicanism. When the Gothic or medieval or avowedly Romantic taste began to gain ground in England after the peace came in 1815, it was at first identified with the *anciens régimes* which had triumphed over France, and with their extreme political conservatism. Indeed it was not until the *next* French Revolution began to get under way – until events in France began to build up to the 'July Revolution' of 1830 – that Romantic artists in any country became generally identified with the radical cause in politics.

It is of course conceivable that England was different. At one time or another most, though not all, of the leading writers of the period in England expressed disapproval of the war with republican France. Blake, Wordsworth, Coleridge, Hazlitt, Byron, Shelley and Keats all did so to some degree, either at the time or in retrospect. On the other hand, Wordsworth and Coleridge also changed their minds, and became powerful spokesmen for the national cause against France; and it is probably significant that all these writers, whatever their individual opinions, were living in the nation that was most deeply and lengthily committed to the conservative crusade. Were these would-be liberals really, like the Germans, unconsciously reflecting their society's hostility to the French Enlightenment and to its radical political consequences? Is the great literature of the Age of Revolution a literature, at the profoundest level, in reaction?

Certainly it is much easier to connect the first wave of European Romanticism with the conservative cause than with radicalism. The English-speaking world's tendency to think of the Romantic as a political rebel is simply an instance of the extraordinary power to survive of those first biographical cults which idealized poets in the 1820s: when we think of a Romantic, we think of Shelley and Byron. Perhaps it has become even easier to believe that Romanticism was part of the revolution in the second half of the twentieth century than it was in the nineteenth. The Victorian Matthew Arnold could say of the culture of the age in question that France under the *ancien régime* gave birth to more radical ideas than the age of Wordsworth. That is not the received view among literary readers now, although it appears to be a more familiar idea among those who write about the visual arts. A group of recent art critics, including Hugh Honour, Robert Rosenblum and Lorenz Eitner, have defined with a new clarity the artistic movement they call Neoclassicism, which began in the middle of the eighteenth century and thus preceded the American and French revolutions. Though this style went through modifications, its assumptions largely set aesthetic standards for both France and England, the two leading protagonists in the French revolutionary wars, until the struggle finally ended in 1815. If the interpreters of this movement are correct, it is *Neoclassicism* that initiates the rejection of previous values, the intellectual and artistic aggression, that for one and a half centuries has been attributed to Romanticism. Eitner, indeed, describes the eighteenth century as a period of 'sharp action and innovation', the first half of the nineteenth century merely as one of 'response and reflection'.

The attraction of this alternative proposition, which permits a redefined Neoclassicism to go on co-existing with Romanticism, is that it allows for a dialogue within the arts, for conflict and even contradiction. Almost every attempt to represent *one* artistic new wave, *one* Romanticism, is hopelessly subverted by the richness of art in the period. For just as there is, politically, no one Romantic rebellion, there is no one style. Critics of Romantic painting, for example, have long since commented on how unlike in this respect it is to earlier movements, like baroque and rococo, which are far more readily recognizable. Romanticism is protean: meticulously detailed in one painting, dreamily vague in another; here copying the medieval or antique manner, there eccentrically new. One celebrated theorist of Romanticism, the intellectual historian A. O. Lovejoy, indeed argued in the 1920s that we should accept an almost infinite diversity as the leading principle of Romanticism. Diversity was, he argued, a reaction against the eighteenth-century ideal in the arts, which was simple and universal; the artists who came after shattered that unity into innumerable individualistic fragments, some of which – like the preoccupation with self, and the demand for particularized fidelity in the description of landscape – seem mutually contradictory. In a recent study of Romanticism in the visual arts, Hugh Honour seems to echo some of the scepticism about the coherence of Romanticism which Lovejoy voiced earlier. At least, he allows that there is no one style and no one political ideology, although there are, he feels, common factors; and he seems to find this common ground above all in that biographical myth of which there is genuinely so much evidence by the 1820s – the Romantic artist's conception of himself as a certain kind of producer. Romanticism inflates the role of the artist, for it is expressive where Neoclassicism is mimetic; it is hostile to external authority, and acknowledges no imperatives other than truth to the artist's experience. 'Tous les systèmes sont faux,' wrote Victor Hugo, another man of the 1820s, 'le génie seul est vrai.'

But on the whole those who have written about Romanticism since the middle of the twentieth century have made more positive efforts than this to see it as a single if complex theoretical movement, unified by certain key aesthetic precepts. A leading scholar of comparative literature, René Wellek, defines these thus:

They all [Romantic poets] see the implication of imagination, symbol, myth and organic nature, and see it as part of the great endeavour to overcome the split between subject and object, the self and the world, the conscious and the unconscious. This is the central creed of the great Romantic poets in England, Germany and France. It is a closely coherent body of thought and feeling.

Wellek is interested in the ideas poets have about writing and about themselves in relation to writing. Though he interprets what the writers themselves say in the light of his own professional training and of his wide knowledge of aesthetics in the period, he nevertheless believes that there *is* a Romantic theory, as opposed to a burgeoning biographical myth or even a growing professionalism. He broadly accepts the validity of the image of the artist first formulated in the early nineteenth century; he thinks that works of art *are* made, semi-miraculously, in the imagination, and that the creative process restores a wholeness lost in common experience. Wellek is supported in his idealizing approach by most of the respected studies of the English literary Romantics, and perhaps most influentially by M. H. Abrams in his book *The Mirror and Lamp* (1953). Abrams virtually echoes Schlegel's argument that modern poetry begins in this era by a decisive breach with classical poetry. The Romantic writer is distinguished from the eighteenth-century writer, he argues, by a changed perception of what a poem is and what it does. For the classicist, says Abrams, the work of art resembles a mirror, which is passively mimetic or reproductive of existing 'reality', and for the Romantic a lamp, which throws out images originating not in the world but in the poet. Art becomes subjective rather than objective, and intuitive rather than rationally planned.

Abrams does not disguise the fact that this bold distinction between the ancients and moderns involves some problems of date. Although he would argue that Wordsworth trumpets the new expressive theory in his celebrated Preface to the *Lyrical Ballads* of 1800, he also concedes that in the same essay Wordsworth adheres to many of the old mimetic ideas. Wordsworth clearly still considers that a number of factors outside the poet's intuition or imagination are important in determining a poem, including the conditions of the outside world, the requirements of the audience, and the artist's conscious, controlling intentions, which will be linked to his preconceived notions of ethics and of art. By Abrams's own yardstick – that the all-important change occurred when a mimetic and objective theory gave way to an expressive and subjective theory of art – Wordsworth is still only a transitional figure. A thoroughgoing dogma of the mysterious, subconscious origin of art has to wait for the 1830s, for the work of J. S. Mill, Thomas Carlyle and John Keble. The doctrine is complete and widely accepted only for the generation *after* 'the English Romantics'.

But, of course, the problem of setting a date for Romanticism is a crucial problem; the very figures we wish to discuss belong to this age of transition. Scholars have been tempted to make the writing of Friedrich Schlegel in Germany and Wordsworth in England a watershed between the old and new, at a date conveniently close to 1800 and to the turn of the century. Yet how is it that Blake, who was designing and writing great works in the 1780s, contrived to be so early? How is it that on the whole English and French painting is thought of as affected by Romanticism so much later than English poetry? In France the Romantic movement is represented taking hold of painters only after the end of the Napoleonic Wars, for example with Géricault's 'Raft of the Medusa' (1819). In England the 'revolution' seems to take place even later, with the work in the 1820s of the apocalyptic John Martin and the impressionistic J. M. W. Turner.

Twentieth-century notions of Romanticism are fed by two intellectual traditions. One tradition tries to understand Romanticism aesthetically, as a theory about the nature and origin of art. The other attempts to see it as a historical phenomenon which must be associated with political and social circumstances. The problem, however, is that these approaches are not independent of one another. 'Common knowledge' about Romanticism proves to be a cluster of assertions about, for example, dates – and that sounds historical enough: Romanticism is said, typically, to have begun with Blake's *Songs of Innocence* (1789) or with Wordsworth and Coleridge's *Lyrical Ballads* (1798); or it has been and gone by 1830. What appear to be aesthetic discussions often rest upon the belief, also ultimately historical, that there is a single coherent Romantic movement. This belief is reflected in, say, the unquestioned coupling in a book or article of Coleridge and Shelley, or in the widely found inference that a work with Romantic traits has found something it ought to have found, that it is profounder and better than work characteristic of an earlier date. Very sophisticated writing about Romantic poems can rest on very simple notions of history. *Poetry and Repression* (1975), for example, by the American psychoanalytic critic Harold Bloom, uses as examples of its thesis a number of difficult poems, including Wordsworth's 'Tintern Abbey', Keats's 'Fall of Hyperion' and Shelley's *Triumph of Life*. The entire complex argument, that poetry originates in the unconscious, derives on the face of it from Emerson, Nietzsche and Freud; but it is also a sophisticated variant of Abrams's account of what Romantic poets believed, and the choice of poems to exemplify it rests on some very basic 'historical' notions. Bloom subscribes to the belief, as have others before him, that a revolution took place in late eighteenth-century intellectual life 'after Rousseau'. Western European men and women came to believe in experience as something that goes on in the head, not as a drama in the world external to the self. On three points this highbrow critic falls in with the vulgar wisdom. He believes that he can approximately date Romanticism. He sees it as a phenomenon firmly linking all the writers commonly thought of as Romantic. He accepts the most important tenets of the Romantic artists' self-image as formulated by about the 1820s, their veneration for the creative process, and their elevation of their own inner experience over prosaic external 'fact'.

The first reason, then, for studying Romantic literature against its historical background is that we already do so. Generalizations about romanticism and 'the Romantics' rest upon hazy historical beliefs, which have become fuller with time, and now demand to be questioned and checked. But there may be more positive, universal and better reasons for studying literature in its context.

The majority of modern critical works subscribe to the cult of the Romantic writer in all kinds of indirect ways. It is common to read and write biographies and critical studies of single writers, in isolation, which proceed as though the poet alone is the creator of his poetry. We are regularly in danger of treating the relationship between author and text as a closed system, when really the process of literary production must be open at both ends. The writer takes in words, thoughts and structures from a babel around him, and his text is a giving back into the same discussion, part, in short, of a social process.

Books have a longer gestation than a few weeks or months, a larger cradle than one man's study. A book is made by its public, the readers it literally finds and the people in the author's mind's eye. Literature, like all art, like language, is a collective activity, powerfully conditioned by social forces, what needs to be and what may be said in a particular community at a given time – the field of the anthropologist, perhaps, rather than the psychologist. This is not to deny that psychology, along with philosophy, has much to contribute to the study of literature. It is merely to observe that, self-evidently, authors are not the solitaries of the

Romantic myth, but citizens. Within any community tastes, opinions, values, the shaping stuff of art, are socially generated. Though writers are gifted with tongues to articulate the Spirit of the Age, they are also moulded by the age. Culture is a social phenomenon, and its larger manifestations are not therefore to be understood without recourse to the disciplines of those who study society, whether anthropologists or sociologists or historians.

It could be useful to check some of our generalizations about literary history around 1800, but this alone is hardly enough. We might do that and still not have asked the central question: in quite what sense is English literature at the end of the eighteenth and the beginning of the nineteenth centuries a product and a part of social experience? In order to counter the isolationism of so many of the commonest approaches of the literary scholar, we need both an awareness of the historical process, and a feel for the community which generated art and provided its public. Clearly the reader must look beyond this essay for a connected narrative of the social and political history of the period; a chronology and notes for further reading follow the text. As for the books under discussion, a full-scale treatment could have found space to make more of popular as well as highbrow literature; of influential authors whom we do not think of as literary but our ancestors did, such as Joseph Priestley, William Godwin, T. R. Malthus and William Cobbett; of all that vast band who are no longer currently much read, Walter Savage Landor, Robert Southey, Tom Moore and the rest. These play only a minor part, sometimes regrettably, but there would have been arguments for omitting them from a book twice as long. The space has gone instead to those writers whom the modern general reader and student is most likely to know at first hand. For writing about literature, whether its bias is historical, linguistic, philosophical or psychoanalytic, must aim to pass the test of adding to experience which is still current. The great writings of the early nineteenth century are not merely pieces of historical evidence, fossils in the ground, but living texts that we too are engaged with. Just as they had no first author, they have not found their last reader. To see these works within their cultural context is also to acknowledge their place in a world we still inhabit.

1   The Arts in an Age of Revolution: 1760–1790

Students of literature, even advanced ones, are apt to see late eighteenth century Western society as a serene and static world, rudely galvanized by the storming of the Bastille in 1789. But this is an old-fashioned and simplistic impression; more analytic recent scholarship suggests that in reality social and economic pressures were building up from the 1760s, if not earlier. The strains were reflected politically, in revolutions (in America and France) and attempted revolutions. The latter took violent form in Geneva (1782), Holland (1794), Poland (1794), Ireland (1798) and Naples (1799), while in England campaigners for parliamentary reform were able to use constitutional outlets in the 1760s and 1780s. It is a period of rapid change or expectation of change, and its restiveness is conveyed in literature and the other arts long before there is violence in the streets of Paris.

Western Europe and America were one community in the later eighteenth century, communicating eagerly by means of better transport and proliferating books and periodicals, sharing common attitudes and broadly similar systems of government. Political customs and institutions might seem superficially different in England and France, Spain and Prussia, the small Swiss republics and the sprawling Austro-Hungarian empire, but socially they had much in common, since all were aristocracies. In all these societies, power resided in the hands of a small, or fairly small, set of people who had inherited their socially superior status. The European aristocrat did not derive his income from trade, which was perceived in all countries as undignified – even though he might acquire money from trade by marriage, and he might make money through investment. The classic sources of money were landed rents and government office, with, in some countries, Church office too. Representative aristocrats sat in corporate institutional bodies in which the rules of membership were either by law or *de facto* hereditary. Such aristocratic assemblies included the parlement of Paris and the surviving French provincial estates, the diets and assemblies of the Habsburg countries and Poland, the Dutch and Belgian estates, and the British Parliament.

The English have inherited the view that eighteenth-century England was not Europe. It is true that over the centuries landownership in England had evolved into a peculiarly commercial pattern, which substituted for the relationship of lord of the manor and peasant the relationship of landlord and tenant. It is also true that, especially in the century since the English had executed a king, their aristocracy, gentry and middle classes had interpenetrated more than on the continent of Europe. Not only were these classes not legally distinct, as they were elsewhere; gentlemen were liable to engage in money-making projects, and tradesmen to buy land, so that to a foreign observer the English upper classes might well appear relatively egalitarian. Actually the English political system was neither as open nor as distinctive as Montesquieu, its French admirer of the 1730s, perceived it. Though the rules of membership were less formally drawn than in other countries, the eighteenth-century Mother of Parliaments was the key institution of a genuine oligarchy. It was in effect self-recruited, within members of its own class. Very few elections were contested. Over half of all the men who sat in the House of Commons between 1734 and 1832 had had a close relative there before them. After 1790 the proportion actually increased.

A flourishing economy contributed to the firm hold on power of the English ruling orders. Since the end of the Seven Years War with France in 1763 England had seized new overseas markets and trade had boomed. The new technology contributed to an expansion of mining and of industry; the landowners led the way, and by putting their money into mining, canals, the new water- and steam-powered 'manufactories', were the first to benefit from the take-off in economic growth. The British aristocracy was enjoying a strikingly vigorous phase, though this too was not untypical. For, far from being static and degenerate, the European aristocracy was in aggressive mood and, instead of retreating before those who sought to curtail its absolute privileges, was pressing confidently for more power between 1760 and 1790.

Social change is one man's opportunity, another man's disorientation. Perhaps the most significant agent of change in the second half of the eighteenth century was the sharp rise in the population. Estimates are subject to a wide margin of error, but it seems certain that, for Europe as a whole, the population grew during the century, and more rapidly after 1760 than before. In some countries, such as Spain, Italy and France, the increase may have been merely steady, about 0.5 per cent per annum; in others, such as parts of Scandinavia and the Low Countries, Russia, England, Wales, Ireland and parts of Germany, numbers probably grew twice as fast. A rising population is probably symptomatic of favourable circumstances, such as higher standards of living and improvements in housing, medicine and public health. Yet in itself it is likely to create problems. In some European countries the poor found themselves with too many mouths to feed, while their betters had more sons for whom to find openings. The middle classes began to murmur against being excluded from opportunities in the public domain; the aristocracies, to entrench themselves and become more exclusive. In Venice, in Switzerland and in France it became harder at this time to qualify for parliament or to become an officer in the army.

In England, for the time being, aristocratic expansiveness seemed to work in the interests of all: the great Scottish commentator on society, Adam Smith, had some reason to argue in *The Wealth of Nations* (1776) that it did so by a natural law. Better farming methods kept the surplus population fed; the enclosures which were a feature of the agrarian revolution meant that the extra people could not be accommodated in the villages, but technology helped to create employment in the new manufacturing areas of the Midlands and the North West. Though the American War of 1775–82 disturbed trade, the decades after mid-century were on the whole prosperous, and there is little evidence of sustained hardship or of radical feeling among the mass of the population. In England, as in other European countries, the country-dwellers especially were unpoliticized. Only later, in the 1790s, did sections of the artisan class, tailors, cobblers, printers, weavers, independent tradespeople, become actively radical in London and in the new urban centres like Sheffield, Leeds and Manchester. Apart from this the most observable political tensions of late eighteenth-century society were to be found within the educated classes at the upper end of the social order.

The first two campaigns for reform in the period came from the gentry and the City, not the unpropertied: they were waged against patronage and corruption, that is against a small oligarchy's effective monopoly of places in the public service. In the late 1760s wealthy Londoners and gentlemanly progressives combined forces in the pressure on Parliament for which John Wilkes was the figurehead; in the early 1780s a group of Yorkshire landowners led by Christopher Wyvill formed an association to campaign for an extension of the franchise. In a campaign which was to have considerable implications for intellectual life, the Dissenters in 1788–90 lobbied for the removal of the Corporation Act of 1661 and the Test Act of 1673, by which they, like the Catholics, were barred from public office.

Throughout the eighteenth century the Dissenters provided an element of pacific dissidence in English society, a tradition of individualism and 'levelling' that went back to the Civil War, though it tended to stress not rebellion but the more constitutional heroics of 1688. Polemicists like

John Toland (1670–1722), a Deist patronized by wealthy freethinkers and Dissenters, and the Unitarian minister Joseph Priestley (1733–1804) wrote about civil liberties and about theology, a field in which they played down religion's magical and liturgical aspects, and stressed instead the moral and the rational. Priestley, for example, denied the doctrine of the Trinity and wrote of the humanity of Jesus Christ. He was intensely interested in the individual mind, in its powers of consciousness and conscience, and the educational syllabus he advocated in the 1760s was designed to train critical, independent-minded citizens, like the Dissenters themselves. It is indicative of a relatively buoyant and open society that the Dissenters seemed likely to bring effective pressure upon the Parliament from which they were excluded. Their first attempt to have the motion to remove their disabilities put in the Commons by a sympathetic MP was buoyed up by the recent celebrations of the centenary of England's own Glorious Revolution in 1688. It appeared not to excite much public animosity from the Anglican majority, and failed by only 122 votes to 102. After this, though, the issue became more controversial. In those parts of the country, such as Birmingham, where the Dissenters were campaigning vigorously, 'Church and King' clubs sprouted in reaction; Priestley, who lived in Birmingham, became a figure of notoriety there, as the most polemical of Dissenters. When the motion on behalf of Dissent was moved in the Commons for the third time, by Fox in March 1790, it was eloquently opposed by the formidable Edmund Burke, who feared that the Dissenters were too sympathetic to French innovations, and detested the doctrine of 'natural rights' on which Fox had based their case. This time the motion was rejected by 294 to 105. During the next two years the cause became hopelessly unpopular, as the French Revolution took a more extreme course, and the Dissenters' criticisms of the Church hierarchy and the law became readily confused with French atheism and anarchy.

Meanwhile, as in other European countries, the entrenched governing class was also threatened from above. The Seven Years War had left most European governments in debt; governments, that is the monarchs and their bureaucracies, were obliged to impose from the centre a more efficient method of tax-collection, which inevitably meant more taxation of the rich. Faced with pressure from two sides, the English aristocracy became more self-aware, and its spokesmen invented the terms with which it might defend itself. Like other aristocratic assemblies, the House of Commons resisted reform with fine and sincere rhetoric about royal tyranny and the need to uphold ancient liberties. These 'liberties' were genuinely traditional, but they were also, as in other countries, confined to the upper classes. The Whigs defended them against George

III, just as the French nobles defended them against Louis XVI's reforming minister Turgot. 'It is our business ... to maintain the independency of Parliament,' said Charles James Fox of this struggle in 1771, 'whether it is attacked by the people or by the crown is a matter of little consequence.'

The arts do not exist faithfully to reproduce political realities or real-life political arguments. In life, Louis XVI and his ministers might have a just and even enlightened case. Certainly the Emperor Joseph II, who reigned over the Habsburg dominions from 1780 to 1790, attempted to impose his political and economic reforms in the name of progress. George III was not necessarily a tyrant for wishing to tax the Americans, still less for attempting to curb the power of the great Whig magnates. But it availed Louis, Joseph and George nothing when they hired journalists or artists to put their case for them; the result was neither good journalism nor good art. Editorial-writing, and also political philosophy and literature, have little to do with political practicalities, or with the complex balancing of interests and pressures that in the real world lie behind decision-making. They have everything to do with what for want of a better word has to be called ideology. When a group acquires a sense of its corporate identity – when it wishes to defend it, or, better still, to impose it on others – it may begin to project in its culture something that approaches an idealized self-portrait. It may seem to us now a paradox that the oligarchs themselves came to talk and write so much about liberty, and that the individualistic rhetoric of the Dissenting minority was splendidly echoed in the House which refused them equal civil rights. Elsewhere among European aristocrats ardent, if notional, libertarianism is a feature of this confident, expansive age.

We shall see that in England from 1792 there was a very marked political reaction, towards a conscious conservatism, which in the next decade made itself felt deeply and decisively in the arts. Between 1760 and 1790, when political feeling ran less high, it was reformist sentiment that was common and even fashionable among the gentry. Thus the last decades of the *ancien régime* are, perhaps ironically, much more 'liberal' in most European cultures than the post-revolutionary period of 1790 to 1820. There is no mistaking the excitement generated in the arts and in intellectual life from about 1760. As news, ideas and books spread across Europe and America with new rapidity, so the journals and newspapers sprang into being to comment on them. England published 90 in 1750, 264 in 1800; 1,350 new papers were launched in Paris between 1789 and 1800. Political events especially evoked comment; the American Revolution was for example a great issue and a source of radical stimulus in Continental Europe. Late eighteenth-century culture took on the air of a vast international debate, an informal Congress of the educated classes everywhere. Regardless of who voted or who was represented in a legislature, public opinion was a force, and it incorporated a notion of the public which was wider and more amorphous than the restricted number of families who technically held the reins of power. This opinion, to look at the matter one way, ran ahead of political reality, and most of the gentlemen keen to talk about rights in the period of the Enlightenment afterwards proved less willing to share them with anyone else. Yet the talk itself significantly expressed the privileged man's self-confidence, his impatience with constraint, his aspiration, being relatively rich, to get richer. The restless, assertive opinion-mongering of newspapers, essays and pamphlets is the tone of a large class of readers, who are also the consumers of the arts.

The most obvious feature common to all the arts of Western nations after 1750 was the refusal to validate the contemporary social world – even though, to the retrospective eye, those who lived in society were never so prosperous, powerful, or (presumably) happy. The art of the late eighteenth century fell decidedly out of love with material possessions: there was little of the affectionate rendering of silks and fripperies of the rococo art fashionable earlier in the century, and none of the greedy, acquisitive dwelling on things which afterwards characterized the nineteenth-century middle-class taste which has become known as Biedermeier. The strongest single tendency of late eighteenth-century art was to reject the ephemeral in favour of the essential, and the search for purity often took the form of a journey into the remote. The settings of poems, plays, paintings and even novels evoked a condition of society that was primitive and pre-social, in contrast to the luxuriousness which was seen as the characteristic of contemporary life in Western Europe. Heroes from simpler worlds visited civilization for the purpose of making adverse comparisons. Voltaire created one classic Outsider, the Huron, in his book of the same name, and Goldsmith another, the Chinaman Lien Chi Altangi, who is also described, in a phrase both levelling and universal, as a Citizen of the World. A real South Sea islander called Omai was a hit in Dr Johnson's London, for like his fictional counterparts he appeared to represent essential Man, as the Parisian in his salon or the Londoner in his drawing-room was too degenerate to do. Alternatively the moralizing writer had recourse not to remote places but to the remote past. Gray wrote about the thirteenth-century Welsh in *The Bard*, and drew in his *Odes* on even more distant and heroic Nordic mythology. James Macpherson 'discovered' the lost work of the early Gaelic poet, Ossian, and in the process manufactured a primitive world in which heroes exhibited the primal qualities of high courage, chivalrous love and humanity. The most popular locations for this fashionable nostalgia were primitive Greece and Rome (as opposed to Periclean Athens and Augustan Rome, both now too urban), the Dark and Middle Ages, and the fine flowering of the civilization of 'medieval' Europe, from the fourteenth to the sixteenth centuries.

The mid-century reaction against frivolity, detail and polish finds various expression in all the arts. The painter becomes less likely to place his subjects in what is visibly an aristocratic park or (especially) a boudoir; more likely to choose natural, homely scenes, or to simplify his portraits so that the human qualities and not the status or possessions of the sitter are stressed. Pope's Belinda and Eloisa give way to the anonymous rude forefathers of the hamlet in Gray's *Country Churchyard*; John Gay's urban setting in his 'Town Eclogue', the *Trivia*, finds fewer followers than James Thomson's country setting in *The Seasons*. Architecture undergoes a process of purification, sometimes to surprisingly abstract extremes. In heavy public buildings in the Doric or Egyptian manner it reaches after effects of solidity and permanence. Particularly in the 1790s, the primitivist inspiration produces buildings (like the pavilion in the park in Goethe's Weimar, the Romische Haus) which evoke a half-excavated temple dreamed up out of an ancient past; or, as in the designs of the Frenchman Ledoux, they bypass known history altogether, and are refined to elemental shapes, the cube, the circle and the pyramid. In music, Gluck writes a classical opera, *Alceste*, and in the dedication advocates 'noble simplicity' and condemns 'superfluous ornaments'. Haydn is inspired by the folk dances of his own Eastern Europe, and by the literary rusticity of Thomson's *Seasons*.

It is easy to miss the underlying logic in the shifting tastes of the period, partly because in practice taste was often compromised. A house and a garden are designed for ordinary (if rich) people. In theory the taste of the upper orders had shifted towards the simple, but in practice the wealthy were unwilling to forego the refinements of modern urban living. Horace Walpole can be thought of as theoretically a primitivist, since he wrote a Gothic novel and built a Gothic house; but he undeniably lived like a highly sophisticated man of the eighteenth century, and the cluttered interior of his house, Strawberry Hill, now seems so chic as to call his admiration for the Dark Ages in question.

But this is not only a conflict between theory and practice. Walpole's literary utterances, like those of other writers, sometimes appear inconsistent. In spite of the attention he had lavished on the Gothic, when he was writing as a critic he could say chastely, 'One must have taste to be sensible of the beauties of Grecian architecture; one only wants passions to feel Gothic.' The most celebrated man of letters of the day, Samuel Johnson, clung as a poet to the urbane couplet, and came under attack from some of the primitivist critics of the day for being old-fashioned and over-elaborate. But Johnson as a critic prized simple emotion above the rules, and when it was his turn to consider Thomas Warton's taste for the antique, he thought *that* over-elaborate:

> Whereso'er I turn my view,
> All is strange, yet nothing new;
> Endless labour all along,
> Endless labour to be wrong;
> Phrase that time has flung away,
> Uncouth words in disarray;
> Trickt in antique ruff and bonnet,
> Ode and elegy and sonnet.

Very different styles of the period originated in a common impulse and tended to fail because they were not executed rigorously enough. The better critics disagreed over style, but in fact usually agreed on the principle that was wanted, a clean reduction to essentials.

The real common ground between 'antique' styles as superficially diverse as the classical and the Gothic can best be demonstrated by showing how interchangeable they often were for the men of the period. Architects like Wyatt and Nash would use both the Gothic and the Grecian style. The Herefordshire gentleman Richard Payne Knight built himself a Gothic house, Downton Castle, but he was also an expert on Greek coins, art and antiquities, and his first work was his 'Essay on the Worship of Priapus'. The furniture-maker Thomas Chippendale designed a Greek chair, a Chinese chair, and a Gothic chair, all of which were decorative variants on what we might call a classic outline.

But this word 'classic' has become the major stumbling-block in our understanding of late eighteenth-century literature. Literary histories tend to teach a golden age of classicism, which they sometimes call Augustanism, from Dryden in the late seventeenth century to Samuel Johnson about a hundred years later. According to the received view, this style aspires in principle to imitate reality, though not its accidentals but the underlying principles of Nature. Its calm, static formality is an appropriate expression both of contemporary theories about the world – the belief in a harmonious universe – and of contemporary practice, an ordered, hierarchical political system.

This theory of a stable eighteenth-century classicism evolved in the late nineteenth century: it is in fact the natural corollary of the concept of Romanticism, which was supposed to have superseded classicism. It probably reflects a prejudiced, outdated and inaccurate stereotype of the late eighteenth century, as an era of stasis rather than of rapid expansion and change, for it hardly squares with observations of the arts in the second half of the century, which do not characteristically celebrate a hierarchy: they tend to be strongly humanitarian, sympathetic to the simple and the weak, and thus, if anything, 'levelling' in their social implications. Use of terms like 'Augustanism' and 'classicism' tends indeed to obscure the fact that in literature as in the visual arts a reaction and even a revolution against some of the social implications of early eighteenth-century art was already occurring by about 1750.

It might be easier if the literary critic were to borrow the art critic's terminology: to think, say, of Dryden's *Annus Mirabilis* or *Alexander's Feast* as baroque poems, and of Pope's *Rape of the Lock* as characteristically rococo. Certainly the latter conveys the same refined if discriminating delight in a world of exclusivity and elegance as the similarly exquisite scenes of the French painter Watteau, the great master of rococo. In literary matters both Dryden and Pope legislated for a society which they saw as arrived at a cultural high tide; behind them were the crudities of the Elizabethans and Goths, ahead perhaps the mob. This cultural superiority, the explicit appeal to a refined élite, ceased not long after Pope's death to be the fashionable orthodoxy. Though Samuel Johnson defends Dryden and Pope as poets and poetic arbiters in his *Lives of the Poets* (1779–81), he does so defensively, in the face of a turning tide of taste and the influential critical attacks of men like Joseph and Thomas Warton. As Hugh Honour and other art critics have shown, the preferred style now was simple, serious and grand, and the art of the first half of the century, Pope's included, came to be seen as over-ornamented, clever as opposed to feeling, and meretriciously flattering. It presented images too likely to favour the modern civilized world in general, or the great man for whom it was made.

How to define this radical reaction of the middle of the century remains a problem. Art critics call it Neoclassicism, after the strong revival of interest in ancient Greek and Roman art that occurred at about the moment in question. Undoubtedly Rome became an international centre for painters and critics from the 1750s, and (under the influence of the delineator of Roman ruins, Piranesi) a renewed source of visual inspiration. Meanwhile the most important aesthetician of the revival, the German J. J. Winckelmann, advocated the study of Greek models, not in order to copy them – Winckelmann denounced mere copying – but so that the artist could emulate the ancients in conveying the real simplicity of Nature. Winckelmann's praise of ancient art's 'noble simplicity' and 'quiet grandeur' was no justification for modern versions that were merely inert – though such existed – and his advice would never have been followed if it had been understood at the time in these terms. The student of the academies of Paris and London who passionately preferred line-drawing, *à la* Flaxman, to the colour of Rubens, or who perfected his notion of the human form by contemplating ancient statues like the 'Apollo Belvedere' or the 'Laocoön', did not see himself as following an old-established taste, but felt the excitement of a radical departure.

An understanding of the mid-century classical revival in the visual arts is very necessary to a student of another art, like literature, since the underlying issues of taste and of meaning were more cogently debated for the visual arts than in writing about literature. And yet even the freshly defined and flexible Neoclassicism of Winckelmann is clearly only a symptom, neither cause nor essence, of a much wider movement of taste. Even in painting and in architecture explicit *classicism* is accompanied by a strong vogue for the Gothic and for the arts of primitive societies, and in music and in literature these other revivals are more significant than the interest in Greece and Rome. The art critic Robert Rosenblum has suggested that we should think of the mid-century movement not as Neoclassicism but as 'historicism'. Perhaps alternatively these enthusiasms for the remote past are all aspects of primitivism, and have their roots in a more general principle still, a revulsion against sophisticated urban life in favour of a dream of the pastoral.

For there surely is a general principle behind the ubiquitous practice of imitating a variety of models: the effect is seldom merely antiquarian or academic. A book which often appears both of these things – Horace Walpole's pioneer Gothic novel, *The Castle of Otranto* (1765) – provides an interesting example of how 'imitation' might work in literature in the hands of an artist with some theoretical sophistication but only moderate practical abilities. Walpole not only succeeded in conjuring up some of the longest-lasting motifs in fiction – the vast, unknowable castle, with its subterranean vaults, its murderous, lecherous lord, the visitations of the supernatural; he also surrounded his story with what were to become favourite trappings. At first he claimed that the manuscript genuinely belonged to its supposed period, and had recently come to light after a most complicated process of transmission. Later, with every appearance of sincerity, he told a friend that the most striking scene appeared to him in a dream (a clue which seems exciting to the modern reader, mindful of Coleridge's 'Kubla Khan' and other nineteenth-century works of mysterious provenance). In spite of all this, Walpole's 'Gothic tale' is also a far from unique example of the revival of the English literary 'primitives' – that is, literary models of the late Middle Ages and the sixteenth century. In the era adorned by Garrick, Shakespeare was entering upon his golden age in the theatre. *Otranto* looks uncommonly like an attempt to graft on to the novel – that modern form concerned with money, possessions, status, circumstance – the heightened passions, elemental situations, and stylized poetic techniques of the Elizabethan dramatists.

The castle setting recalls *Hamlet* and *Macbeth*, but it also, more technically, recalls the cockpit of the Globe theatre. For, as the line taken in both Walpole's Prefaces confirms, he is in large measure conducting a kind of exercise in literary criticism, whereby he means to prove the superiority of Shakespeare to his traducer Voltaire, of primitive art to the modern art of 'cold reason'. His pastiche of Shakespeare includes an approximation of the 'mixed' effect, whereby low characters mingle with high and comedy with tragedy. But more important, the whole work is conducted along the lines of a Shakespearean play. While not conforming to the unities any more than Shakespeare does, its action has the tight and sequential quality of stage action. It is divided into five chapters, after the five acts, and the action unfolds with dramatic propriety. The first chapter is an exposition for the main plot: the doom of Manfred's line is prophesied, and his son Conrad killed by supernatural means (effects which mimic the other-worldly visitations of the first acts of *Hamlet* and *Macbeth*), after which the villainous Manfred begins his career of crime by forcing his attentions on the heroine Isabella. Chapter II introduces a subplot – Matilda's love for Theodore – which will be picked up again in Chapter IV. Chapter III returns to the supernatural omens – the plume nods, and a mysterious procession of knights appears – and to the main plot, which is concerned with the downfall of Manfred. And so on. The entire effect may be more reminiscent of Beaumont and Fletcher than of Shakespeare, but there is no doubt that the 'kind ' involved is the drama, and the period no later than the Renaissance. Recent critical attention has focused on obvious Gothic properties, like the gigantic helmet, and the castle setting, and has tended to view *the imitation of a classic original* (in this case, a Shakespearean tragedy) as either incidental or out of keeping. Yet it is exactly in keeping with other imitations of classic models in all the arts of the period, and with the principle of imitation as defined by Winckelmann. Walpole translates his action into a mythical past, and substitutes for the ordinary novel's documentary realism a poetic simplification, in order to get at a kind of essence of human experience, the emotional core at the heart of all relationships – love, and terror. *Otranto* may not be a perfectly successful experiment, but it is neither aberrant nor confused.

Otranto is one kind of reduction of the large, cluttered naturalistic novel of contemporary life of the first half of the century. Laurence Sterne's *Tristram Shandy*, 1760–7, more effectively assaults the same target. A happy, wholesale challenge to *a priori* assumptions about man, education, biography, fiction-making, writing and reading, it stands for the period's characteristic fundamentalism in its wittiest variation. In representational literature the age of Sterne is no longer a period for the unselfcritical naturalism of Defoe or even for the lengthy literalism of Richardson. The earlier novelists' clutter of detail perhaps attributes too much importance to the epiphenomena of the external, sophisticated world; certainly that effect of fussing now runs counter to contemporary taste. The novel commands less critical esteem than didactic tales like Voltaire's *Candide* or Johnson's *Rasselas*, with their ironic commentary, their elegant simplicity and their pathos. Even when writing more discursively, the sentimentalists Mackenzie, Goldsmith and Radcliffe eschew detailism in drawing the external world, and when they create their protagonists they show more concern for representative, elemental human responses (love, family feeling, pity, fear) than for particularizing character. It is often suggested that theirs is not a good age for the novel – by whatever standards that judgement is made – and less often recognized that the sentimentalist was experimenting with radically different aesthetic priorities from those of the realists who came before and after.

The change to an emotive style parallels or follows the choice of certain characteristic topics. Representative men and women are studied in some of the common crises of life: they are counters for human sympathy, as befits the prevailing humanity and seriousness of tone. Graveyards become a favourite setting for reflection, deathbeds a favourite subject. Among countless celebrated paintings of noble or pathetic departures are Benjamin West's 'Death of General Wolfe' (1771) and J.-L. David's 'The Death of Marat' (1794). Richardson responds to a similar taste when he dwells on the death of Clarissa (1749), and Wordsworth, at the other end of the period, with his elegiac treatment of the Forsaken Indian Woman (1798). Johnson's *Vanity of Human Wishes* (1749) has a series of deathbeds, all stylized until they fit a universal pattern. His Wolsey and Charles XII of Sweden are not portraits, as they would have been in the hands of Pope before him or of Scott after him. Nor are they in the old epic sense heroes. The late eighteenth-century artist portrays human figures in order to crystallize human experience. He draws men and women, not gods, kings or leaders.

Clearly so general a shift in aesthetic principle is not to be explained solely within the arts; eighteenth-century culture was reflecting a deep and widespread change of feeling, a pervasive mood of rejection of current society. The artefacts and styles which went out of fashion were those that reflected unacceptable aspects of contemporary life – luxury, formality, hierarchy – and to proscribe these is a matter of social values.

Again, it is from mid-century that the reading public becomes familiar with a type of social criticism that contrasts the modern world unfavourably with earlier times. Jean-Jacques Rousseau's *Discours sur les sciences et les arts* (1750) is one classic of this genre, Adam Ferguson's *Essay on the History of Civil Society* (1767) another. Rousseau measures the vices of civilization by the yardstick of a pre-social 'state of nature', while Ferguson compares the modern nation-state with simpler social organisms like the Roman republic or the Highland clan. Other historical myths become politically potent. The reformers Priestley, Price and Cartwright all claim that Anglo-Saxon England enjoyed a freedom and equality lost when the Normans imposed their 'yoke' of religious and secular law, and an aristocratic social hierarchy. The term 'Goths' loses its abusive connotation: the Germanic peoples in general come to be thought of as noble and free, until they too fell under the yoke of priests and kings, the corrupting tyranny of Catholic Christendom. Horace Walpole, though no more a democrat than Samuel Johnson, echoes in *Otranto* a deeply significant historical myth of the day when he makes a villain out of a corrupt Italian tyrant, Manfred, and a hero out of a manly freespoken peasant with the significantly Gothic name of Theodore.

The omnipresence of a deep vein of social criticism, which informs the work of creative writers of all shades of political opinion, cautions us not to attribute too much influence to individual thinkers. The name of Rousseau in particular is too frequently invoked to 'explain' the taste for primitivism in other intellectuals and artists. In fact a thinker probably becomes 'influential', that is, read, admired and echoed, because he has ideas in common with others, rather than because he initiates them. And yet, though philosophers and historians are not primarily sources for other intellectuals, their common preoccupations are nevertheless instructive. Their works illustrate that outside the creative arts proper, the late eighteenth century was characterized first by its impulse to see society in a grand and simple historical perspective; second, by the tendency latent in the recourse to history, to find thoroughgoing fault with the contemporary world.

The œuvre of Adam Smith admirably represents the intellectual bias of the period. Though only *The Theory of Moral Sentiments* (1759) and *The Wealth of Nations* (1776) appeared, Smith apparently intended to produce a complete cultural history and social philosophy. On his deathbed he ordered the destruction of his unfinished manuscripts, which included (according to his own account five years earlier) 'a sort of Philosophical History of all the different branches of Literature, of Philosophy, Poetry and Eloquence', and 'a sort of Theory and History of Law and Government'. The evidence suggests that between them these enterprises would have depicted the entire evolution of man in society, interpreting it as on the whole an upward progress. But no perfectibilarian could have seen in Smith a sanguine propagandist of the age of commerce, nor a prophet of the millennium to come. He was much too aware of the evils of life in an advanced society, among them the narrowness of the commercial spirit, the greater nobility in the values of more martial ages, the deadening of intelligence due to the division of labour. Even more sobering, he did not conceive that social advancement had been brought about by the efforts of individual men. On the contrary, few had willed or foreseen the consequences of their generally petty, selfish actions:

A revolution of the greatest importance to the public happiness was in this manner brought about by two different orders of people (the nobility and the merchants), who had not the least intention to serve the public. To gratify the most selfish vanity was the sole motive of the great proprietors. The merchants and artificers, much less ridiculous, acted merely from a view to their own interest and in pursuit of their own pedlar principle of turning a penny wherever a penny was to be got. Neither of them had either knowledge or foresight of the great revolution which the folly of the one, and the industry of the other, was gradually bringing about.

(*The Wealth of Nations*, 1.369–70)

According to Smith's pupil Dugald Stewart, one of the lost manuscripts was to have shown that progress is best served by a negation of effort, the mere absence of interference with the spontaneous historical process: 'All governments which thwart this natural course, which force things into another channel, or which endeavour to arrest the progress of society at a particular point, are obliged to be oppressive and tyrannical.' So much for an older culture's trust in kings, leaders, heroes: neither leadership nor conscious effort makes much sense in the complex, impersonal modern world. Translated into personal terms, Smith's is a disturbing view, which neither discerns individual excellence, nor leaves much scope for it. He is a progressive, but in a rare spirit of intellectual detachment. He combines a belief in advanced society with a disbelief in its laws and hierarchies, its social and economic planning. Unlike the vision of the great social family Burke was to propound in his *Reflections on the Revolution in France* (1790), Smith conceives society as an aggregate of moving atoms, the analogue to the physical scientist's conception of a universe which is continually in flux. The openness and political ambivalence of Smith's conception is important, for it represents better than Burke the daring and expansiveness and even, potentially, the desolating vulnerability of the late eighteenth-century imagination.

Gibbon's completed masterpiece, *The Decline and Fall of the Roman Empire* (1776–88) is much nearer to Smith than to Burke. As well as a history, it is an achievement of English Neoclassicism: an elegy for an advanced society, the Roman Empire, measured by the heroic simplicity, freedom and individualism of its primitive precursor, the vanished Roman Republic. Gibbon's critique of Empire has a continuous contemporary reference since, as the sardonic record of the imposition of bureaucracy, hierarchy, tyranny and state religion, it could relate to any modern nation. In Gibbon's world would-be heroes, like the Antonine Emperors and Julian the Apostate, turn out to be no more than cogs in a great system. Gibbon's ironic portrayal of an advanced society in action nicely illustrates Smith's pessimistic thesis. But his implied nostalgia for the primitive republic, together with his foretaste of republics that were to come, the medieval Florentine and still-surviving Swiss, give his work a much more poetic colouring, and even a polemical edge. Though a member of the gentry, and for eight years a Whig MP, Gibbon celebrates the kind of ideal – plainness, republicanism, individualism – that is so typical of his era, and potentially seems so subversive of its institutions.

Ideas which gain currency in a culture – whether a theory of perception or a notion of society – presumably themselves originate in changing circumstances, though the ideas may also contribute to further change. No period is static, but change may have been especially rapid in the second half of the eighteenth century, and perceptibly so to contemporaries. The growth in the English population and its shift towards the Midlands and North were trends which left plainly discernible traces; they are reflected in literature by frequent contrasts between an innocent idyllic countryside and a corrupt town. Perhaps Cowper's *Task* (1785) or Thomas Day's *Sandford and Merton* (1783–9) or, later, Wordsworth and Jane Austen ultimately reflect a group consciousness and a nostalgia for a predominantly agrarian world. Equally striking from mid-century to about 1790 is the pervasive appearance, in the arts and in other records, of the crowd: not a crowd made up of strangers, as in a London street, still less a threatening mob, but a room full of acquaintances or potential acquaintances at a ball or party.

The letters, journals and lives of the later eighteenth century confirm that it was an age of remarkable sociability. This may seem a curious generalization, as though societies are commonly solitary or parties ever unpopular. But it was after all a period when more people were gathered in towns than ever before, and more of them were leisured; upper-class women, in particular, were released by wealth and servants even from many domestic duties which might in an earlier period have occupied their time. Every reader of Boswell's *Life of Johnson* or of Horace Walpole's *Letters* has noticed how much of the London literary man's daily life was spent in groups, in conversation of a generally fairly serious kind; the pattern was anticipated in fiction in Richardson's *Sir Charles Grandison* (1754). As we shall see, even more serious and purposeful conversations were organized in the provinces to exchange ideas and information; Manchester had its Literary and Philosophical Society, Birmingham its Lunar Society, and similar groups met regularly over many years in Derby, Liverpool, Lichfield, Bristol and Norwich. Several London coffee houses became the venue for discussion clubs with a membership that from the sociological point of view is interestingly mixed. At Slaughter's Coffeehouse in the 1760s the gentleman and amateur inventor Richard Lovell Edgeworth met the surgeon John Hunter, the artist Joseph Banks, the sailor-geographer Captain James Cook, the Swedish botanist Daniel Charles Solander, and the engineer John Smeaton, but, Edgeworth afterwards recorded, 'the society became too numerous and too noble, and was insensibly dissolved.' A radical-sounding group gathered fortnightly from 1764 at St Paul's Coffeehouse and after 1772 at the London Coffeehouse: Benjamin Franklin came to this supper club, and met there the well-known Dissenters and polemicists James Burgh, Richard Price and Andrew Kippis. But again the social principle was heterogeneous, and the Tory landed gentleman's son James Boswell attended too.

Even the architecture of late eighteenth-century England contrives to bear witness to the period's gregariousness. Mark Girouard has observed how from before mid-century a town house was likely to be given a suite of rooms through which a large concourse would circulate, instead of a single great room as a ceremonial centre. The new plan (of which Norfolk House, London, is an example) no longer emphasizes the elevation of the master of the house, and the exclusivity of his friends. It reflects a new pattern of entertaining, in the direction of balls, ridottos, assemblies and masquerades. The letters and essays of the time, together with the novels of Smollett and Fanny Burney, and the water-colours of Rowlandson, convey the atmosphere of the period's favourite crowded social occasion, in which society is necessarily heterogeneous.

The single country house must stand as the visible emblem of a hierarchical world in which the lord is at the apex of the social pyramid. The townscape of Georgian Bath is an expressive monument to a new ideal which, though certainly not democratic, is nevertheless open, receptive, and generous in its understanding of who the sociable classes are. Eighteenth-century Bath acted as a magnet to the nobility and gentry, and its design – in terraces, straight or curved, and in the Circus – suggests that within that world of gentry there is a kind of equality. No axial vistas lead to a central feature. The focal points are the Baths and the Assembly Rooms, between which the gentry stroll about, undifferentiated by rank. One is reminded of Jane Austen's Elizabeth Bennet, who can say proudly of herself and of Darcy, the owner of Pemberley – 'He is a gentleman. I am a gentleman's daughter.' To contemporaries, the Bath of Beau Nash achieved a desirable social levelling at the expense of a stiff older convention, that perhaps of a Lady Catherine de Burgh. Goldsmith, in his life of Beau Nash, praises his achievement in getting rid of a 'Gothic haughtiness'.

The post-1790s generation did not revert to the old sense of formality and hierarchy; but nor did it retain the open townscape with its suggestion of accessibility. The Bath Jane Austen describes in *Persuasion* (written 1816) is more snobbish and exclusive than the open, socially promiscuous Bath of her *Northanger Abbey* (begun 1797). Individual houses began to be designed in the new century for smaller groups of people, family and more intimate friends, to pursue quiet hobbies together: library, morning room, music room, afterwards the smoking and billiard rooms. Jane Austen's preference for a village setting and a domestic circle, unlike the wide-flung social world of Fanny Burney's *Evelina* (1778), apparently reflects both a changed reality and a changed spirit of the age.

From 1760 to 1790 a fluid, expanding society is mirrored in artistic forms and styles. The prevailing impulse these convey is of impatience with constraint and a desire to return to fundamentals; Adam Smith most clearly expresses the link with contemporary circumstance when he lauds unfettered individual energy and assails society's effort to limit or regulate it. Yet the arts in the same period can betray a more introverted and pessimistic mood, which is sufficiently common to seem equally characteristic. Unease, disturbance, an obsession with death, a gloating and often perverse sexuality: these traits, in novelists as different in their background as Richardson, William Beckford, M. G. Lewis and the French Marquis de Sade, appear to speak of a state of mind so different from that of the prevailing culture that it is sometimes dubbed pre-Romanticism. The Gothic fantasists have often been interpreted as expressing a reaction against the optimism and confident rationalism of majority taste. In so far as some of them (Beckford and the painter Fuseli, for example) are sophisticated figures, the attribution to them of intellectual, almost philosophical, motives of this kind becomes tempting. But it is worth exploring whether the link between social experience and artistic expression is not more generalized, itself more of a social phenomenon, than this. It may be that the dark vein in the contemporary arts relates, like the more confident trends, to aspects of social life which touched most people, if not all: the disruptive, desolating aspect of change, increased mobility, loosened ties within the large old family units; at the same time, evidence everywhere that urban life, however sophisticated, had made no secure advances over poverty and hunger, crime and injustice, disease and premature death.

The focus of some eighteenth-century novels and drawings on human irrationality and cruelty arouses in the modern reader a specially modern curiosity about the inner life, acknowledged and suppressed, of the individual author. Did Richardson indulge in sadistic fantasies about his heroines during the prolonged passages in which he contemplated their rape? Beckford in *Vathek* (1786) would seem peculiarly interested in the bodies of young boys, while Fuseli in his drawings of the same decade appears to make a fetish of women's hair. But then the Gothic romance, and disturbing graphic images like Fuseli's or Piranesi's, may speak not for emotions private to the author, but for collective anxieties.

The taste for Gothic coincides suggestively with a taste for new, very emotional or millenarian religious cults, both in England and on the Continent. Methodism is a phenomenon of the mid-eighteenth century: later came a host of minor cults and, about the turn of the century, prophets and Saviour-figures such as Richard Brothers and Joanna Southcott. Seen from an orthodox religious point of view, cults of this kind may be no better than magic. But then the anthropologist might argue that for most people religion is officially-sanctioned magic, and that both represent the recourse to an ineffective means of help when no effective means offers itself. And help all too commonly had to be called upon, against the common conditions of human life, illness, poverty and early death.

It may be, as the historian Keith Thomas has argued, that by making a stricter distinction between orthodox Christianity and magic the religious reforms of the Reformation deprived the populations of Western Europe of certain magical comforts which medieval Catholicism offered its believers. The devout medieval victim of misfortune could ask for the intercession of the Saviour, the Virgin or an individual saint; he could try to drive out the Devil with exorcism; he could use rituals to protect himself at every important transition of life, including the last rites and absolution on the threshold of another world. Without these comforts, both the vulgar and the educated in the sixteenth and seventeenth centuries had recourse to witchcraft and astrology. Even in the 'rational' eighteenth century, a population which was not offered scientific explanation for its ills, and had no scientific protection (for medicine offered little until the twentieth century) had the same need of reassurance which earlier generations sought from a more naïve Christianity or from witchcraft. And in this connection it is striking how Gothic fiction, with its strangely recurring motifs, has an almost ritual aspect.

The commonest of all plots of the eighteenth-century Gothic novel involves a frail protagonist in terrible danger. She (more commonly than he) is placed in a hostile, threatening, mysterious environment, usually so prodigiously large that it dwarfs her; she is made prisoner; she is threatened by individuals who should protect her, parents and parent-figures. It is a nightmare, and perhaps the reason for its potent appeal is that it enables the reader to live vicariously through nightmare. It is not so terrible as it would be if one were asleep. It is not nearly so terrible as it would be in life. Facing up to one's fears is a needful process, and emotionally satisfying. Besides, there is something comforting, again almost magical, in anticipating the worst. It is a common intuition that the known evil never comes. If all eighteenth-century popular fiction – not merely the Gothic – rests ultimately on the simple black-and-white fables common to oral literature in many cultures, it may well be because in these reiterated adventures by surrogate figures there is reassurance and even the illusion of protection.

At first sight there is no reason to connect the eighteenth century's literary Gothic with the general population. As it happens, the handful of writers who first excelled at this kind of writing were anything but vulgar: Walpole and Beckford were rich men, unusually so for authors – it perhaps took social confidence to write something as extravagant as *Otranto* or *Vathek* – and Clara Reeve and Ann Radcliffe were gentle-women.

And yet throughout the period the belief was frequently expressed that the public for both Gothic and Chinoiserie was a relatively vulgar one. Of architectural ornaments in these two styles, the journal *The World* sneered in 1754 that 'from Hyde Park to Shoreditch scarce a chandler's shop or an oyster stall but has embellishments of this kind'. Half a century later taste in cheap novels and in cheap stage melodrama ran decidedly to the Gothic, though before 1800 it had sharply lost caste with the critics and with respectable readers. In Dickens's day violent effects, fear, suspense, the isolation of characters in a threatening environment, were all still symptoms of the author aiming at a vulgar mass market.

The Gothic taste is not so much aberrant as an extreme instance of a development characteristic of the period: art openly designed for an expanded public. The role of the public in determining its art was implicitly admitted at the time: neither Neoclassical theory nor contemporary practice in various styles and genres put much emphasis on the individuality of the artist. The period is sometimes known as the age of sensibility, and sensibility can be thought of as self-expression by an effete class, or as a weak trial run for Romanticism. It is, in fact, in a key respect almost the opposite of Romanticism. Sensibility, like its near-synonym sentiment, echoes eighteenth-century philosophy and psychology in focusing upon the mental process by which impressions are received by the senses. But the sentimental writer's interest in how the mind works and in how people behave is very different from the Romantic writer's inwardness. In representational literary forms such as drama and the novel, the responses of characters in interesting situations are carefully observed; but the responses of the reader are also borne in mind, and the reader's capacity to identify with a character seems more salient than the presence of the author. A developing interest in narrative, expressed in poetry for instance in the many ballad imitations, further masked the writer's direct emotional involvement in his fiction. Writing directly about the self seems to invite self-expression, yet Gibbon's decorous *Autobiography* (1796) represents the taste of the period as fairly as Rousseau's daring experimental *Confessions* (written 1765– 70); but even Rousseau conveys the sense (as De Quincey in his *Confessions* of 1821 does not) that his growth to manhood might be anyone's, mankind's rather than Jean-Jacques'.

There is surely, then, a functional explanation for the special tone of sentiment, affective and emotional without seeming private. The burgeoning enterprise of Western Europe was turning art and literature into commodities on an unprecedented scale, and distributing them internationally. In the long run the new conditions – by which the rich patron and the coterie were replaced by the impersonal exhibition, the print, or the book running through many editions – probably tended to isolate the artist from his audience and thus to contribute to his solipsism. In this early stage, the innovations surely seemed above all an opportunity. The period's emphasis on simplicity and ease and on direct emotional effects suggests that artists were rising to the occasion, along with other entrepreneurs, responding to a new conception of a public which was potentially no less than mankind itself.

Our Romantic and post-Romantic interest in the *writer* intrudes when we encounter literature which keeps a partnership with the *reader* so steadily in mind. Though the period produces so much work which is technically inventive, vigorous and intellectual, we only intermittently think of it as avant-garde: the very word conjures up a picture of the bohemian artist, and suggests that belief in art as the vehicle for the artist's self-expression which began to become typical after 1800. For the same reason we overlook the political radicalism of the later eighteenth century. Romantic rebelliousness is more outrageous and total, the individual rejecting not just his own society but the very principle of living in society – which means that the Romantic and post-Romantic often dismisses political activity of any kind, as external to the self, literal and commonplace. Since it is relatively uncommon for the eighteenth-century artist to complain directly on his own behalf, he seldom achieves such emotional force as his nineteenth-century successor. He is, on the other hand, much more inclined than the Romantic to express sympathy for certain well-defined social groups. Humanitarian feeling for the real-life underdog is a strong vein from the 1760s to the 1790s, often echoing real-life campaigns for reform. The cast-lists of dramas, novels and some poems of the period repeatedly include discharged and disabled war veterans, war widows and orphans, prostitutes (especially if they have been seduced and abandoned by a wealthy profligate), foundlings, chimney sweepers' boys and prisoners (for lesser crimes against property or for debt). Some of these topics have an implicit political reference. War, particularly, was unpopular among many sections of the community, since it was felt to defend or enrich those who already had a stake in America, the West Indies or India, at the expense of ordinary manufacture and trade and, of course, of the poor, who provided the soldiers. The manufacturers of the Midlands and North West sympathized firmly with the Americans in 1775, and resented going to war with them, just as Blake's London artisan class did. When literature dwells on the sufferings of war's English victims, it inevitably sounds like opposition to authority, or perhaps literally Opposition to Government. One of the archetypal sentimental novels, Henry Mackenzie's *Man of Feeling* (1771), is pointedly topical when it criticizes the consequences of a war policy – press-ganging, conscription, the military punishment of flogging, and inadequate pensions – and when, like the same author's *Julia de Roubigné* (1777), it attacks the principle of colonialism. An interest in such causes was the logical outcome of art's frequently reiterated dedication to humanity. It was a period when the cast of villains was drawn from proud men representing authority, downwards from the House of Lords, the bench of bishops, judges, local magistrates, attorneys, to the stern father; when readers were invited to empathize with life's victims, especially poor but true-hearted lovers, and even to shed a tear with Burns for a cowering field-mouse, or with Sterne for a trapped fly or a dead ass.

We must hesitate before equating the kind of 'opinion' thus apparently refracted through art with 'public opinion' expressed through more conventional channels. It would be rash indeed to confuse these universal but disconcertingly stylized liberal sentiments with anything like a will to practical reform. Yet to some extent the interpretation of this unusually open kind of art requires a reading of its readers. If the public played an enlarged role in the moulding of art, we ought to be developing the techniques to understand this better: for we do not know much about how the reader in the age of sensibility understood his participatory role, nor whether his intellect or opinions were commonly engaged along with his sympathies, nor who read what. Robert Darnton has written an absorbing study of the distribution to French readers of one of the most explicitly liberal books of all, the *Encyclopédie*. He shows how the quarto edition, which sold for one third of the price of the original *Encyclopédie*, went preponderantly to members of those groups who were shortly to be among the sufferers from the revolution – landowners, rentiers, office-holders, clergy and the like – and more rarely to the entrepreneurs in commercial centres like Lyons. There is no single work in England of controversial significance comparable to the *Encyclopédie*, so that information about the circulation of any one book or type of books might not seem historically so revealing. Aesthetically, however, such information matters a great deal, for if a kind of compact existed between the book and its readers, we need to recover the terms of that lost understanding. To read individual books sensitively, and to make precise discriminations between one style and another, the student of literature in eighteenth-century England needs the knowledge of the reading public which the historian can give.

Sufficient records were kept and private letters and diaries written to enable us to achieve a kind of cultural map or groundplan for some at least of the better-defined circles of readers. Particulary interesting are the wealthy groups, often dominated by Dissenters, in the burgeoning provincial centres of Manchester, Liverpool, the North Midlands (Derby and Stoke), Birmingham and Bristol. At least as much is recorded about more private circles of lesser gentry and clergy rather than manufactur-ers, in and around cathedral cities like York and Lichfield, and resorts like Bath. Even without a special effort to assemble evidence it is clear that the tastes of the two types of provincial centres diverge. York, Lichfield and Bath are in the vanguard of the cult of sensibility; the manufacturing cities, with their professional involvement in the new science and technology, and their more pragmatic interest in a policy of peace, cultivate a variety of styles, among which the taste for sensibility is not salient.

The potter Josiah Wedgwood is conveniently representative; the position of his factory in North Staffordshire, between Manchester and Birmingham, enabled him to maintain contact with fellow scientists and entrepreneurs in both the other two centres. Wedgwood was patron to two local painters in a new vein of realism, the faithful rendering of prosaic subjects from a middle-class range of experience: George Stubbs, who portrayed horses with anatomical exactitude, and Joseph Wright of Derby, who painted 'conversation pieces' of families like Wedgwood's in their daily settings, as well as subjects associated with the new science and industry. Wedgwood's own artefacts, his mass-produced china, combine two aesthetic concepts. On the one hand they are practical utensils designed for daily use. On the other hand the prevailing stylistic influence is strongly classical: Wedgwood employed the strongly Neo-classical John Flaxman and borrowed design-ideas from the new Italian archaeological finds – the Greek key motif, the figures in bas-relief on his Portland vase, the flat Greek perspective and the emphasis on line rather than on colour. In acknowledgement of this large, generalized source of inspiration he called his factory Etruria.

It would of course be an error to assume that in fostering the new realism Wedgwood was being somehow progressive, while in turning to the Greeks he was not. Wedgwood's social and cultural life had an international dimension, and he maintained contact with political liberals in France and America. The kind of classicism Wedgwood went in for had strong intellectual links with the France of Voltaire and the *Encyclopédie*: its connotations were with reason and against obscurant-ism. In Germany, where French literature exerted a strong influence – since the German aristocracy preferred to speak and read French – the Enlightenment or classical French literary taste was perceived as more fashionable and more radical than homely burger literature, with its limited horizons and its tendency towards piety.

What is interesting about provincial England and about Wedgwood in particular, however, is the fact that classicism coexisted so comfortably with more homely tastes in the arts, which were indeed flourishing in just the same circles at the same time. Just as they fostered the anatomical realism of the painter Stubbs, Midlands circles began to demand and even to supply writing that recorded the external world with scientific fidelity. Several of Wedgwood's farflung acquaintances, including Anna Letitia Barbauld, *née* Aikin (a member of the Norwich Dissenting circle), Joseph Priestley, R. L. Edgeworth, Thomas Day and Thomas Beddoes (a Bristol radical of the 1790s), began to write for and about children, in response to their period's deep interest in the early growth of conscious-ness. By the late 1790s, Maria Edgeworth's innovatory realistic tales for children were making a contribution to fictional techniques in general, through their precise rendering of daily life and their close, sensitive perception of the thought-processes of their youthful protagonists. In 1800 Maria Edgeworth went on to produce *Castle Rackrent*, the fore-runner of a nineteenth-century genre, the naturalistic tale of provincial life. Social realism in prose fiction would appear to have been grounded in the habits and interests of the entrepreneurial class, centred in provincial cities like Norwich, Birmingham and Bristol.

In verse the cities produced less innovative work, though Sheffield fostered the competent middle-class poets James Montgomery (1771–1854) and, in the next generation, Ebenezer Elliott, 'the Corn-Law Rhymester' (1781-1849). It was left to more isolated country dwellers to bring the external world into poetry with a new precision: William Cowper, living in Olney, Buckinghamshire, in the 1780s; beginning in the same decade, George Crabbe, the self-taught surgeon from Aldeburgh, Suffolk; William and Dorothy Wordsworth, in the Quantocks and the Lakes, from the 1790s; and John Clare, the agricultural labourer's son from Northamptonshire, in the 1820s. At least it seems worthy of note that the concern for documentation so common in the early nineteenth century is confined in the eighteenth to particular circles, on the whole non-metropolitan and non-gentry.

There is some evidence that in other respects, too, the provinces in this period were more go-ahead in the arts. London writers might continue to use Pope's couplet, if the Johnson circle is anything to go by; as dramatists Goldsmith and Sheridan might ridicule the incursions of sentiment. The fact remained that outside London it was sentiment which was winning and keeping adherents. The cult of sensibility is associated with genteel figures, often provincial clergy and their families, like the circles of Anna Seward and Christopher Anstey. It finds expression in for example the occasional poetry of the *Gentleman's Magazine*, or in the 1780s taste for sad, melodious sonnets by Charlotte Smith and the Revd. William Bowles. Bath, the home of such groups, becomes an alternative capital of genteel taste, amusingly captured in the observations of Fanny Burney and Hester Thrale. But by about 1790 heterodoxy becomes more offensive, and there is no room for a second capital. The attacks on sentiment begin to develop an edge, part snobbish and part alarmist. The Della Cruscan circle of genteel English exiles in Florence, which Mrs Thrale joined in 1786, became an object of much ridicule for their affected sentimentalism, partly because they were associated with liberalism and partly, surely, because they were felt to be new men socially, that is provincial and parvenus. Jane Austen's Lucy Steele in *Sense and Sensibility*, a novel first sketched in 1795, has a provincial vulgarity and pretentiousness, and is also an ardent sentimentalist: the two traits may have appeared to the genteel conservative Jane Austen to go together.

Again, and for similar reasons, the most dedicated efforts to revive earlier English poetry seem to be associated with figures outside London, or, in London, not of the upper classes. This is, like sentiment, an anti-Johnsonian and anti-Augustan trend, as the London schoolboys Coleridge, Southey and Lamb perceived in the 1780s. Recalling the time in the first chapter of his *Biographia Literaria*, Coleridge distinguishes firmly between 'the school of Warton and the school of Johnson', and indicates that the middle-class schoolboys of Christ's Hospital were afire with the new fashion for the former – for 'the manly simplicity' of 'our elder poets', and against Pope's inheritance, which the young Coleridge thought of as a concern with men and manners in an artificial state of society.

The recovery of genuine early popular poetry would appear to have been a largely non-metropolitan activity. The provinces produced the antiquarians – the Northamptonshire vicar, Thomas Percy, who published his *Reliques of Ancient English Poetry* in 1765, and Joseph Ritson from Tyneside. In the 1770s and even more in the 1780s there is a rage for imitating these ballads, which lend themselves so readily to the portrayal of essential human feelings. Not quite all the new balladeers were provincial. William Blake, whose *Songs of Innocence* appeared in 1789, was a London printmaker. But it seems fair to say that on the whole the working men who succeeded in publishing poetry in this generation and the next were non-city dwellers, rustics – Burns and later Hogg in Scotland, Langhorne, Bloomfield and Clare in England. One factor in this achievement was that the rural poets had ready to hand a form which enabled them to utilize their backgrounds and the rhythms of their regional dialects. But it seems likely that in the English provinces and in Scotland the educated orders were also more responsive than Johnson's London to popular modes and to those who practised them.

Sometimes literature in the new and fashionably simple styles is radical in tone. Burns in the 1780s is a leveller: 'a man's a man for a' that.' Blake's sympathies in his *Songs* of the same decade are with the poor and oppressed, and against war. In his series of novels of the 1780s and 1790s, the Derbyshire papermaker Robert Bage regularly lampoons the aristocracy, contrasting its failings with the sober virtues of the middle classes. In Book IV of *The Task* (1785), Cowper criticizes the wealthy and represents them as the corrupters of the poor:

> Excess, the scrofulous and itchy plague,
> That seizes first the opulent, descends
> To the next rank contagious, and in time
> Taints downwards all the graduated scale
> Of order, from the chariot to the plough.

But it would be unsafe to jump to the conclusion that the message of writing such as this was always perceived as actively radical. The morality of Cowper at least among this group made a strong appeal to the conservative, traditionally Christian strain in the gentry and the prosperous middle class, which responded to the coming Evangelical movement, and sought a spiritual regeneration within individuals rather than by disturbing the present hierarchical order of things. It is no accident that Cowper was a favourite of Jane Austen's. His kind of concern with the simple and humble of the earth, the blessedly meek, need not be in the least politically inflammatory.

If one were now to assess dispassionately the ideological tendency of the artistic idiom of the 1780s, one might well conclude that the more rousing (contemporary progressives would have said 'energizing') radical statements emerged from artists who belonged in the Greek revival, Neoclassicism proper, the *lingua franca* of the international Enlightenment. In painting, the stark primitivism of this manner, its grand gestures, its focus on the single human image, seemed to lend themselves to a very basic, and, after 1790, very pointed political message. Although in his *Songs* Blake might evoke the homely ballad, the eloquent, suffering human figures of his Neoclassical paintings and prints indicate how that cultivated manner might be even better adapted to transmit his revolutionary ardour. The dignity and heroic aspirations of this style had polemic advantages, among the various styles which enacted the rejection of civilization in favour of primitivism, and so were notional models for revolution in the social and political spheres too. Not that Neoclassicists and painters of heroic historical topics necessarily themselves saw in their work a pointed political reference. It seems appropriate that the Frenchman J.-L. David supplied the archetypal painting of the revolution with his 'Oath of the Horatii', a literally classical subject, the three brothers dedicating themselves to the service of the republic – for David painted it in 1785, before the French republic existed and before the artist had articulated his own radical sympathies.

All the more innovatory styles of 1760–90 were to fall under suspicion for political reasons in an England at war with a revolutionary enemy. Alarmists during the next decade at different moments detected subversion in an entire range of fashions acceptable in the 1780s, from the cult of tears to the folk ballad, from criticism of lords, clergymen, lawyers and fathers to praise of widows, asses and needy knife-grinders. The Revd. T. J. Mathias's *Pursuits of Literature* (1794–7) is a satirical verse anthology of literary fashions which had come to seem subversive or at least unsound. In her juvenilia of the 1790s and in her three novels begun in that decade, Jane Austen derided the taste for sensibility as selfish and indulgent. Like other Christian critics, Coleridge in 1797 violently censured M. G. Lewis's Gothic *Monk*, and increasingly found the rage for Gothic literature feverish, sickly and subversive. In their poetry, Coleridge and Wordsworth at the same time began to turn away from

Enlightenment universalism to a concern with the private and domestic.

In England the least suspect of these cults of the Enlightenment during the first decade of counter-revolution was, strangely enough, the antique. The explanation for its surprising ideological neutrality for the English counter-revolutionary generation may be that the classical had been disseminated more widely down the social scale in England than in Germany, and was not so explicitly associated with Voltairean France and with a progressive, freethinking element in the aristocracy. Before the war was over, allusions to the Greek and Roman republics certainly began to convey, as we shall see, an emphatic message of pro-French or radical sympathies; but for the informed public at large, and for critics in particular, the notion of the classical also retained far safer connotations – with the traditional, established educational syllabus at the public schools and at Oxford and Cambridge, or with the concept of 'correctness' and submission to an inherited system of rules.

The more fervid alarmist reaction against sensibility and the Gothic is not easy to account for; unless, through their known appeal to a less cultivated, more middle-class readership, they carried a distinct whiff of *popularity*. Enlightenment openness, its wide and instant appeal to its audience, took on sinister overtones in the age of the *levée en masse* and of sympathetic, provocative toasts at English reformist meetings to 'our sovereign lord, the people'. Poetry in a popular style might be dangerous if it became an ideological weapon in the popular cause: as indeed intermittently it was, for example in Burns's indignant response to the savage sentences handed down on a group of Scottish radicals in 1793 – 'Scots wha' hae wi' Wallace bled'. Thus, though a cultural witchhunt was a feature of the second half of the 1790s, it became rabid only where attempts to subvert the population at large were suspected. Godwin's *Political Justice* (1793) and *Memoir of Mary Wollstonecraft* (1798), together with what was known of the work of radical feminists like Mary Wollstonecraft and Mary Hays, were felt to constitute an outrage specifically because they were taken for efforts to subvert the institution of marriage and the chastity of the female; and the susceptible, under-educated female reader was an object of particularly tender critical solicitude. Tom Paine's *Rights of Man* (1791–2) and even Wordsworth's far less overtly offensive *Lyrical Ballads* (1798) became notorious because they were directed, or appeared to be directed, at a simple (and thus politically unsound) public. The real relationships between artworks and their sectarian readership in the 1780s were probably very different, for our limited evidence has been sufficient to show that neither the Gothic nor sentiment was a characteristic taste of the group who were most actively incubating reform in that decade – the Dissenters. Hysteria has its own logic; the hitherto dominant *public* was transformed by political events in the 1790s into the prime object of fear, the *people*. The necessity to reconstitute the arts without the people became a driving force behind creative endeavour in the post-revolutionary decade.

2 Art for the people in the revolutionary decade: Blake, Gillray and Wordsworth

A representative artistic venture of the late eighteenth century in England was inaugurated in November 1786 at a dinner party given by the London printmaker and entrepreneur, Josiah Boydell. The host was the nephew of Alderman (later Lord Mayor) John Boydell, who had already made a small fortune from commissioning an engraving of Benjamin West's 'Death of Wolfe'. The new idea was to build a gallery to house an exhibition of scenes from Shakespeare's plays, painted by the best artists of the day. The public would be invited to subscribe to the series of engravings made of the paintings, and to buy a lavish new illustrated edition of the text.

The Boydells were out to take their share of what had become an important international commodity, of which England had been hitherto an importer. The reputation of Shakespeare, growing throughout Europe since mid-century, provided the perfect opportunity to put English engraving on the same footing as that of France. For the painters whom they meant to commission, the Boydells' hopes were equally grandiose. Shakespeare's plays afforded the subject matter for a national school of historical painting in the most elevated and prestigious of contemporary styles.

The first part of this venture in marrying art to commerce – the Gallery – opened in 1789 and seemed a considerable success. The most eminent of living artists, Sir Joshua Reynolds, the first President of the Royal Academy, was struck by the diversity of the effect achieved, which he took as evidence of a truly Shakespearean variety among his contemporaries. Reynolds himself exhibited, along with West and James Barry, the two other leading historical painters, and most other artists of note, including Thomas Stothard, Joseph Wright of Derby, and Angelica Kauffmann. Some reputations were enhanced, notably that of Henry Fuseli, who brought to Shakespeare (whom he loved) an idiosyncratic combination of *Sturm und Drang* intensity and Michelangelesque power. Side by side with sophisticated painters trained in international styles were artists working in a more homely native tradition. Francis Wheatley, who supplied scenes from *The Winter's Tale* and *The Comedy of*

Errors, was the son of a master-tailor, who had served his apprenticeship decorating Vauxhall Gardens; posterity knows him for his 'Cries of Old London' (1792–5), which for two centuries has graced many a table mat and chocolate box. Robert Smirke, who also rose from humble origins, provided twenty-six pictures, mostly featuring comic characters, and, in the age of Maurice Morgann's celebrated essay on Falstaff, gave that character a permanent visual image. It seemed in the early days that the enterprise of the 'commercial Maecenas', as Boydell grandiloquently became known, was enriching the artist, and bringing him in immediate, unprecedented ways to the public. Those who flocked into the Shakespeare Gallery in the early 1790s, those who from 1791 began to receive the large and small prints on subscription, were indeed the public, the ultimate patrons of a new age.

And not before time. The question of who should patronize the arts in an age of humanity had been raised in the England of Wilkes, as it had in the France of Diderot. Wilkes in the Commons in 1777 demanded more generous funds for the British Museum, better facilities for the public to use it, and the establishment of a national gallery of paintings. Diderot's theories, that art should contribute to public morality, and that the artist should not be subject to a hierarchy under a cliquish Academy, were soon to be advanced in the French National Assembly by the leading radical artist, the Neoclassicist J.-L. David. The artist's ideal public role and his commercial opportunity to sell his pictures may logically have been two distinct issues, but they did not always appear so. In England as in France, in these lucrative but also highly competitive years, aspiring painters and engravers were often radical, because they associated the entrenched and dictatorial leaders of their profession with the 'System' in general.

The Boydell experience testifies to the confident, commercially based sense of expansion in the arts at the end of the 1780s. But, as Boydell reflected sadly in 1804, while he prepared to sell off the paintings for far less than he had paid for them, the boom had been shortlived. He blamed above all the war with France in 1793, which cut him off from the international market on which he had relied. 'The unhappy Revolution ... cut up by the roots that revenue from the Continent... Flanders, Holland and Germany, who, no doubt, supplied the rest of Europe, were the great marts: but alas! they are now no more!' The firm contributed to its own troubles by adopting cheap engraving techniques, and by failing to keep careful records of subscribers. But when by 1796 it became clear that the Boydell scheme was in trouble, it also seemed that the very idea of such an ambitious popular enterprise had fallen out of fashion. In part it was tainted by the aura of radicalism surrounding individual artists like

Barry, Fuseli, Smirke and Joseph Banks. More fundamentally, the heterogeneity, the exuberance, the hint of the primitive, the sense of a nation's life at all levels – the very essence at that date of a *Shakespearean* revival – had lost its public appeal.

Commercially the curve of Blake's career resembles that of the Boydell project, though Blake was not, to his chagrin, employed by Boydell. His first employer was the engraver James Basire, who had a commission from the patrician Society of Antiquaries to make a visual record of the tombs of Westminster Abbey and their contents. As an apprentice, Blake was set to delve into England's primitive past, and it gave him a number of fashionable topics for water-colours, among which the oppression of two women, 'The Penance of Jane Shore' (*c*.1779; another version, 1793) and 'The Ordeal of Queen Emma' (*c*.1793) are subjects highly typical of the age. The imitation of earlier models again provides a rationale behind his varied first literary production, *Poetical Sketches* (1783), which, as is often the way with juvenilia, can come near to pastiche: of the Gothic (*Fair Elenor*), of the ballads made popular by Percy and Chatterton (*Gwin, King of Norway*), of Elizabethan narrative poetry and drama (*An Imitation of Spenser*, the Shakespearean *Blind-man's Buff* and *King Edward the Third*). *The Songs of Innocence* (1789–90), especially in their early versions, also have that deliberate naïveté which marks the era of essentialism.

The Westminster Abbey experience might well have induced Blake, like many other artisan-artists, to develop in the most obviously native primitive tradition, the Gothic. As a writer he did indeed remain deeply influenced by the fundamentalist forms most accessible to him in youth, especially the Old Testament, the translation of the Icelandic *Edda* affixed to Mallet's *Northern Antiquities* (1770), and Macpherson's Ossian epics (1762–3). As a graphic artist he found other models of the primal. He knew and was much influenced by Henry Fuseli, whose decisive training had been in a Rome saturated by the theories of Winckelmann and Piranesi. Fuseli made an internationalist of Blake, who himself hoped to travel on the Continent in 1783–4. Like other ambitious students, he evidently thought in terms of an art marketable to the educated and wealthy, and he put himself through a classic apprenticeship to the best models. His most famous design, 'Glad Day' or 'Albion Rose' (1795), is, as the sketches dating from about 1780 show, derived from the 'Vitruvian figure', which was used by the Roman architect Vitruvius and by his followers in the Italian Renaissance to demonstrate the proportions of the human body. In the original diagram the figure stands within a circle, itself within a measured square, and implies that

Man is the measure of a mathematically proportioned universe. Small wonder that a recent art-critic has remarked of this borrowed concept, that it 'places Blake right in the midstream of the humanist, rational, academic tradition, however much he might later rebel against its restricted vision'. Classical Antiquity gave him one of the most central of his images, the nude male figure, dominating and expressive. Classicism seemed to guarantee moreover a cultivated public who could read the language of his pictures.

But, as the Boydell enterprise suggests, the readiest market was probably felt to lie in prints and books, items which could be displayed in the well-to-do home, aimed at what we might think of as the coffee-table public. Early in the 1780s Blake set up business with his wife Catherine as an engraver and printmaker. Their business foundered, and Blake's subsequent failure in 1786–90 to be employed by Boydell, suddenly the major patron of the day, was more serious still. Yet from 1789 the times still must have struck Blake as auspicious for his own experiment, books for which he supplied text, illustrations and engraving. The great series of illuminated books, from the *Songs of Innocence* in 1789 to the *Book of Los* in 1795, marks the central phase in Blake's career, which includes most of the best literary work and leads naturally to the great series of coloured prints of 1795, 'Elohim Creating Adam', 'Satan Exulting over Eve', 'God Judging Adam', 'Nebuchadnezzar', and 'Newton'. Blake's years are thus the Boydell years, and the play of market forces to which both were subject enables us to see them as fellow-victims rather than as rivals.

The years of Blake's great achievement also correspond with the revolutionary ferment. His apprenticeship had been served in the era of gentlemanly reform, the 1780s, when the dignified individualism to which reformers and oligarchs both subscribed was matched, as we have seen, by the tone and preoccupations of the contemporary arts. His maturity coincided with the rapid growth of a radical movement, its extension into parts of the urban working class, and its disintegration. Within a few years, the first half of the 1790s, the radical artist fell out of step with his identifiable public, and lost his place in the cultural mainstream.

At the beginning of the decade enthusiasm for reform and fellow-feeling for the French revolutionaries was marked at all levels of the population except perhaps the very lowest. Aristocrats from the circles around Charles James Fox and the first Marquess of Lansdowne, and gentry and manufacturers all over the country formed associations like the London Friends of the People; sometimes their zeal (as was the case with Erasmus Darwin's at Derby) outran that of the local populace. But it was also significant that artisan radicals now made autonomous groups, in London most numerously but also in other growing centres of population like Leeds, Sheffield, Nottingham, Manchester and Glasgow, and their concerns were no longer limited to piecemeal parliamentary reform. Blake, the journeyman engraver and son of a hosier, knew many members of London radical circles and shared the social origins of the more artisan. He was not, apparently, a paying member of the London Corresponding Society, run by the shoemaker Thomas Hardy, nor of the more intellectual and urbane Society for Constitutional Information (S.C.I.), which in 1792 was revitalized by John Wilkes's old associate, the philologist John Horne Tooke. Blake's friend and fellow-engraver William Sharp was, however, a member of the S.C.I., which from 1792 to 1794 had some claim to be the powerhouse of London radicalism; Sharp was one of the Londoners taken up for treason in 1794 (though in the end he was not indicted) along with Horne Tooke, Hardy, the lecturer John Thelwall and the playwright Thomas Holcroft. While Sharp evidently had more the temperament of an activist, Blake seems always to have been on the fringes of the same worlds: he and his wife for example attended meetings in 1788–9 of a religious sect with advanced ideas, the Swedenborgian New Church, of which Sharp seems to have been a member. Blake had links, again, through his publisher Joseph Johnson with a group of London middle-class writers, artists and intellectuals whose sympathies in 1790–2 were strongly pro-French, including Fuseli, Priestley, Tom Paine, William Godwin and Mary Wollstonecraft. Blake's ambience helps to explain why the illustrated books he produced during the heady years of radicalism, 1790–4, are *revolutionary* works. *The Marriage of Heaven and Hell, The French Revolution, The Visions of the Daughters of Albion, America, Europe* and *The First Book of Urizen* emanate at a particular time from a society which believes it is seeing the end of an old world and the coming of a new dawn.

At this time especially it would be a pity to read Blake as though he were singlehandedly the author of his own text. The corporate author is the urban sub-class which emerged through its opposition to Britain's national policy. The Dissenters were the first to give definition to the movement, with their parliamentary campaign of 1788–90. After 1790 interest in the French reformers grew, to culminate in 1792 as the French declared a republic and affirmed their support for people everywhere who wished to throw off their rulers. The very internationalism of the revolution now suggested (to English alarmists, at least) that its sympathizers in England were enemies of the English state and potential revolutionaries. Divisions in English political life reached a rare bitterness after 1 February 1793, when England entered the war against revolutionary France, for English radicals vociferously continued to oppose hostilities against a popular, libertarian opponent. Blake's books contribute to the controversy because they are angrily pacifist, and explicitly opposed to government and to all symbols of authority. Their remarkable settings interpret imaginatively the internationalism and universality of mankind's hour. While in a few years Coleridge and Wordsworth, in response to the loyalist reaction, would emphasize local loyalties, English places and customs, family and friends, Blake conveys no feeling for the English plot of ground. Instead he ranges to America, Europe and Africa, but also out to the furthest known point of the solar system, to the planet discovered in 1781 by Herschel, Georgium Sidus or Uranus; backwards in time to the Creation of the world, and onwards to the Last Trump. It is an artist's projection of a moment when boundaries appeared to fall, when fraternal greetings and delegates were sent by the London Corresponding Society to the French Revolutionary Assembly, and man's civil history until the present day seemed bound in one great cycle, now to be decisively broken, of oppression and revolt.

English radicalism moved through a number of phases in the decade in which Blake, with the idiosyncrasy of genius, gives back its flavour. The Dissenters' campaign for reform of the late 1780s was not only constitutional in its methods but still traditionally English in spirit. Its spokesmen (and Blake in his art made one) traced the roots of English liberty back to a simple past, Anglo-Saxon times, before the imposition of the twin hierarchies of aristocracy and church, when Englishmen were free and equal. A theologian like Priestley conveys the Dissenters' stubborn individualism when he rejects all authority but the Bible, his reason and his conscience. *Political Justice* (1793), by the former Dissenting minister, William Godwin, can be viewed as a pioneering work in a new intellectual movement, anarchism; but, with its emphasis on the 'sacred and indefeasible right of private judgement', it also draws deeply on the old feeling inherited from the Commonwealthmen and the sects. Blake expresses it with simpler force in his vivid sense of identification with the Isaiah who had not actually seen God, 'but . . . as I was then persuaded, and remain confirmed, that the voice of honest indignation is the voice of God, I cared not for consequences but wrote' (*Marriage of Heaven and Hell*, p.112*).

It is a quality of feeling which links Blake with the native tradition of Priestley and his fellow-Dissenter Richard Price, or even the ambivalent

---

* Editions used for quotations are listed with books for further reading on p.198 below.

Anglo-American Paine. Unlike Godwin, Blake seems largely untouched by sophisticated French scepticism in the vein of Holbach and Voltaire. Though he follows fashion in using mythological material, Blake mythologizes in a far less rational spirit than the current generation of French intellectuals, freethinkers like Volney and Charles Dupuis, who were anthropologizing religion out of existence. The native English reforming tradition was pragmatic, in keeping with its hopes of constitutional progress, and this presumably explains why Blake remained so far resistant to the kind of inquiry into mythology and comparative religion which commonly had as its aim the dethroning of religion altogether. But he was no more susceptible to apologists for religion, even when they presented an imaginatively seductive case. Blake was acquainted with the antiquarian Thomas Taylor, who in his book *The Mystical Initiations of Hymns of Orpheus* (1787) gave a fanciful account of such Alexandrian neo-Platonists as Plotinus, Porphyry and Iamblichus. Coleridge claimed in 1796 to find these early Christian mystics (in Taylor's interpretation of them) deeply satisfying, but Coleridge was writing in disillusioned times; earlier Priestley and Paine taught their admirers to suspect traditions that involved the handing down of secrets and mystery, on the grounds that they lent themselves to 'priestcraft' and 'imposition'. When in his *Book of Thel* (1789) Blake mimics the neo-Platonic myth that the soul journeys out of light into a human world of darkness, suffering and loss, he exposes that state of innocence as a virginal fear of engagement, and proclaims the real world to be one where matter is acceptable, even holy. Indeed other writings confirm that Blake's position in the early phase of English radicalism, up to say the Treason Trials of autumn 1794, was roughly that of the intellectual circle, dominated by Dissenters and ex-Dissenters, which Blake mingled with at Joseph Johnson's house. His *Visions of the Daughters of Albion* (1791–3) upholds two of their libertarian campaigns, the emancipation of slaves and the emancipation of women. *The French Revolution* (1790–1) and *America* (1791–3) are mythologized historical narratives celebrating the two actual revolutions. But above all Blake shows himself the spokesman for his group and age in the masterpiece of these years, *The Marriage of Heaven and Hell* (1790–2).

In its dramatized conflict between null, hypocritical, law-abiding Angels and energizing revolutionary Devils, *The Marriage* is a direct rendering of current political tension. It has a strong scent of specific allusion, in the style of contemporary caricature. The Puritan Milton, and Milton's heroic rebel Satan, provide a convenient classic base for the action, imagery and language. Fuseli in 1790 was planning to rival Boydell's Shakespeare Gallery with a Milton Gallery, which was to have manifestly radical connections. Fuseli's illustrations were to be engraved by Blake and by William Sharp; the text would be given to the humanitarian poet, William Cowper, to edit; Joseph Johnson was to be the publisher. The edition never appeared, but when in *The Marriage* Blake writes with humorous approval of those most celebrated rebels of literature, Milton's Devils, and when he alludes gleefully to a printing house in hell, he is unmistakably bringing to mind the radical literary scheme of his own politicized coterie. His handling of the Angels reveals who he thought the enemy were, and so defines his political position even more clearly.

In the early 1780s the millenarian religious group influenced by the Swedish philosopher and mystic Emmanuel Swedenborg (1688–1772) had set themselves up in London as an informal organization, the Theosophical Society, rather than as a Church. At this stage the Swedenborgians had a decidedly progressive appeal (evidently felt by Sharp and Blake) both because of their informality and because of the radical emphasis of their doctrine that Christ, the Man, was Divine. In 1787, however, the English Swedenborgians opted to form a church, in the process of doing which they gradually acquired such symptoms of institutional status as baptism, the ordination of ministers, and a catechism for the children. Moreover, their effective leader in London, Robert Hindmarsh, the minister of the New Church at East Cheap, was by 1792 assiduously attempting to clear Swedenborgianism of its earlier taint of radicalism by entering a protest in the minutes of his church's annual conference, 'against all such principles of infidelity and democracy as were then circulating in the country'.

A branch of the New Church was set up in Birmingham, where Joseph Priestley was the most celebrated of Dissenters, and in the late 1780s relations between Priestley and the Swedenborgians were cordial. But Priestley, for whom the tests of a doctrine were reason and scripture, remained a Christian in a very different tradition. His well-known and characteristic *History of the Corruptions of Christianity* (2 vols, 1782) had after all contained an analysis of the accretions of early Christianity, which to Priestley included the deification of Christ as well as the idolatrous cults of saints and angels. It was a book which represented the Established Church as essentially decadent, a typical institution of an advanced society, and the agent of an élite caste of governors and priests whose interest was always to exclude and manage the mass of mankind. In 1791 Priestley issued a pamphlet criticizing the New Church on some characteristic grounds: he found Swedenborg irrational (in his belief that he was specially inspired) and unscriptural (in his assertion of the divinity of Christ).

In that same summer of 1791 popular feeling hostile to Dissent, or rather to those Dissenters who were known radicals and reformers, flared up in Birmingham, incited, it was widely believed, by the local clergy. On Bastille Day, 14 July 1791, a loyalist mob wrecked Priestley's home at Fairhill with its books, papers and scientific equipment, and Priestley, along with some others of his persuasion, spent several days virtually in hiding for fear of further violence. The Revd. J. Proud, stated minister of the Swedenborgian Temple of the New Jerusalem in Birmingham, reacted to these events by anticipating his London colleague, Hindmarsh, and publicly disassociating himself from Priestley's politics.

The Marriage of Heaven and Hell is among other things a topical assault on the backsliding from progressivism of the Swedenborgian Church, represented by Blake's angels. Blake is aware of the dispute between the Swedenborgians and Priestley, and he takes Priestley's side. They are Priestley's written criticisms that he uses when he sneers at Swedenborg for his pretensions to originality ('he has written all the old falsehoods' (p.119)) and to divine inspiration (Swedenborg's conversations with supernatural beings are parodied in the 'Memorable Fancies'). Blake also appears on occasion to glance at the pivotal Swedenborgian belief in Jesus as identical with Jehovah. But the last read like sidelong references rather than criticisms, for Blake's quarrel with the Swedenborgians is far less doctrinal than Priestley's; it reflects the total situation of the New Church, its realignment on the side of authority in place of its old inspirational radical simplicity. It is probably fair to suppose that the satirical attack of *The Marriage* draws strength from the political, intellectual leadership offered by the whole of Priestley's career, that thirty-year campaign in favour of individualism and against priestcraft, authority, and 'corruptions'. Ironically it is the recent renegade from the libertarian position, the aptly named New Church, that becomes in Blake's hands the representative of all corrupt Church institutions, its 'angel' that stands for all clerical rule-makers:

A MEMORABLE FANCY

Once I saw a devil in a flame of fire, who arose before an angel that sat on a cloud; and the devil uttered these words:

'The worship of God is honouring his gifts in other men, each according to his genius, and loving the greatest men best. Those who envy or calumniate great men hate God, for there is no other God'.

The angel, hearing this, became almost blue, but mastering himself he grew yellow, and at last white pink and smiling, and then replied,

'Thou idolater, is not God One, and is he not visible in Jesus Christ? And has not Jesus Christ given his sanction to the law of ten commandments; and are not all other men fools, sinners, and nothings?'

The devil answered, 'Bray a fool in a mortar with wheat, yet shall not his folly be beaten out of him. If Jesus Christ is the greatest man, you ought to love him in the greatest degree. Now hear how he has given his sanction to the law of ten commandments: did he not mock at the Sabbath, and so mock the Sabbath's God? Murder those who were murdered because of him? Turn away the law from the woman taken in adultery? Steal the labour of others to support him? Bear false witness when he omitted making a defence before Pilate? Covet when he prayed for his disciples, and when he bid them shake off the dust of their feet against such as refused to lodge them? I tell you no virtue can exist without breaking these ten commandments. Jesus was all virtue, and acted from impulse, not from rules.'

(pp. 120–1)

It was characteristic of libertarian thinking in the eighteenth century that Swedenborg had turned his attention to the question of sexual liberty and the religious code. In his *Delights of wisdom concerning conjugal love* (translated into English in 1789), he had cautiously implied that where a legal union had failed, men's sexual drives would lead them to take adulterous partners, and that in certain circumstances such unions ought to be accepted. In 1789, after a sharp struggle, the East Cheap Conference rejected the proposition that such licence ought to be permitted to its congregation. But the acceptance of the natural, together with the rejection of the Church's authoritarian insistence on elevating soul above body, is deeply engrained in radicalism at this period, especially where the French influence is strong. 'Energy is the only life and is from the body' (*Marriage*, p.105). Here again, the Blake whose circle of acquaintance included Godwin, who in *Political Justice* (1793) argued against the institution of marriage, and Paine, the scoffer at religion of *The Age of Reason* (1794–5), can weave the particular incident into the general revolution. The time has come for breaking the tablets of repression, the stony laws, which a church only thirty-three years old has already inscribed:

Empire is no more! And now the lion & wolf shall cease.

CHORUS

Let the priests of the raven of dawn no longer, in deadly black, with hoarse note curse the sons of joy. Nor his accepted brethren whom, tyrant, he calls free, lay the bound or build the roof. Nor pale religious lechery call that virginity that wishes but acts not.

For everything that lives is holy.   (p.124)

Broadly speaking Blake's position would seem at this time to have resembled that of the anticlerical and sexually libertarian Paine and Godwin, along with the anti-institutional Priestley, but his cast of mind has none of their educated rationalism. His roots are clearly in the artisan world, Protestant, radical, Bible-reading, to which the Swedenborgians appealed before they organized themselves. Blake retained the Biblical tone and the artisan flavour, but over the next few years, as English radicalism broke up and changed its quality, he lost his intellectual circle. The government moved against radicals ineffectually in the Treason Trials of 1794, but much more successfully with two 'Gagging Acts' of November 1795, which drastically restricted what public meetings could be held and what could safely be said at them. The years before 1797 saw a losing struggle by the lecturer John Thelwall to maintain contact with the provincial groups and to preach his temperate message: an end to the war, a start to egalitarian Painite reform (as opposed to violent revolution). Already the middle-class supporters of radicalism had largely fallen away. By 1797 almost all the mass following had dispersed as well, and the remaining radicals were increasingly violent and desperate men, largely out of touch and probably out of sympathy with the English population, often Irishmen implicated in plots for real revolution in Ireland. Driven underground by repressive legislation, they now came near to meeting the stereotype which English alarmists had long believed in. Cells of jacobin conspirators plotting to overthrow the state existed in 1798 and 1799, though the fear they excited was out of all proportion to their strength.

Blake's roots in radical Dissent are deeper and stronger than his connection with the French-type intellectualism of men like Fuseli, so that his position must have been affected by the changing religious alignment of the English radical movement. After the hardening of opinion against all progressives in the second half of 1792, it was clear that the Dissenters could no longer expect a favourable vote in Parliament; the great majority took the route of the New Church, declared their loyalty, and dropped out of the campaign for reform. Paine fled to France in 1792; Priestley emigrated to America in 1794; the other leading Dissenting polemicist, Richard Price, had died in 1791. By 1793 what was left of the radical movement was becoming increasingly identified with the republican, regicide and atheistic French. The radical classics of the mid-1790s, Godwin's *Political Justice* and Paine's *Age of Reason*, seemed subversive at a profounder level than any campaign for legal relief the Dissenters had ever engaged in, for they challenged secular and religious authority at its very roots, in the individual's simple habit of belief. English radicalism had been so deeply involved with Protestant sectarianism for at least two centuries that the development was likely to constitute a crisis for a man like Blake, regardless of government repression and of the mounting ill-will of the loyalist majority. His friend Sharp took up with two of the millenarian cults which now began to burgeon, becoming a follower of the prophet Richard Brothers in 1795 and of Joanna Southcott in 1801. In preaching an imminent Second Coming, the Kingdom of God soon to be established on earth, these cults offered a promise of Utopia, an end to hardship, injustice and the present order of things, but by divine rather than human agency. It is clear that many artisan radicals who had been exalted by the visions of Glad Day in the late 1780s and early 1790s now followed this route. Belonging to a newly formed sect offered many of the same comforts as belonging to a Painite reading circle – friendship, mental stimulus and mutual help from fellow idealists; the hope of a better life to come, here rather than hereafter. At the same time such loosely organized religious groups were reassuringly homely, simple and traditional, drawing upon the Bible and upon folk wisdom and folk practice. Joanna Southcott, a domestic servant from Coleridge's Devon village of Ottery St Mary, gave advice about cures for sickness in the spirit and language of a local Wise Woman, which is almost what she was. Though Blake did not receive Joanna's seal, his work in the first decade of the new century has the flavour of private world-building, of internalized religious comfort, that she and prophets like her communicated to their followers.

Events so ordered it that as an artist Blake passed through sharp transitions in a short decade. His earlier graphic art, with its affective topics, its visual reduction to a linear minimum, had belonged, like his ballad style in the *Songs of Innocence*, to the common idiom of the Enlightenment. The language of the *Marriage of Heaven and Hell* was in its way a culmination of the stylistic manner of the 1780s. Behind the 'Proverbs of Hell' especially were Fuseli's *Aphorisms on Man*, translated and adapted from the aphorisms of Fuseli's Swiss friend Lavater, and in this age of essentialism the aphorism arrived at the irreducibly minimal. It escaped from the analytical, prosy element of extended form; it was subject to no law but the artist's inspiration. Blake had learnt his style, and however some of his opinions might change he could not revise his fundamental notions of art. In his idiosyncratic way he continued to practise the Neoclassical doctrine of imitation, though increasingly with the Bible as his model. The *First Book of Urizen* (1794) is his imitation of Genesis and Exodus, for which the Biblical alternative name is the First Book of Moses. He calls a group of his works the Prophetic Books.

But as opinion fragmented in the 1790s, and the old expansive belief in one market, national, even international, was lost in bitter divisiveness, Blake's great strength, his brilliant capacity to adapt Neoclassical precept to his own experience, became his vulnerable Achilles heel. The Bible, that characteristically artisan source of inspiration, must have given him a quaint, homespun air to wealthy buyers brought up in rationalist or even sceptical ways of thinking, and accustomed to jeer at manifestations of popular feeling like Methodism. How much more socially acceptable to the art-consuming classes was the classicism of Fuseli and Flaxman, with their impeccable cultivated spheres of reference, the Renaissance and ancient Greece. And how infinitely more reassuring their politics: for Fuseli quickly became apolitical, and Flaxman was a conservative. Blake alienated one kind of potential patron with his 'enthusiasm', another with his black and bitter popular humour, a third with his obscurity, and by mid-decade almost all the world with his radicalism.

As an artist working for the market, Blake crashed about the time Boydell did, in 1795. He published no more substantial original work for a decade. The later 1790s are the years of his great book illustrations, of Young and Gray, but the *de luxe* edition of Young's *Night Thoughts* foundered because of the economic climate. Though Blake continued intermittently to exhibit at the Royal Academy until 1808, he seems to have sold nothing there after 1785. As a poet he turned his attention, with *Vala, or the Four Zoas* (begun 1797), to the development of an increasingly private mythology, which is less topical than the earlier work and indeed begins to seem effectively de-politicized. In 1800 he retired to a depressing, neurotic isolation in a country cottage, funded by the gentlemanly, Whiggish man of letters William Hayley, and henceforth consolidated his reputation for religiosity and downright crankiness. His imagination was increasingly possessed by the Old Testament and by the world of arcane Biblical learning, including that very school of Alexandrian, neo-Platonic immaterialists, the favourite topic of his acquaintance Thomas Taylor, which Priestley and the younger Blake would have anathematized as a corruption of the Church. True to the reticence of the counter-revolutionary period, Blake began to value the mystery and secrecy which in his revolutionary period he denounced as the characteristic of priestcraft.

Many of Blake's subsequent admirers have not merely preferred the later work, but seen its mystery and compensatory world-building as the heart of this great artist. They have turned his work into a single comprehensive system, devised by Blake on his own, instead of seeing it as a reflection of group experience which underwent profound transformations. The later books, *Vala, Milton* and *Jerusalem*, are enormously powerful and deeply expressive of their age: 'Romantic', perhaps, in the new German sense, like very few other English productions of the immediate period. But in their turning away from the material world of political action and the senses five there is also the shadow of a collective frustration and postponed, if not lost, hope. The natural world of immanent magic in *The Book of Thel* is replaced by a fallen world through which the exiled soul travels in pain. Blake has foregone the delight in individualism, the energy, the prospect of fulfilment both sensual and political, that makes the poems and illustrations before 1795 so exhilarating. Intellectually he retained the configuration of the British radical in the changed circumstances of the long-drawn-out Napoleonic Wars. He detested the war with France and to the end saw it as a conspiracy of the English aristocratic and commercial interest. Nevertheless, his later work in fact shares the pietism and (in scriptural contexts) the literalism that overtook so many of the followers of the defeated radical movement during the ascendancy of the counter-revolution.

It was certainly not Blake's politics that attracted what patrons he found after Hayley. The clerk Thomas Butts kept him going in return for the bulk of his output from 1799 to 1810: Blake executed for Butts a series of more than eighty tempera and water-colour illustrations to the Bible, small enough to hang in a modest home. They are less preoccupied than early work with the authoritarian figure of God the Father; more with a merciful Christ. After 1818 he was helped by John Linnell, another painter, who found enough commissions to occupy Blake until his death in 1827. The Linnell circle of artists included John Varley and the more substantial figure of Samuel Palmer (1805–81), men who shared the intense religious enthusiasm which was experienced so widely in all classes in the early 1820s. It was the inspirational side of Blake that they cultivated, and made for the first time acceptable in upper-class circles such as those frequented by Henry Crabb Robinson, the friend of Wordsworth, whose diary is testimony to Blake's success. Blake seems to have teased his distinctly gullible admirers, by evoking for their benefit rather more visions than he really had, but he also responded to their tastes. It is significant that his last two series of book illustrations are for his most esoteric, learned texts, the latter of which was associated in the postwar period with orthodoxy and submission to a divine order: Virgil's *Pastorals* (1820–1) and Dante's *Divine Comedy* (1824–7). Certainly Blake was critical of much that he found in Dante, particularly the role assigned to the Church; but the critique of institutions so central to *The Marriage of Heaven and Hell* has given place to the exaltation of spirituality. The appeal of Blake's later work to his young contemporaries is nowhere more clear than in the case of his woodcut engravings to Virgil, the most influential work he ever did. The old primitivism is perfectly matched here with the new piety. Small wonder that Samuel Palmer, who now seems so representative an early Victorian, found his inspiration in them:

They are visions of little dells, and nooks, and corners of Paradise; models of the exquisitest pitch of intense poetry. I thought of their light and shade, and looking upon them I found no word to describe it. Intense depth, solemnity, and vivid brilliancy only coldly and partially describe them. There is in all such a mystic and dreamy glimmer as penetrates and kindles the innermost soul, and gives complete and unreserved delight, unlike the gaudy daylight of this world. They are like all that wonderful artist's works the drawing aside of the fleshy curtain, and the glimpse which all the most holy, studious saints and sages have enjoyed, that rest which remaineth to the people of God.

A parallel to Blake's career, which is also a commentary upon it, is afforded by the work of James Gillray. He was born in Chelsea in 1756, the third child of the sexton of Chelsea's Moravian community. His father, James Gillray the elder, had been raised in Lanarkshire in the Scottish Kirk, but had converted to the intensely Evangelical Moravians, who believed in the depravity of man and in the anticipation of death as a deliverance from earthly bondage. The only formal education Gillray is known to have received, which ceased when he was eight, was at the Moravian academy in Bedford.

Professionally Gillray seems to have aspired, like Blake, to become an accepted engraver of serious subjects. Though he was drawing caricatures all through the 1780s, taking advantage of the brisk state of the market, he did this anonymously until 1789, and did not regularly sign his caricatures until 1792, when he had virtually abandoned his 'serious' aspirations. In the autumn of 1791 he settled down to etch more or less exclusively for the printseller Hannah Humphrey, and for more than a decade and a half he produced a steady stream of topical political satires at the rate of one a week or ten days. Throughout this period, until about 1808, he dominated his profession, and indeed was known throughout Europe both for his technique and for his trenchant commentary. His fellow-cartoonist David Low has called him the father of the political caricature, a new art-form for the age of mass politics and of public opinion.

Gillray's ideological position is something of a puzzle. During the 1780s he seemed willing to satirize anything or anybody. Early in the revolutionary period his sympathies are reported to have been with the revolutionaries: in 1831 John Landseer recalled him in the 1790s in his cups, kneeling and reverentially proposing a toast to the jacobin David, the 'first painter and patriot in Europe'. Landseer believed that Gillray joined the government side in 1796 because he was bribed to do so, and threatened with prosecution if he did not, for an objectionable cartoon concerning the royal family. Certainly a government stipend was secured for him in 1798 by the group, headed by Frere and Canning, which ran the Tory satirical weekly, *The Anti-Jacobin*. Gillray himself laconically ascribed his conversion to commercial motives: 'Now the Opposition are poor, they do not buy my prints and I must draw on the purses of the larger parties.' It nevertheless seems likely that Gillray, who depended on sales direct to the public, was producing art after his own heart in the polemical series which expresses like no other artefacts the British mood during the first decade of the French revolutionary wars.

The ideological mainspring seems to have been the growing popular nationalism after 1792, the zeal to defend John Bull against the Gallican enemy. Hence, no doubt, Gillray's burgeoning popularity afterwards in Germany, when the common cause against Napoleon produced symptoms of similar xenophobia. The very period when the Neoclassical and pro-French Blake was finally cut off from the public saw Gillray's triumph, and it is to an astonishing degree a popular one. Half a century of high-minded aspiration about art for the people ended, on one of its routes, at the window of Mrs Humphrey's shop in St James's Street, where the crowd eagerly gathered for a free display of Gillray's latest prints.

Gillray was capable of the sophisticated cross-reference, the allusiveness or intertextuality which was the by-product of the Neoclassical period's belief in imitation. He could construct large allegorical prints in the grandest Renaissance manner ('The Apotheosis of Hoche', 1798), or, as in his 'Weird Sisters' (1791), mimic an actual painting by Fuseli. But these effects, though enhanced by his public's familiarity with established art, did not absolutely depend on it. The aim was not burlesque but redeployment, the harnessing of the older work, with many of its characteristic effects intact, to a new purpose. Now Gillray bestowed grandeur on a protagonist like Pitt; now he borrowed distortion and disturbance from Fuseli. The command over technique which is evident in his greatest period, from 1795 to 1803, also shows in the controlled relationship between means and end. These were years not so much of government manipulation of public opinion, by such means as *The Anti-Jacobin*, as of genuine anti-jacobin hysteria. Gillray could not have been hired to engrave as he did. He was moved to it, as a man of the people.

French historians of their revolution speak of the brief period of the *levée en masse*, in 1792, when all classes were effectively revolutionized. In England, beginning about the same time, there was a comparable movement of opinion, but in the conservative direction. There was no difficulty in finding the loyalist mob in Birmingham in 1791 to sack Priestley's house in the name of Church and King. By 1792 the gentry were marshalling tenants, servants and local labourers in troops of Yeomanry, a kind of Home Guard, which never needed to go into action against the threatened invasion, but was nevertheless effective in whipping up national sentiment. The crisis of the 1790s was felt as the war to the death of traditional enemies – the European nation-states – with this difference from tradition, that the strongest of them, France, was further armed by the potent weapon of her new popular ideology.

No nation at war with France overlooked the contagious potential of the concept of the sovereignty of the people. The fact remained that in most societies, England among them, it was not the masses but the educated classes that had hitherto shown most symptoms of the revolutionary illness. They had been conditioned over more than a generation by their cults of simplicity and humanitarianism, of the peasant, the slave, the noble savage; by the protracted assault on institutionalized religion, and on other forms of establishment 'imposture'; by the fashion, among many Englishmen as well as on the Continent, of hearty approval of the American War of Independence; by the habit of criticizing advanced society, and the equally widespread habit of believing in man and in his future. In these circumstances it is not surprising that the English conservatism of the 1790s often takes the form of a profound suspicion of ideas and of the type of man who holds them. Burke's *Reflections on the Revolution in France* (1790), the first classic of the counter-revolution, is among other things a polemic against intellectuals: it claims that it is presumptuous for individuals to seek through reason to challenge the state, a mystic organism symbolized by the domestic hearth as well as the throne and the altar. The radical intellectual becomes a bogey-man upon whom grandiose power is bestowed. In London, in Vienna and in the German states feverish fantasies of subversion circulate. The French Revolution is held to have been brought about by conspiracies of intellectuals organized in secret societies, and for a while, especially in the years 1797–8, the word 'philosopher' becomes a term of abuse in popular fiction, drama and journalism, connoting atheist, seducer, plotter and revolutionary.

Fear makes men cruel. At home in England, the government seems with hindsight to have over-reacted to the danger of subversion, yet the abortive Treason Trials of 1794 and the prosecutions resulting from the 'Gagging Acts' of 1795 fell far short of the bloodbaths elsewhere. The Irish peasants who rose in 1798 were not so lucky: it is worth remembering that England committed twice as many troops in Ireland as she ever engaged on the Continent and that one foreign observer, witnessing their vengefulness, could call them the 'worse-disciplined troops in Europe'. The fate of the common Irish was matched by that of the republican aristocrats of Naples who in 1799 surrendered with guarantees, but fell into the hands of the stalwartly counter-revolutionary English admiral, Horatio Nelson. Indeed, the Queen of Naples urged Nelson to treat the city just like a rebel town in Ireland, and so he did, with a series of summary trials and executions explicitly intended as a deterrent to international jacobinism.

But no event tells us as much about this savage and compulsively irrational decade as the art of James Gillray does. Gillray's prints are visual evidence of the wave of feeling that made counter-revolution as genuine a popular sentiment in England as revolution was in France. Indeed, the caricature thrown up in France by the radical revolution of 1789–94 is in many ways similar, though it is technically inferior, to that of Gillray. Which of the two is more consciously 'popular' in its tastes and clientèle? For all its levelling sentiment, there is surely nothing in French caricature to rival the mistrust of the aristocrat – shifty and decadent – that Gillray conveys in his presentation of the Foxite Whigs. Gillray's is an art without a hero. Even his portrayals of Pitt, Nelson and Admiral Sir Sydney Smith – war heroes all – are undercut by a wariness that seems latent in the artist's attitude, a cynical suspicion of the heroic pose. It is as though the very idea of heroism is suddenly imposture, for Gillray's common people are no more given than his aristocrats to idealistic self-denial. They sit stolidly by, sweaty aproned artisans in his imagined reformed House of Commons; they loiter, dropsical and poxy, in his street scenes. Like their archetype, his bovine John Bull, Gillray's common people appear to exist only to be conned by their betters. Though his women can superficially resemble Rowlandson's voluptuous beauties, they are far less enticing, for the flesh has little appeal in the Moravian purgatory which is Gillray's universe. Neither perfectibility nor the Brotherhood of Man has meaning for him either. His imaginative vision refutes Tom Paine. It is a more vivid debunking, pursued to a similar end, than the Revd. T. R. Malthus's statistical demonstration in his *Essay on Population* (1798) that Godwin's optimistic dreams of human progress to happiness are unlikely to be fulfilled. Gillray's portrait of society is as harsh as Godwin's in the novel *Things As They Are, or Caleb Williams* (1794); unlike most conservatives, Gillray implies no commitment to Things As They Are, but simply a leery knowledge that they are unlikely to get better. The shocking, ugly pessimism of his images belongs to the hour when the Brave New World seems lost. He is terrifyingly convincing, partly because, unlike Blake, he is immediately readable and specific, peopling London streets and interiors with recognizable personalities. A mere publicist, parroting Burke's flattering sentimentalities about the Nation's mystic continuity, or about the paternalistic bond uniting the people with the King, could never have had the popular impact that Gillray had. He is cruelly vindictive: his vigour is borne out of mockery of the idealistic revolution and the educated men who made it or sympathized with it. The populist reaction he expresses is as pungent as it is unmistakably representative.

The very power, energy and aptness of Gillray, as an artist for the time and for the people, throws into relief the problems of some of his rivals. Though Gillray was rewarded with an official pension, he did not need it. He could sell direct to the public. He succeeded with a coarse-grained, chauvinist and misanthropic art which was in total contrast to the dominant styles of the previous thirty years – an art also, at least in aspiration, meant for mankind. What became of the international cultural movement so characteristic of the second half of the eighteenth century, as Europe was plunged into the revolutionary wars, with their attendant symptoms of instability, xenophobia, paranoia and pessimism?

Though the artists of the Enlightenment might express themselves in a variety of forms – among which homely middle-class realism was as typical as the grandest classicism – they tended to share a number of principles. Of these the most fundamental were a rejection of the complexities of advanced society, a reiteration of human values (often conveyed in painting, poetry and the novel by focusing upon a single central human figure), and an emphasis upon reaching out to an audience which is as wide as mankind itself. If Blake was the greatest graphic artist to employ this 'essential' style in England, Wordsworth was the greatest writer. It is as easy to miss Wordsworth's representativeness as it is to miss Blake's. Both are often taken to be initiating a new artistic tradition, rather than joining an established one. Yet the fact is that Wordsworth was brought up in the mainstream of Enlightenment culture, and he realizes its potential better than any poet anywhere, with the possible exception of Goethe.

The essential point about his early writing is that, just as visual artists reject the rococo for a new simplicity, the Wordsworthian juvenilia are based on models, most of them fashionable from mid-century, which are associated with naturalness and often also with a culture earlier than that of the present day. Wordsworth himself is explicit about this. In the 'Essay, Supplementary to the Preface' (1815) he reviews eighteenth-century literature, denigrating the tradition of Dryden and Pope and its apologist Johnson, while clearly identifying a preferable alternative tradition in the nature-poet and Spenserian James Thomson. He is thus consistent; and his early writing is conventional, though the convention is a relatively new one. *An Evening Walk* (written 1789) and *Descriptive Sketches* (written 1791–2) are in the loose, flowing couplets appropriate not to satire but to discursive writing. *Guilt and Sorrow* (written 1791–4) recalls both Thomson and the Elizabethans in its use of the Spenserian stanza.

The blank verse drama *The Borderers* (written 1795–6) models itself on the greatest of the Elizabethans, Shakespeare. Typically, then, Wordsworth is a primitive. We need not be inhibited about seeing his taste as orthodox, or linking it with his period's endemic historicism. He himself makes the connection with all kinds of fashionable simplifications, including admiration of the ancients, when he praises the 'manly classical simplicity' of Thomson.

Since Thomas Percy's *Reliques* (1765) the archetypal popular form had been the ballad. Many literary imitations of the folk ballad were adulterated by an essentially modern sensibility and by over-ornamental language; Wordsworth himself objected on these counts to some of the work of Percy and of the German Gottfried August Bürger. As late as 1815, he still stood out for his version of the primitive and essential, though long before this – in fact, from the early 1790s – opposition to the ubiquitous ballad was mounting on a completely different score. William Gifford's *Baviad* (1791) and T. J. Mathias's *Pursuits of Literature* (1794–7) are satires, written significantly in couplets, against the fashion for infantilism. They give early warning that the growing political backlash would have its cultured dimension. Their claim that the Neoclassical cult of simplicity is linked with the cause of the Rights of Man is symptomatic of the politicization of literature throughout the revolutionary and Napoleonic period. It explains how Wordsworth's adoption of the idea of a collection of ballads, in 1797, is already ominously late. To publish ballads in 1798 – moreover, to add a Preface in 1800 which insists that there is one language for poetry, the language of the people – here is already a solecism, compounded by a theory about as controversial as could well be conceived.

We should dismiss at the outset the belief, still widely held, that Wordsworth's contributions to the *Lyrical Ballads* of 1798 represent an altogether new kind of poetry. Wordsworth's experiments with subjects from among the lower orders of society, in metres appropriately taken from popular poetry, follow thirty years of public interest in this matter and this manner, and are thus characteristic of the culture of the Enlightenment. A further question which has preoccupied some critics, though it is surely in the long run less significant, is the question of the authorship of the *Lyrical Ballads*. Should we regard them as primarily an experiment in a truly simplistic poetry, by Wordsworth; or are they a joint undertaking, with Coleridge, which has perhaps more complex or private ends in view?

The *Ballads* are literally a joint venture. Wordsworth took up the project with Coleridge after they became neighbours at Alfoxden and Nether Stowey in Somerset in 1797, and Coleridge's contribution, 'The

Ancient Mariner', even became the most celebrated of the collection. Yet it seems reasonable to concentrate discussion on Wordsworth's kind of ballad – 'The Thorn', 'Goody Blake and Harry Gill', 'The Idiot Boy', 'We Are Seven' – and on Wordsworth's purposes, as outlined in his Preface of 1800. The main reason for this is that there is no evidence dating from the 1790s that Coleridge at that time was concerned with literary experiment; it was, on the contrary, a matter of some comment and amusement among his friends that the tenor of his thought and its vehicle were often far apart. What distinguishes the Wordsworthian side of the *Lyrical Ballads*, on the other hand, is its consistency of subject-matter and of manner. Here at the end of the century, at a time when belief in a rigorously pared 'true style' was old and in certain manifestations suspect – here in the celebrated Preface to the *Lyrical Ballads* is a remarkably complete statement of what the artist's Neoclassical revolution might mean for the poet dedicated and consistent enough to carry it through in terms of his principal tool, language. It is one interpretation of Neoclassicism's fundamental spirit (though not Blake's) that the artist should imitate Nature – not sophisticated life, not life refracted through literature, but human existence in its simple, essential forms. At the same time, the object is not a series of detailed, individual portraits, but something stylized and universal.

The principle that great art returns to essentials is Wordsworth's starting-point. His subjects typically include 'characters of which the elements are simple. Belonging rather to nature than to manners, such as exist now, and will probably always exist' (p.128). True to the humanist sympathy of classicism, he does not approach human nature dispassionately: what is most essential and most human is what is virtuous. When the mind is moved by 'the great and simple affections of our nature' (p.126), like mother-love, or the imminence of death, it is shown in its 'beauty and dignity'. 'One being is elevated above another' (p.128) by his capacity to experience these essential feelings. Equally in keeping with recent artistic practice is Wordsworth's extreme seriousness. Though in general a moralist rather than a behaviourist, he does display the scientific observer's interest in how 'language and the human mind act and react on one another', and, more generally, in uncovering 'the primary laws of our nature'. He has the Neoclassical artist's fresh sense of addressing a whole public, not a narrow clientèle, and his awareness that previous kinds of poetry have been taken to be more trivial than this, and far beneath so adult a preoccupation as an enquiry into the human mind. For this reason he rejects partial or accidental features of poetry, adornments like 'beauties' of style, and reductive notions – for example, that poetry has to do with emotion rather than with reason or the moral sense. If ever a phrase has been taken to define Romanticism in our popular notion of it, it is that part of the Preface that declares poetry to be 'the spontaneous overflow of powerful feelings'. But in its context that very sentence has Wordsworth, like a true son of the Enlightenment, putting rational thought, moral intention and social utility above the subjective, emotional side of the mind, and above the claims of self-expression. He has been writing of other kinds of poetry, both the conventional and the personal – 'false refinement and arbitrary innovation':

> From such verses the Poems in these volumes will be found distinguished at least by one mark of difference, that each of them has a worthy *purpose* ... If in this opinion I am mistaken I can have little right to the name of a Poet. For all good poetry is the spontaneous overflow of powerful feelings: but though this be true, Poems to which any value can be attached, were never produced on any variety of subjects but by a man who being possessed of more than usual organic sensibility had also thought long and deeply. For our continued influxes of feeling are modified and directed by our thoughts, which are indeed the representatives of all our past feelings; and ... by contemplating the relation of these general representatives to each other we discover what is really important to men.
>
> (pp.124–6)

As a whole the passage stresses the controlling activity of the writer's intellect and moral sense. The word 'spontaneous' usually signifies in eighteenth-century philosophic writing not 'unpremeditated' but 'voluntary' or 'of one's own free will' (as opposed to by external constraint). That key 'Romantic' phrase carries a more cerebral connotation than appears at a later date. In its context it is moreover subordinated to purposes characteristic of the Enlightenment.

Why, then, does Wordsworth seem to claim originality, and seem to fear that his 'experiment' will not be acceptable to his reader? He is original in the thoroughgoingness and consistency with which he tries to apply Neoclassical precepts, and above all in his concentration on what for him are the ultimate principles, simplicity of language and truth to personal experience. His phrasing implies that while he expects informed readers to grant most of his premises, he knows that they may find it hard to adjust to a rigorous enforcement of them, at least where they affect style. And here Wordsworth means to be rigorous. He condemns the avant-garde mannerisms which have begun to adhere to some adaptations of popular literature, like the newly fashionable melodramatic German ballads – even though he risks giving offence on the Germanic, since his partner Coleridge has an evident taste for what he describes himself in a letter of 1803 as language and sentiments deployed merely because they are 'wild, and original, and vehement, and fantastic'. Wordsworth also deplores Erasmus Darwin's attempt in *The Botanic Garden* to use poetry to transmit newly-discovered principles of science. Using Wordsworth's strict and logic test of a generalized, universal 'truth', the truths of science are not yet suitable matter for poetry, because they are not yet part of 'the impressions which we habitually receive' (p.141). These last two caveats show that Wordsworth articulated the classical taste in a version less up-to-date than some; but where language was concerned he was more extreme than virtually all. He represented strands of thinking and of taste typical of the last half-century, particularly the preference for the simple subject and style and the aspiration to speak on serious subjects to the public at large. But his was an extrapolation from the common body of art in the 'true style' that in its accessibility and strong, clear emphasis might almost have been calculated (though it was not) to bring out that movement's subversive potential. If Wordsworth's contributions to the *Lyrical Ballads* had appeared a decade earlier – and there is nothing in them that could not have been written in 1788 – they would hardly have attracted attention, except for their merits. As it was, literary excellence was an additional offence. It made Wordsworth more readable, and therefore more dangerous.

Modern literary criticism is by comparison with earlier periods exceptionally literary-centred. Modern interpretations of the *Lyrical Ballads* have accordingly approached the matter of the shock they caused as aspects of the evolving literary relationship of Wordsworth and Coleridge, or as questions in the history of aesthetics concerning poetic diction and the theory of imagination. The actual reception of the *Lyrical Ballads* was not personal, nor theoretical, nor in our terms literary. The two great contemporary interpreters of Wordsworth's *Lyrical Ballads* and of his Preface to it were Francis Jeffrey and Samuel Taylor Coleridge, and it is worth grasping the grounds of their criticism.

Jeffrey was the editor and most prolific reviewer of the *Edinburgh Review*, which he helped to found in 1802. His influential position ensured that from 1802 to 1817 he was the leading critic of the age. In private Jeffrey was ready to admit that he was moved by Wordsworth's ballads. In public he attacked them, using ridicule as his main offensive weapon. Coleridge waxed indignant over this discrepancy between Jeffrey the individual reader and Jeffrey the critic, but Jeffrey was neither corrupt nor bigoted and in fact his position is defensible in terms of his own critical theory. He belonged to the Anglo-Scottish intellectual tradition which saw literature as a product of a particular society and as a social fact, an influence, within a society. He did not dislike Wordsworth's experiment absolutely but he did dislike it in the context of the time, when England was at war with revolutionary France, and fears of subversion from within had never been fully laid to rest. The prime factor governing Jeffrey's public judgement was thus openly ideological. His interpretation of Wordsworth's experiment was neatly summed up in an aside he made when reviewing a book which the Anglo-Irish novelist Maria Edgeworth deliberately designed for a mass audience, her *Popular Tales* of 1804. Jeffrey extolled the Edgeworth book (for modern tastes one of her weakest) because it advised the lower orders to be thrifty and diligent:

This is an attempt, we think, somewhat superior in genius, as well as utility, to the laudable exertions of Mr. Thomas Paine to bring disaffection and infidelity within the comprehension of the common people, or the charitable endeavours of Messrs Wirdsworth [sic] & Co. to accommodate them with an appropriate vein of poetry. Both these were superfluities which they might have done very tolerably without.

(*ER*, iv (1804), 329–30)

Jeffrey links the Wordsworthian ballad with Paine's *Rights of Man*, the most notorious of all books of the 1790s directed at a mass audience. The implication is clearly that the influence of Wordsworth is likely to be similarly in the direction of 'levelling' proper social distinctions. Now Jeffrey was no Tory backwoodsman, but a liberal Whig. Lest we should think that there is eccentricity in his reflections on Wordsworth's ideological tendency, it is worth noticing that most of the collection's reviewers between 1798 and 1807 praised poems which use an elevated language and subject, like 'Tintern Abbey', and attacked those using a 'mean' language and subject, like 'The Idiot Boy'. Though Darwin's conscious intentions were more subversive than Wordsworth's, he was less generally frightening, because he did not profess to write for the people; similarly, Pitt found Godwin less alarming than Paine, who had such a wonderfully universal idiom. That the controversy over Wordsworthian language was inseparable from the issue of the extent (and political sympathy) of the greater reading public is demonstrated by the tone of Coleridge, Wordsworth's co-author, when he returned to the question of the *Lyrical Ballads* in 1817.

Coleridge's *Biographia Literaria* was a book deliberately written for an hour of public peril. Never since 1798, when the original *Ballads* appeared, had revolution seemed as real a danger in England as it did in 1817. The danger would come from below, from rioters, machine-breakers, the unemployed or underpaid and hungry work-people. But it was fomented, or so the propertied classes felt, by some educated men. The journalist William Cobbett, who addressed himself in cheap newssheets direct to the populace, was the focus of special anger and fear, as a traitor to his order. Coleridge's *Biographia* is addressed to that order, the intellectual élite, for the purpose of urging it to fulfil its social responsibility. Coleridge opposes to Cobbett's example and to the old French-style materialism and radicalism a new intellectual fashion, that of the German counter-revolution, with its nostalgia for medieval social institutions, that is for a hierarchical society bonded together in one church. It is often alleged that the *Biographia Literaria* is formally shapeless, and that no logic can be found to link the discussion of German philosophy in the first half with that of Wordsworth's early work in the second, but the book's ideology is a unifying factor. Coleridge commends the German example, which is religious, and so exalted that it is meaningful only to a small educated élite. He criticizes Wordsworth's 1798 experiment because its simplicity and universalism are associated with the radical, levelling tendency of the pre-revolutionary Enlightenment.

In the celebrated chapter xxii, where Coleridge sums up the case against the Wordsworth of the *Lyrical Ballads*, he begins by proclaiming that taken as a whole Wordsworth is a very different kind of poet – as Christian, as difficult, and hence as élitist, as the most timid could wish:

It is high time to announce, decisively and aloud, that the *supposed* characteristics of Mr. Wordsworth's poetry ... whether they are simplicity or simpleness; faithful adherence to essential nature, or wilful selections from human nature of its meanest forms and under the least attractive associations; are as little the *real* characteristics of his poetry at large, as of his genius and the constitution of his mind. (ii.95)

Jeffrey's persistent campaign had unfortunately made the *Ballads* notorious, and far more salient than Wordsworth's greater and safer later work. Coleridge was thus moved to level against the unfortunate *Ballads* a far more elaborate case than ever Jeffrey did. He lists their defects – the inconstancy of style, the matter-of-factness, the 'ventriloquist' deviation into a dramatic technique. Now Coleridge's criticisms are compatible with some of the tenets of the new German literary theorists, especially Friedrich and A. W. Schlegel, whose preference for 'Romantic' as opposed to classical art was beginning to be known in England. Perhaps the *Biographia Literaria* threw some light on the topic of Romanticism – but a more common, familiar frame of reference must have seemed more salient to his first English readers. What Coleridge essentially disliked about the style of some of the poems, and about the argument with which Wordsworth defended his diction in the Preface, was that it took the common people, their experience and language, as its proper standard. This was a translation of the idea of the sovereignty of the people into first the moral and then the cultural sphere. Wordsworth had never sufficiently acknowledged its wrong-headedness. Indeed, he had repeated it even in his later work, even in his most ambitious poem, when he perversely made the leading character of *The Excursion* (1814) a *pedlar*. 'Is there ... one sentiment', cries the exasperated Coleridge, 'that might not more plausibly ... have proceeded from any wise and beneficent old man, of a rank or profession in which the language of learning and refinement are natural and to be expected?' (ii.108). He finds a similar tendency towards a subversive levelling of rank in the sentimental drama which had been popular at the end of the eighteenth century, and this genre was often avowedly radical.

The whole secret of the modern Jacobinical drama (which, and not the German, is its appropriate designation) and of all its popularity, consists in the confusion and subversion of the natural order of things ... in the excitement of surprise, by representing the qualities of liberality, refined feeling, and a nice sense of honour ... in persons and in classes of life where experience teaches us least to expect them. (ii.193)

The strategy of the *Biographia* is to describe first the Christian culture Coleridge wants the English upper orders to revert to, and then to draw attention to the sundry aberrations of the last twenty-five years, with Wordsworth's *Lyrical Ballads* as the most prominent. It is a rich critical treatise, but above all it identifies and denounces the tail end of the movement to popularize the arts which had characterized the second half of the eighteenth century.

Of course it is an irony that later critics have persisted in seeing the *Lyrical Ballads* as heralding a new kind of poetry – when the ablest contemporary critics saw them as the epitome of an older, if recent and short-lived kind, which became unacceptable once England's destiny was to champion the counter-revolution. It is even odder when we reflect that Coleridge was broadly right both in his ideological characterization of the *Ballads*, and in his observation that they do not represent the work of Wordsworth as a whole. Before he wrote them, Wordsworth was proving by his *Borderers* that he was no conscious apologist for revolution. One leading character in this drama written in 1796 is typical of the period: Oswald (who is given the name of a real man, an English jacobin in Paris while Wordsworth was there in 1792) is one of those sinister, subversive intellectuals who haunt the propaganda and fiction of conservative Europe in the pre-Napoleonic period, when revolutionary ideology still seemed to be spreading irresistibly. *The Borderers* can be read as a stylized account of the French Revolution. Its hero, Marmaduke, is led on by the disaffected Oswald to wish to kill the old, blind, helpless Herbert, a father-figure who might stand generally for the *ancien régime* or more specifically for Louis XVI himself. Long ago, Oswald claims to have been similarly misled into killing the captain of a ship by the ruffianly crew, who wanted to get rid of 'a tyrannic Master whom they loathed'. The play explores the part played in the revolutionary crime by intellectuals; it depicts the wickedness, prematurity or arrogance of revolutionary political action and those who seek cerebrally to initiate or justify it. When Oswald thinks that Marmaduke has killed Herbert, he congratulates him for defying 'misty rules', and trusting instead his 'independent Intellect'. It is an unfavourable portrait of the self-reliant modern individualist, in terms similar to those in which he was drawn by Burke, the great apologist for the counter-revolution. 'We know that *we* have made no discoveries; and we think that no discoveries are to be made, in morality; nor many in the great principles of government, which were understood before we were born ...'. Wordsworth echoes the most quoted of all passages in Burke's *Reflections*, the extravagant paragraph which describes Marie Antoinette as dauphiness, 'glittering like the morning star ... I thought ten thousand swords must have leaped from their scabbards to avenge even a look that threatened her with insult.' Marmaduke recalls Burke's phrasing when he reflects that the heroine, Idomenea, has been

made an Orphan

By one who would have died a thousand times
To shield her from a moment's harm.   (ll.2298–2300)

If the action of *The Borderers* resembles the revolution stylized, or even allegorized, the dénouement for each of the principals is pure moral fable. Herbert's descendant, Idomenea, comes into her own again, as in real life the Bourbon dynasty had not so far done after the death of Louis XVI. The villain Oswald is killed, while Marmaduke goes off to be a hermit, as a religious penance for his part in Herbert's death. And this last is Wordsworth's prophecy or programme for the future for himself as intellectual.

For during the next years he adopted the public mantle of the poet of counter-revolution, celebrating the Burkean conservative ideology of personal humility and service, domesticity, hearth and home, the English plot of ground. Not that he was uncritical of English society. His journey to France in 1802 during the short-lived Peace of Amiens to see his former mistress Annette Vallon showed him much that he disapproved of in both nations. 'I could not but be struck', he said in a letter, 'with the vanity and parade of our own country, especially in towns and cities, as contrasted with the quiet, and I may say the desolation, that revolution had produced in France':

> Milton! thou shouldst be living at this hour:
> England hath need of thee: she is a fen
> Of stagnant waters: altar, sword and pen,
> Fireside, the heroic wealth of hall and bower
> Have forfeited their ancient English dower
> Of inward happiness: we are selfish men . . .

It is no part of the ideological poet's role to flatter; though indirectly it *is* flattering, and legitimizing, to call upon your readers to imitate the conduct of great men in a heroic period. The same appeal, to old-fashioned domestic virtue and simple principle, as opposed to commercial instinct, is to be heard in another conservative writer, Jane Austen. But Wordsworth's call is larger and more ambitious, more genuinely to the nation as a whole. She is an author of the gentry; he, of the whole nation temporarily roused in opposition to the French and innovation.

His choice of mode indicates the largeness of his thinking. In his sonnets Wordsworth adopts the grand, heroic tones of another poet-prophet, Milton. It is of course splendidly unifying to address the English people in their present difficulties in the accents of the greatest republican writer:

> Plain living and high thinking are no more:
> The homely beauty of the good old cause
> Is gone.

Alternatively, at his very greatest Wordsworth retains the familiar subjects and simple treatment of his own ballads and of so much else in the primitivist late eighteenth-century vein. His best poems, including 'Michael', 'Resolution and Independence', 'The Ruined Cottage' and the Lucy poems, are the very apotheosis of a style which prefers to portray the essential man in a natural setting. Wordsworth carries over into the new. major phase of his writing the characteristics of Neoclassicism – simplicity, gravity, humanity and public spirit – which in his hands are at first fortified, not undermined, by the counter-revolution's taste for hearth and home. He also retains his preference for the unsophisticated among his predecessors, as no one can doubt who has studied the 'Essay Supplementary to the 1815 Preface', with its censure of Pope, Gray and Johnson, its praise of Percy's ballads, Burns, and above all Thomson. Yet it is clear that for Wordsworth the solution to the sufferings of Margaret, the Cumberland Beggar and the Leechgatherer are not now to be found in simple social action. Unlike the sentimental writers and

Southey and unlike his own earlier self, Wordsworth from 1797–8 ceases to see others as social phenomena; they are objects for contemplation, images of apparent alienation which the poet's imagination translates into private emblems of his troubled communion with nature. In Books x to xiii of *The Prelude*, the great poem he began now and published in 1850, Wordsworth himself analysed the all-important transition from external to internal goals, which to him seemed to follow disillusionment with the Revolution, but to us looks equally like a response to the deep new current of conservatism in English thinking. Looking back with an increasingly orthodox religious perspective, he felt that there had been a period in which his eye, dwelling on external things, had meant too much. Gradually his vision internalized itself: he perceived that significance lay not in the simple object in the world of Nature, but in the power of his imagination to work upon the impression he retained, fully to appropriate to his own thought these 'spots of time'. Thus a pagan, external this-worldliness is transformed into a habit of mind compatible with acceptance of religious truth. *The Prelude*, which enacts an intellectual and spiritual journey in terms of the poet's own experience, is also a national epic, since it explicitly weighs the social, secular ideology sustaining the Revolution against the ideology of the conservative powers, which focused more and more effectively upon the emotional appeal of traditional religion.

Understanding of Wordsworth has always been bedevilled by paradox. A great national spokesman, who arrived at the height of his powers at a time of remarkable unity for the English propertied classes, he was mistaken (largely thanks to Jeffrey) for the leader of the Lake poets, a disloyal coterie. Later in the nineteenth century and in the twentieth, his true stature as a religious poet emerged; but later notions of what it means to be religious are not limited to the specific situation in which Wordsworth came to be a religious poet, and so put fresh difficulties in the way of his meaning. It is not simply that Wordsworth's religion is often nearer to the eighteenth-century Anglicanism of Bishop Butler than to the nineteenth-century Anglo-Catholicism of Cardinal Newman. It is also that in the context of 1800 to become domestic, withdrawn, quietist, meditative and very consciously English was to make a choice which carried a specifically political connotation. Or was it precisely a choice at all? Probably it was by instinct that Wordsworth bowed to reality – an egalitarian revolution that turned into a dictatorship – and to the prevailing atmosphere, which made private or religious men of so many artists and intellectuals all over Europe about 1800. Perhaps the really distinctive thing about him was that he succumbed to the conservative intellectual tide so much more slowly than Coleridge. He was unusual, and so was found suspect, because he stubbornly retained so much of the Enlightenment spirit, especially its simplicity, its universality, and its validation of essential human experience.

Yet in keeping that Enlightenment focus upon the public, in aspiring to speak of and to mankind, Wordsworth also set himself the central problem of his career. To appreciate it we only have to return to the comparison with Blake and Gillray. They both hailed from the urban artisan class: Gillray had the common touch in everything he did, Blake had it in an elusive but real sense denied to Wordsworth, the land-agent's son and Cambridge graduate. But Blake and Wordsworth were alike in having been trained in artistic absolutes which could not survive unchallenged the crisis of the 1790s. Even to write in a style meant for mankind became a divisive and inflammatory gesture. Cruelly, it was also useless, for the international style of the Enlightenment was in reality neither universal nor popular, but the *lingua franca* of an aristocracy, a fact which became increasingly significant as class consciousness grew with the new century. Blake and Wordsworth faced the same trials – obscurity or notoriety, and the special problem of adapting for a suspicious, segmented society a kind of art that was in origin public and corporate.

Wordsworth made some adjustments that Blake did not. By 1800 it became as apparent to him as to the infinitely more vulgar Gillray that the popular artist of the war period must be anti-French and must have a specifically English appeal, after the internationalism of the recent mode. Paradoxically, however, Wordsworth was cut off, above all by the outcry that greeted his Preface, from the rich vein he had recently unearthed in his search for a popular and genuinely native poetry. The cry of 'jacobinism' that greeted the *Lyrical Ballads* must have helped to drive him away from the kind of specificity that was available to the impeccably anti-jacobin Gillray. In addition he faced from 1808 the problem Gillray never had to face, since Gillray collapsed in that year into alcoholism or insanity. The letters and memoirs of the time – Jeffrey's, for example – demonstrate how from about 1809 the cohesive wartime mood began to give way to the usual party divisions, as the danger from France became less threatening. If Wordsworth's orotund public pronouncements henceforward seem more strained than his sonnets of 1802, it is largely because the imaginative concept of a public that was also a people increasingly lost credibility. Great though he was at making his private experience read like universal experience, Wordsworth came to feel his want of what Gillray after his own manner found – a common medium of communication, a language, made up of precisely those elements of the simple, the commonplace and the dramatic which Coleridge deplored.

3 The Rise of the Man of Letters: Coleridge

Coleridge is universally felt to be a great writer, but it is hard to define his greatness precisely in terms of what he wrote. He is the author of poems almost everyone has heard of, but he produced relatively little, and that little lacks the commonly recognized characteristic of major status – a distinctive philosophy expressed in a distinctive manner.

After 1802 he is a prose writer, but few if any can have claimed him as a prose stylist. His sentences tend to be laboured and tortuous: arguably they are appropriately so, since his meaning is complex and as time goes on he is more and more anxious to direct his message only to those qualified by education to understand him. Yet the same principles that determined the Coleridgean manner, often not so much exalted as portentous, moved other writers, like De Quincey and Carlyle, to more colourful experiments with prose.

Is he, then, a thinker? Specialists in the different fields he essayed have argued convincingly that he is not a philosopher nor a Bible scholar of the first rank. Many more would be found who would hail a great critic. Some Coleridgean passages, from the lectures, the table talk, the notebooks and the letters, are undoubtedly very fine, though the greater part are the insights of an observant and acutely sensitive reader. As a critic Coleridge is not merely unsystematic; he is seldom even sustained. Furthermore, it can be shown that in, for example, the celebrated critique of Wordsworth in the *Biographia Literaria*, his interests are not primarily those of the literary analyst, nor of the prophet of Culture in Matthew Arnold's grandiloquent sense, but those of a polemicist arguing a cause which many of Coleridge's modern admirers might not find wholly sympathetic. Perhaps this hardly matters. Nuggets of great critical writing can be extracted from the temporalities, and if need be reunited with the strands in Coleridge's thinking which have worn better than his politics. Nevertheless, extrapolating Coleridge's critical writing from its actual context creates further problems of interpretation for his modern reader, for distortion enters in if it is treated as writing wholly or even mainly concerned with literary issues, such as language or the imagination.

Coleridge's first decade of maturity, the 1790s, was on the face of it the most literary. From his schooldays he was reading and writing poetry; from early manhood he was publishing it, and by 1800, when he was twenty-seven, he had written 'The Ancient Mariner', 'Kubla Khan', and the two parts of 'Christabel', as well as the best of the conversation poems – that is, almost everything for which he is remembered as a poet. But the main impulse behind his activity in the 1790s was perhaps the desire to comment on public affairs. His most ambitious project was his journal of 1795, *The Watchman*, though he also came before the Bristol public as a lecturer, and during the years 1795–8, when he thought of becoming a Unitarian minister, he frequently preached on subjects both religious and political. After the failure of his journal, the generosity of the Wedgwood brothers, Josiah's sons, who in 1798 promised him £150 a year, enabled him to give up the idea of the ministry, and to devote himself instead to issues of religion, ethics, politics and literature on a more national or universal scale. It is clear that both Coleridge and his most sympathetic friends thought it was his vocation to be, in a phrase, a professional intellectual.

Coleridge is in fact one of the first representatives in England, and perhaps the most important early representative, of a distinct new type. It is worth exploring, since it may be that the search for 'Romanticism' is not so much the quest for a certain literary product, as for a type of producer. We have seen that one of the circumstances which made the last decades of the eighteenth century seem distinctive was the proliferation all over Western Europe and America of books, newspapers and journals. Once controversy on a national and international scale became part of a civilized diet it was always a factor to be reckoned with. Even in countries governed by secure aristocracies, 'public opinion' is identified as such, and acknowledged as an inevitable influence upon government. In Britain in the 1820s, for example, reform of the legislature would have been a remote possibility if it had been solely a technical question of obtaining the majority for it in the two aristocratic chambers of Parliament. Nevertheless, as the decade wore on, reform became a certainty, because 'the country' was felt to require it. Before mass suffrage, the referendum and the opinion poll, there was no scientific way of measuring public opinion. But newspapers were felt to express it, so that by the late 1820s the leader-columns and feature articles of the major newspapers and journals had acquired not direct political power, but most significant influence, before which power might be obliged to retreat.

One of the innovations of our period, then, is the emergence on the scene of the modern journalist – not as a reporter only, but as a critic, watchdog and self-appointed spokesman for the individual citizen.

Perhaps the first models for the type were the *philosophes* of eighteenth-century France, who not only wielded an enviable influence, but evolved an appropriate rhetoric: that dignified, disinterested public tone, so typical of discourse in the Enlightenment, which is with us still in the leader-columns of *The Times* and the *New York Times*. Thomas Babington Macaulay (1800–59) has been called the pioneer modern leader-writer, and in terms of the refinements of the craft the description may be just. Yet as the role of sage, unacknowledged legislator or fourth estate of the realm could be clearly discerned a generation before Macaulay, so too could the outlines of the characteristic posture.

The new journalistic air of sublime assurance is nicely pinpointed in Sydney Smith's joke about the *Edinburgh Review*, that, given the solar system to assess, it would surely damn it: – 'bad light – planets too distant – pestered with comets – feeble contrivance – could make a better with great ease.' The man of letters made it his object to carry weight, to wield a kind of moral authority that had nothing to do with political power and perhaps reached beyond the power of individuals in the modern state. Journalists quickly learnt the most appropriate tactics, and independence, integrity, idealism and humane concern become the leading characteristics of Coleridge's persona as a leader-writer for the *Morning Post* (1800–2) and as editor-proprietor of *The Friend* (1809–10), just as they appear, in a more homely idiomatic guise, in the image of the labourer's son William Cobbett, the greatest English journalist of the day or perhaps any day, in the *Political Register* (1802–35).

In the same era that the new intellectual acquired a manner, he was forming a character. Social changes, which put pressure on all sections of society, certainly did not spare the artist. It could be said that urbanization and the growth of a literate leisured class gave him an unprecedented freedom and status, as compared with his lot in the days of the aristocratic patron. But the new conditions, an art marketed rather than an art commissioned, also imposed upon the artist-intellectual the symptoms of disorientation. The necessity to communicate with a large public to which no individual could relate created large problems, of form and tone, and also imposed peculiar strains. Like the public posture of confident integrity, a syndrome of private neuroses have remained characteristic of Western intellectuals from that day to this. Alienation is perhaps at the root of them, and it is seen as early as 1750 in that hero and archetype of intellectuals, Jean-Jacques Rousseau, the sensitive, near-paranoid bourgeois ill at ease in an aristocratic world. Rousseau, like so many after him, experienced simultaneously a rage to reject existing society, and a yearning to be integrated with it. With the modern man of letters, modern literary *Angst* was born.

Or was it? Two documentary historians of the Renaissance artist have shown persuasively that the 'artistic type', wild, bohemian and melancholic, was recognized by his characteristics from the time that the arts began to rise in social prestige towards their height in modern (as opposed to ancient) times – that is, in fifteenth-century Italy. Rudolf and Margot Wittkower are sceptical about the 'artistic temperament' as a distinct clinical phenomenon. The notorious irregularity of artists, their unpunctuality in producing work and their wandering habits, were probably linked in the Renaissance to uncertainties built into the system of patronage. Otherwise artists tended to behave as their contemporaries did, though if their names were known their bad behaviour attracted more attention. If weight can be placed on the scarce, difficult statistical evidence about suicide, they were not more desperately disturbed than others – perhaps because their calling had its own rewards. What happened in Europe at the end of the eighteenth century may be at most a further series of social changes, which threw the emphasis on to the writer, even more than the painter and composer, as a man representative of the educated 'professional' class in everything but his eloquence. His new problems in marketing his work to a larger, more urban public were clearly related to the frustrating and alienating experience of other citizens in an increasingly complex and specialized environment. Objectively the writer was not in a unique position, until advancing social sophistication led him, along with other intellectuals, to become aware of the position and role of his type in society. Once arrived at collective self-consciousness, artists inevitably sought to advance their prestige by developing exalted theories about their distinctive creative powers – 'imagination', as opposed both to the 'reason' employed by other brain-workers, and to the more mechanical function implied by the term 'craft'. Somewhat later other members of the new professional cadres – doctors, engineers, academics – similarly learnt devices to dignify their own groups and to control admission to them. Not that the new literary theorists of around 1800 necessarily perceived how far their ideas worked in their own interests. They responded intuitively to their uncertain role and larger, less knowable public, just as the public came gradually to respond to a new kind of art, expressive of unfamiliarity and disturbance.

It is clearly significant that it was in a society where social change was unusually rapid and difficult, the North German state of Prussia, that a new and exaggerated Portrait of the Artist first defined itself. In eighteenth-century Germany divisions between the classes, aristocrat and burger, were rigid and legally enforced. It seems that the population was growing particularly fast in Prussia, and in a relatively small country the inevitable social problems were hard to deal with. A confined, inflexible society could not cope with the numbers of extra mouths to feed or young men to employ. England had its economic take-off, created by and accommodating the surplus numbers. Prussia experienced landless sons and daughters of peasants, roaming about as bands of beggars; or young burgers who went to university and stayed on, because there were no jobs – the bitterest and probably the best-educated middle class in Europe. Since the aristocracy had sons to place too, and since there was little industry, young graduates had few recourses but the Protestant Church – and the profession of letters. Mid-eighteenth century middle-class talent presses into literature in Germany, creating a literary Golden Age, and also a definitive impression of the frustration and and alienation of clever men for whom society has no room.

The *Sturm und Drang* generation of the 1770s produces a literature of protest. Goethe's hero Werther conveys the enforced idleness, the indignation at social exclusion, the sense of waste, of a whole class and generation. Schiller's outlaw Karl Moor, hero of *The Robbers*, is an imaginative symbol for the same sensation. But it is notable that even the *Sturm und Drang* generation is not politically radical in the same practical sense as some of the youthful artists of France and England. In Germany political activism is not possible; there is no substantial, unified polity to act against. There is not even a general reading public to address. It has been calculated that the reading public for books in German was probably only one twelfth that for books in French, a proportion made artificially small because it was the custom for the German aristocracy to speak and read French. Thus the German intellectual has to write, and to find a public, because he has so few other means of advancement, but he has far less confidence than his English or French opposite number that his public exists; still less again, that anything he writes can be translated into meaningful action. Hence the striking tendency of German literature to focus on private experience, inward culture, and frustration, even in the relatively social and outgoing era of the Enlightenment.

Well before the Revolution occurred, German literature thus anticipated what were to seem some of the most characteristic features of the counter-revolution, including inward intensity and a compensatory inclination to prefer thought to action. Germany was socially backward, but its intellectuals experienced prematurely what was henceforth a typical experience for intellectuals in advanced countries – they became conscious of themselves as an alienated sub-group that was neither aristocratic nor any longer quite middle-class. Especially after 1795, certain traits in German literature seem to anticipate the future, and have been taken to offer a kind of cultural leadership. Between 1797 and 1800 a group emerged at Jena and the Prussian capital, Berlin, around Friedrich Schlegel and his journal the *Athenaeum*, men who are sometimes known collectively as the *Frühromantiker*, or early Romantics. It is actually hard to find evidence that for the time being they had much influence in other parts of Germany, let alone outside German borders. If the group's emergence seems momentous, it is not because it was copied but because it was paralleled in the social and cultural experience of Europe in the coming century.

Though a social history of European Romanticism has not been attempted, a Frenchman, Henri Brunschwig, has given an able account of late eighteenth-century Prussia. He suggests that here over-population produced a crisis all the more severe because it followed a golden age. Under Frederick the Great, who died in 1786, Prussia had seemed to many the model state of the *Aufklärung*, an enlightened despotism which institutionalized freedom of speech and religious toleration. Partly as the result of the social pressures towards the close of the century, rational toleration was challenged at all levels of society by an emotional, mystical, irrational religiosity. Among the peasantry there emerged cults of self-proclaimed prophets; higher up the social scale, pietism and pseudo-religious movements like the Freemasons. The same irrationality finds intellectual expression in what Brunschwig calls the cult of the miraculous. Educated men come to see everyday occurrences as disconnected, strange. In private letters as in literature, events are narrated as though they cannot be explained. It is quite different from the inwardness of Goethe's generation, when emotional experience, though central, was nevertheless under the control of the conscious mind. (In this respect Goethe resembles the eighteenth-century Englishman Wordsworth, also no irrationalist.) For the literary generation that matures in the 1790s – Tieck, Wackenroder, Novalis – life is dream, theatre or miracle. Thus the Romantic mentality is not, it seems, made out of politics. Still less is it a response to the work of a philosopher like Kant. It is not merely a reaction against other intellectual products, such as the classical style. More probably it is born from social experience, out of unemployment, frustration and rejection of the outside world.

For some months from the autumn of 1798, Samuel Taylor Coleridge, together with Wordsworth, visited Germany. He thought initially of going to Jena, but in the event preferred Göttingen, which was rumoured to be cheap, and was moreover eminent for its Bible scholars. He did not meet any of the early Romantics, nor, as far as we know, did he hear of them at the time. His debt to Germany is real and continuous, but it does not depend on chance encounters with men or with books. Because Coleridge was himself the product of a social experience so far more common perhaps in Germany than in England, his attitudes resemble those of German intellectuals in key respects, and predispose him to make use of their work.

The tenth child of elderly parents, who made him their favourite, but could not protect him from the jealousy of his siblings nor the dislike of servants, Coleridge at the age of eight lost his much-loved father. He was sent away to Christ's Hospital as a charity-boy; he had already acquired the habit of living in books and daydreams. At school, as afterwards at Cambridge, he underwent the isolating experience of being marked out as a genius. It is noticeable that more than one of Coleridge's contemporaries afterwards saw his own adolescence in similar terms, as a process of alienation from a family, in several cases particularly from a mother, leading to the rootless, classless career of a professional author or journalist. Charles Lamb, youngest surviving child of a clerk and servant, was promoted out of his class when he was sent to the same charity school. Another boy prodigy, Thomas De Quincey, son of a well-off, literate linen draper, ran away from his school and from his widowed mother to live alone on his talents. These three personalities had traits in common with one another and with the German *Frühromantiker*. There was in each case social displacement; subsequently, a difficulty of adjustment to ordinary everyday life, either an overwhelming sense of the ugliness of the contemporary urban world, or an inability to cope. Brunschwig also points out, in the case of the German group, the high incidence of health problems. Poverty, carelessness or contempt for the mundane led them to eat not very sensibly. Almost all the Germans complained of stomach troubles, colics and migraines. Coleridge ate inadequately as a schoolboy, and probably as a result was frequently in the infirmary, with jaundice and stomach troubles. His letters as a young adult racily memorialize a delicate digestion – he records, for example, an incident in October 1795, when he bathed in the sea after smoking, and 'my triumphant Tripes cataracted most Niagara-ishly' (p.163). De Quincey says that it was acute pain in the stomach – which could perhaps have been an ulcer, brought about by irregular eating – that led him to his opium habit. Byron and Shelley both ate crankily and inadequately and both as a result frequently felt ill. Brunschwig guesses that among the Germans anaemia was prevalent. So was nervous tension. Almost all the Schlegel group were, to judge from their letters, manic depressives. All were obsessed with the thought of death, and most proposed suicide, though only Kleist, who was not of the immediate *Athenaeum* group, actually followed Werther's course, put the pistol in his mouth, and fired. These health problems, from toothache and stomach upsets to more lethal complaints, were probably typical for the age-group, class and period: all young adults were at risk from the tuberculosis which killed Novalis and Karl Philipp Moritz in Germany and Keats in England. But, being educated and self-aware, the emerging group of intellectuals found imaginative correlatives for physical suffering, and were moreover abnormally predisposed to the kind of ailment, such as depression, hypochondria and 'nervous fever', which was neurotic in origin.

It is thus in keeping with the group self-portrait that Coleridge and De Quincey became addicted to opium, while Lamb and Hazlitt, though not alcoholics, were prone to self-destructive bouts of heavy drinking. The modern medical attitude to addiction is that it is a symptom of personal insecurity and dependence, rather than itself a cause of those things. What Coleridge, and more particularly De Quincey, wrote about opium has misled generations of readers into believing that it was the reason for their stomach cramps and bad dreams and an alibi for their non-productivity. We now know that the physical disorders and nightmares the two writers catalogue so vividly were unlikely to have been the direct consequences of opium-taking, though they are symptoms compatible with an attempt to withdraw from it. It may be more significant that dreams are prevalent everywhere in the literature of the period, and in the work of other writers cannot be associated with narcotics. Dreams, dream-states and dream-worlds are suddenly a leading feature of literature. In Germany the middle-aged Goethe, though he held aloof from Romanticism and described it as a disease, nevertheless in the late 1790s created in Wilhelm Meister a hero who made an alternative fantasy-world out of the theatre. For Charles Lamb in England in the first decade of the nineteenth century, the theatre and the quaint, dated literature of the early seventeenth century represented precisely such a refuge from the world of external circumstance. Lamb hardly published anything on the literature or the affairs of the present day: his taste was for Burton or Wither, old plays, the lost world of childhood, or eccentric, forgotten old acquaintances – countries of the mind disjunctive with his readers' and his own ordinary existence. Like Coleridge in 'Kubla Khan' – but not at all like Wordsworth in 'The Idiot Boy' or 'Michael' – Lamb values literature as fantasy, otherness; in some sense magical. It is the *mal du siècle:* not universal – for the public, unselfconscious Enlightenment tradition remains strong – but in every European country from the 1790s endemic.

Coleridge's biographical experience may then be taken as a case-history, at once unique and representative. The heady 1790s saw the intellectual making of him, and it is a process which can be traced in his letters and notebooks as well as in the formal writing. In youth, at school and at Cambridge, Coleridge was unstable and immature even for his years: his 'ideapot' bubbled over, his plans were legion and his judgement erratic. His life was made and marred by a series of impulsive actions, including running away when in debt to enlist as a dragoon, his decision to share with Southey in an idealistic property-sharing scheme in America, and his commitment as part of the same scheme to marry Sara Fricker, whom he did not love. Coleridge's letters to his correspondents, many of whom were older and more forceful personalities, reveal his tendency to trust others, to depend on them, to act out of obligation towards them, and (when things went wrong) to be easily and deeply hurt.

Perhaps the main impulse throughout, on the evidence of the letters, was the need to be faithful to the idea of that family from which he had been for years effectively estranged – especially to the memory of his saintly clergyman father, and to the example of his father's representative in his own generation, his clergyman brother George. Coleridge wrote later in the decade that there had been a point earlier when he ceased to be a Christian, but the contemporary evidence hardly supports him. As an undergraduate he sympathized with a Cambridge dissident who opposed the war, the Revd. William Frend, and he became a Unitarian: Priestley was then an intellectual hero, as were two other liberal theologians, Nathaniel Lardner (1684–1768) and the Unitarian John Disney (1746–1816). Coleridge was at his most radical in 1794–5, at the close of his Cambridge career, when he met Southey, just down from Oxford. Then his letters, sympathetically catching fire from the more dominant Southey, speak derogatively of 'aristocrats' and are full of republican and egalitarian sentiments, of a highly idealistic kind: the pantisocrats should take no servants with them to America, should restrict the number of women (because women are conventional, and will teach children to be so), and should disencumber themselves of private property. Though Southey was the prime mover behind the scheme, he proved less absolute on all these points, especially the last. Disillusioned both with the experiment and with Southey as a friend (though left with the wife Southey had foisted on him for pantisocratic purposes), Coleridge gradually after 1795 found his way to the intellectual position which came most naturally to him.

Throughout the 1790s, Coleridge's views reflect public events and opinion with curious sensitivity: he was strongly susceptible to those around him, particularly to his own kind, the intelligent and altruistic. To begin with, the old and deeply rooted tradition of libertarian Dissent ensured that the radical movement was his natural home. Not that there was any longer hope of gaining civil rights for Dissenters, or indeed any other kind of modest parliamentary reform. Especially as it touched middle-class sympathizers, radicalism was, for the time being, conscious-ness-raising and not a programme for political action. Coleridge, always innocent of parliamentary designs or indeed practical politics, was so far typical enough of his moment. But his position became more particu-larized once, after about 1793, English radicalism began to move away from the connection with Dissent, to become instead identified with the French challenge to all forms of Christianity.

The progressive intellectuals of the 1790s in whom the youthful Coleridge took so keen an interest steadily began to naturalize in England what had hitherto been a French tradition. Classics of the assault upon Christianity included for example Erasmus Darwin's *Botanic Garden*, especially Part I (issued in 1791 under the separate title of *The Economy of Vegetation*) with its stress on propagation as the life-force of the natural world. Darwin substituted for the Genesis account of the Creation a pagan version which emphasized the role of sexuality:

> When Love Divine, with brooding wings unfurl'd
> Call'd from the rude abyss the living world . . .
>   (Canto I.101–2)

The theme of the naturalness of sexuality appeared to contemporaries to be picked up in Godwin's *Political Justice*, 1793, a work which affronted religious ethics with its attack on marriage and apparent advocacy of sexual freedom. Paine's *Age of Reason* (1794–5), though not the huge popular success of his *Rights of Man*, struck at the proprieties in what to some minds seemed profounder terms, for it was a frontal attack on revealed religion in the new French mythological manner – 'It is curious to observe how the theory of what is called the Christian Church sprung out of the tail of the heathen mythology . . . The Christian theory is little else than the idolatry of the ancient mythologists, accommodated to the purposes of power and revenue' (p.5). Two French books made up a radical booklist in this vein. Volney's *Ruins* (1791) was a deliberately reductive historical survey of all religions, in which belief of any kind was viewed as a shackle of the mind. A good piece of polemic, popularly written, it was quickly translated into English and played some part in the configuration of English radicalism over the next generation. Charles Dupuis's more ponderous *Origine de tous les cultes, ou religion universelle* (7 vols, 1795), came too late for translation, given the wartime atmos-phere, but for those who could read it in French made a significantly wholesale attempt to reduce all religions, including Christianity, to Sun-worship. Unlike Paine, Dupuis wrote less like a polemicist than a scientist; religion was to him a study not in the objective truths claimed by revealed religion – 'Les Dieux, chez moi, sont enfans des hommes' (p.viii), but in primitive anthropology and mass psychology: 'je ne suis que l'historien des opinions des autres' (p.vii).

Taken all together, these books of polemic rather than of strict science surely had a very considerable influence in the middle and long term. Between them they suggest why the educated scientific mind might henceforth be inclined towards the atheism which Newton had abjured. Whether through burgeoning natural history, the study of the earth's origins, or through anthropology, the study of primitive man's patterns of belief, the intellectual was moving to his modern position, in which belief became a possibility and not a necessity. The great Victorian controversies were anticipated in the early 1790s: Dupuis's chapter 9 could even be issued as a pamphlet in 1873, translated at last ('Christianity: A Form of the Great Solar Myth'). In the short term the appearance of these books must have had a negative influence on the fortunes of radicalism in England, as the moderates of the all-important Dissenting interest were driven into the loyalist camp. Even the stalwart Priestley issued a pamphlet in 1797 in which he disassociated himself from Volney's atheism. By 1798 Coleridge had publicly protested his loyalty to home, hearth and church, and even his qualified support for Pitt's war-waging administration.

He had read each of the freethinking classics. He had also read a book which he felt to be more dangerous than any of them, Lessing's *Über den Beweis des Geistes und der Kraft* (1777), (On the Proof of the Spirit and the Power'), in which Lessing doubted whether the Bible could serve as the basis for a rational faith, and distinguished between miracles witnessed at first hand and miracles relayed by uncertain testimony. Lessing, Coleridge declared in April 1796, was 'the most formidable infidel of all' (p.197). Intellectual admiration of such daring competed in Coleridge with emotional rejection. To Darwin he conceded 'a greater range of knowledge than any other man in Europe', but their meeting in January 1796 was not a success. 'He thinks in a *new* train in all subjects except religion' (p.177); and Coleridge could not understand Darwin's neglect to think about religion in any way at all. Godwin's arguments about moral and political justice, his objections to the coercions of existing society, his advocacy of a form of extreme decentralization or anarchy, seemed to pass Coleridge by, if indeed he really read *Political Justice*. He was obsessed by Godwin's viciousness, an impression he seems to have arrived at on the basis of his attack on marriage. He jeered at Paine for his lack of Biblical sophistication, and wrote encouragingly to his friend the Revd. John Prior Estlin, who published two anti-Paine pamphlets. His opinion of Dupuis, whom he read in November 1796, is not recorded,

except indirectly: a pity, for Dupuis's line of argument is more fundamental and explicit at this time than anyone's, and his anthropologist's
interpretation of religion not as revealed truth but as something subjective, what men have believed, has an affinity with Coleridge's emerging
concept of the all-creating Imagination.

Thus Coleridge rejected in turn the most innovative radical books to
appear in England during his formative years. Once radicalism denoted
atheism he could not be a radical. Instead of identifying himself with
public causes, or pinning his idealism upon a real-life sect or nation, like
the French, he preferred now to internalize it. His 'Ode' of February
1797, 'France', invokes Liberty, which is no longer to be found across
the Channel, among 'factious Blasphemy's obscener slaves', but in
Coleridge's own imagination and in a new empathy with his surroundings,

> . . . on that sea-cliff's verge,
> Whose pines, scarce travelled by the breeze above,
> Had made one murmur with the distant surge!
> Yes, while I stood and gazed, my temples bare,
> And shot my being through earth, sea and air,
> Possessing all things with intensest love,
> O Liberty! my spirit felt thee there.

The problem for a man of Coleridge's profoundly intellectual habits
was that secession from ideological controversy meant or seemed to mean
a retreat from ideas themselves. All over Europe among France's enemies
there was indeed in the late 1790s a strong drift into anti-intellectualism;
in France itself Napoleon would take steps to quell the revolutionary
ferment of ideas. With his acute sensitivity to the prejudices of others,
Coleridge in March 1798 reassured his clergyman brother that his
friendships – notably now with Wordsworth – were the occasion for
supportive discussion and contemplation rather than argument:

In general conversation & general company I endeavor to find out the opinions
common to us – or at least the subjects on which difference of opinion creates no
uneasiness – such as novels, poetry, natural scenery, local anecdotes & (in a
serious mood and with serious men) the general evidences of our Religion. (p.398)

But he was far too intelligent not to sense the philistinism behind the
current mood. With typical fineness of insight he urged Wordsworth in
1799 to write in addition to the significantly named *Recluse* a poem
analysing the dangers of the anti-intellectual reaction:

I wish you would write a poem, in blank verse, addressed to those, who, in
consequence of the complete failure of the French Revolution, have thrown up all

hopes of the amelioration of mankind, and are sinking into an almost epicurean selfishness, disguising the same under the soft titles of domestic attachment and contempt for visionary *philosophes*. (p.527)

The fact was that Coleridge found his own intellectual position horribly compromised by the schism within the radical movement between Christians and Deists, which meant that though he still notionally abhorred 'aristocracy', his profoundest disagreements were with his fellow-liberals. The philosopher in him longed to do battle; the Notebooks of 1795–6 list the many schemes with which he intermittently thought to confront his intellectual opponents in argument:

'Answer to the System of Nature' ... 'The Origin of Evil, an Epic Poem' ... 'Strictures on Godwin, Paley &c &c' ... 'A Liturgy On the different Sects of Religion & Infidelity – philosophical analysis of their Effects on mind & manners'. (*Another list*) 'On Marriage – in opposition to French Principles' ... 'Hymns to the Sun, the Moon, and the Elements – six hymns. – In one of them to introduce a dissection of Atheism – particularly the Godwinian System of Pride Proud of what? An outcast of blind Nature ruled by a fatal Necessity – Slave of an ideot Nature!' (entries 161G.156 and 174 G.159)

All remained unwritten, as did his frequently promised book opposing the ethical system of Godwin with that of Jesus Christ, which might have made Coleridge's central statement of his thinking during the decade. Eventually, in his books as in his personal contacts, he preferred to deal with ideas emotionally. He cast into his memory and was able to match the clever books which had disturbed him with imaginative books which had comforted and delighted him. Thus, though he often declared that he was about to equip himself in the sciences (to refute Darwin and perhaps as time went on his former idol Priestley), he detached himself from the contemporary progressive campaign to educate children in the sciences, to which his friend Thomas Beddoes and Beddoes's father-in-law Richard Lovell Edgeworth were contributing. Coleridge recalled that it was the least rational part of his own early reading which had led him to what he considered the greatest truths:

From my early reading of Faery Tales, & Genii &c &c – my mind had been habituated *to the Vast* – & I never regarded *my senses* in any way as the criteria of my belief. I regulated all my creeds by my conceptions not by my *sight* – even at that age. Should children be permitted to read Romances, & Relations of Giants & Magicians, & Genii? – I know all that has been said against it; but I have formed my faith in the affirmative. – I know no other way of giving the mind a love of 'the Great', & 'the Whole.' – Those who have been led to the same truths step by step through the constant testimony of their senses, seem to me to want a sense which I possess – They contemplate nothing but *parts* – and all *parts* are necessarily little –

and the Universe to them is but a mass of *little things* . . . . I have known some who have been *rationally* educated, as it is styled. They were marked by a microscopic acuteness; but when they looked at great things, all became a blank & they saw nothing – and denied (very illogically) that anything could be seen.   (pp.354–5)

In December 1796, the month when he was reading Dupuis's chilly analyses, Coleridge upheld to the atheist Thelwall the superior beauty and imaginative force of the Hebraic Bible over the classical pantheon. The version of classical lore that interested him was, as he put it, 'from Tauth [Thoth] the Egyptian to Taylor, the English Pagan' (p.260); he ordered from his bookseller Iamblichus, Proclus and Porphyry, the Alexandrian neo-Platonists whom the new scientific anthropologists had sought to explode as decadent obfuscators of genuine primitive religion. Coleridge's reaction to the growing dominance of atheists over English radicalism was, like Blake's, a recourse to a kind of Christianity which blended magic with the comforts of the nursery. He was thus on a course of irrationalism and Christian apologetics before he went to Germany in 1798–9 and equipped himself to read the writers of that already internalized culture who would furnish him with further material: the metaphysician Kant, the Bible critic Eichhorn, and the anthropologist Blumenbach.

Coleridge's rejection of the growing Deist vogue for mythology has enormous repercussions in his literary work. The mythologists saw religion as the imaginative product of early man, his re-enactment in poetic terms of permanent truths about the environment, such as the cycles of the year and the relationship of Sun or Heat or Energy to Matter. For them the diversity and fancifulness of myth was further evidence of its human origins: the same phenomena were reflected in as many versions as there were cultures, religions, and individual poets or myth-makers. Coleridge saw the implications and resolutely lined himself up with the One God of the Hebrews against the pagan many. He experienced religion as something intensely personal; Jesus, whom he loved, was a Man; the Old Testament, divinely inspired, was a sequence of narratives about human beings with whom he could empathize, 'living educts of the imagination' (*Lay Sermons*, p.31). Some contemporaries would see in the plenitude of ancient mythology, its legion of allegorical fables, externalized, fanciful, yet also truth-telling, a potent example for art. In Germany Friedrich Schlegel, who was deeply versed in Greek literature, developed an aesthetic which fully allowed for the various, the objective and the dramatic. Erasmus Darwin, insufficiently skilfully, produced in *The Botanic Garden* a poem that was at once intellectually meaningful and richly diverse and fantastic, itself a deliberately constructed mythology. Shelley and his contemporaries would achieve a poetically more acceptable equivalent in the next generation. But for the time being English horizons were, as Coleridge himself so revealingly confessed to Wordsworth, shrinkingly personal and domestic. Lamb in the same turn-of-century mood abjured the systematic history-writing of the Enlightenment, of Hume and Gibbon, and returned to the agreeable fireside gossip of Bishop Burnet; later, in selecting Elizabethan and Jacobean plays, he would reject masques and pastorals, 'with their train of abstractions', in favour of a human dimension –

to show in what manner they felt, when they placed themselves by the power of imagination in trying situations, in the conflicts of duty and passion, or the strife of contending duties; what sort of loves and enmities theirs were; how their griefs were tempered, and their full-swoln joys abated. (iv. xi–xii)

Coleridge's deeply introverted and fideist traits were apt for the hour, and it was in 1797–8, the fiercest year of the English counter-revolutionary reaction, that he produced almost all his corpus of great poems. 'This Lime Tree Bower my Prison', 'Frost at Midnight', 'The Ancient Mariner', 'Kubla Khan' and 'Christabel' express the intensity and freshness of the process the letters reveal, that discovery of the self and elevation of the self's truth against the disturbing systems of generalized external 'truth'. All Coleridge's greatest poems are rapt, intent and exclusive; they invoke one protagonist, one imagined world. It is a mistake to see the development of Coleridge's poetry as fundamentally determined by the ideas or personal example of Wordsworth or of any other external 'influence'. His commitment through his Christian beliefs to the cause of humanity, peace and freedom, and the fragmentation in the mid-1790s of the English movement to support that cause affected Coleridge independently, and the problem was more emotional for him than for Wordsworth. Coleridge's experience had led him to long above all for a secure place among a tight circle of family and friends and before the public. The Pantisocratic scheme, which would have made an ideal community, had failed him; the wider radical movement had failed him; all those still suspected of radical opinions were unpopular; his marriage with Sara Fricker brought him scant security or companionship. In his early adulthood Coleridge was experiencing not community but alienation, and his best poetry is the record of it.

'The Ancient Mariner' (1798) depicts a man in whom moral isolation is inseparable from a sense of guilt. After a nightmare in which, alone of his kind, he seems unable to die, his climactic experience is the return to his own country, where, a haunted outcast, he can never be accepted into the common pattern of other men's lives. Ghastly, possessed, his appearance at the wedding is as ominous and unwelcome as that of the bad fairy at a christening, yet, far from representing mankind's enemy, he is man himself at his most vulnerable, the archetypal victim. But Coleridge's other poems of 1797–8 envisage some relief from the vision of unending horror. 'This Lime Tree Bower my Prison' opens in a mood of misery and self-pity, because Coleridge is temporarily separated from his friends. Sara has accidentally scalded his foot, so that his visitor Charles Lamb and his neighbours William and Dorothy Wordsworth have set out on a keenly anticipated walk without him. Coleridge imagines with wonderful precision what they are seeing in the dell to which he has directed them –

> there my friends
> Behold the dark green file of long lank weeds,
> That all at once (a most fantastic sight!)
> Still nod and drip beneath the dripping edge
> Of the blue clay-stone.

The contemplation of nature vicariously, through sympathy with his friends, leads him to an equally intent apprehension of his own surroundings:

> And that walnut-tree
> Was richly tinged, and a deep radiance lay
> Full on the ancient ivy, which usurps
> Those fronting elms, and now, with blackest mass
> Makes their dark branches gleam a lighter hue
> Through the late twilight.

Their shared response to the same natural world links him with his friends; the bower encloses him, he is at home. And the most perfect of his poems, 'Frost at Midnight', is similarly reassuring. Contemplation of his sleeping baby and the quiet fire sends his train of thought outwards to their natural surroundings, in which the child will find the home which Coleridge's family denied him when they sent him away to school.

The intense focus upon the intimate and local which Coleridge achieved in his poetry during this brief phase was not peculiar to him. Burke in his *Reflections* (1790) had already spelt out the ideological implications of such a focus:

To be attached to the subdivision, to love the little platoon we belong to in society, is the first principle (the germ as it were) of public affections. It is the first link in the series by which we proceed towards a love to our country and to mankind.

Coleridge did not need prompting from Burke, for his own nature evidently responded to motifs, especially marriage and parenthood, which were all the rage in the popular art of the late 1790s. In scores of novels coldhearted seducers appear from London or Paris to break up the happiness of hitherto virtuous rural families. An etching by Rowlandson, 'Disturbers of Domestic Happiness', nicely epitomizes the theme: three ruffians, one of them bare-legged, literally a *sansculotte*, have broken into a house and gather menacingly around two graceful fainting figures, a young woman and her little girl. It is no coincidence that in the very years of Coleridge's absorption in such themes, Jane Austen, like many another women novelist, developed her preference for the tightly enclosed, familiar, intimately English range of subject, 'three or four families in a country village'. The shift from a public to a private focus is in response to political events and has an acknowledged political significance–loyalism–a fact which is well demonstrated in Coleridge's most ideologically explicit 'private' poem of this sequence, 'Fears in Solitude. Written in April, 1798, during the alarm of an invasion'. Here Coleridge opens in what is by now a favourite setting, an enclosed dell, 'a green and silent spot, amid the hills', from which all views of the outer world are excluded. But his thoughts wander out to contemplate, shrinkingly, a violent disturbance in this invisible vista, a French invasion bringing with it 'uproar and strife'. His thoughts reluctantly engaged with external reality, Coleridge considers what has brought England into her present peril. He blames first the inherent defects of her own oligarchic system: the blasphemous oath-taking (a reference to the tests which excluded Dissenters and Catholics from public office, that is a reiteration of the complaints of Dissenters in their campaign of 1788–90) and the aggressive colonial wars. But he also blames the French who, impious, cruel and sensual, 'poison life's amities'; he now finds them so much more profoundly guilty that he urges his countrymen to unite against them. In a divided nation, he himself has been accused by a bigoted faction of disloyalty –

> But O dear Britain! O my Mother Isle!
> Needs must thou prove a name most dear and holy
> To me, a son, a brother, and a friend,
> A husband, and a father! who revere
> All bonds of natural love, and find them all
> Within the limits of thy rocky shores.

His sense of these bonds of natural love brings him back to a sharply particular observation of the dell, where

> now the gentle dew-fall sends abroad
> The fruit-like perfume of the golden furze . . .
> . . . And after lonely sojourning
> In such a quiet and surrounded nook,

This burst of prospect, here the shadowy main,
Dim tinted, there the mighty majesty
Of that huge amphitheatre of rich
And elmy fields, seems like society –
Conversing with the mind, and giving it
A livelier impulse and a dance of thought!
And now, beloved Stowey! I behold
Thy church-tower, and, methinks, the four huge elms
Clustering, which mark the mansion of my friend;
And close behind them, hidden from my view,
Is my own lowly cottage, where my babe
And my babe's mother dwell in peace!

It is the demonstration that attachment to the little platoon we belong to in society is attachment to society itself. Thus the minutiae of Coleridge's actual life in this rich year were made to illuminate public issues. Hyper-emotional, acutely responsive, he caught the fear in the public mood and availed himself of a moment when his own insecurity could be made the correlative for England's. If his creative period as a poet was brief, it was partly because his emotional life ceased to make natural material for public poetry. He went abroad to Germany with Wordsworth in October 1798, perhaps (though this would be ironic) to avoid conscription; when he came back, the failure of his marriage was more evident and William and Dorothy Wordsworth had removed to the Lakes, breaking the intense but fragile bonds on his local spot of ground.

The truth was that, unlike Wordsworth, Coleridge had a very narrow range as a poet. Wordsworth's attitude to the world he contemplated had a general philosophical dimension; it lacked the neurotic intensity and feverish topicality which were Coleridge's strength and weakness. Though Coleridge believed in philosophical poetry (for Wordsworth) and saw the dangers of anti-intellectual domestic poetry (for Wordsworth again), he himself lacked the strictly professional resources to get out of his self-made enclosure. Wordsworth retained in large measure the liberating externality of the Enlightenment writer, even if he now struggled to internalize and spiritualize his relations with Nature. Coleridge, more introverted to begin with, lacked this range, just as, lacking Wordsworth's craftsmanship, he could not sustainedly make language itself the medium for conveying the world of thought. For all his rich talent, for all the metrical inventiveness of a poem like 'Christabel', Coleridge the poet was not myriad-minded like Coleridge the man. The vein of his poetry ran out because it could not be adapted to a sufficient variety of ends. It worked while its seclusiveness seemed meaningful, and after that it was solipsistic.

For a very considerable difference of approach divided Wordsworth and Coleridge, even in their *annus mirabilis*, and in spite of their mutual agreement (in Coleridge's phrase) to 'snap [the] squeaking baby-trumpet of Sedition' (*Letters*, p.397). Each was writing a play in 1796–7, and the comparison between the two works is instructive. Wordsworth's *Borderers* (which biographical evidence suggests was written first) and Coleridge's *Osorio* share elements of plot and character beyond the point of coincidence. In both there are two male protagonists, one of whom tempts the other to a crime against the woman he loves. But *The Borderers* is a public play, an allegory meant quite explicitly to convey Burke's suspicion of the modern radical intellectual, and of intellectualism itself. In *Osorio* the same underlying nexus of ideas appears to be present, but without *The Borderers* the reader might have difficulty in making it out. The element of allegory – that essentially intellectual device – is drastically reduced. It is as though this is a critique of intellectualism and abstraction so total that ideas themselves have had to be omitted. What is left is personal – the psychological experience, a sensitive, empathetic, even heartfelt rendering of guilt between brothers. Coleridge has pushed to an expressive extreme art's retreat from ideas. Though his medium, the drama, implies the existence of an objective social world, he writes as though the world outside his tormented hero's consciousness is hardly his concern. The signs are strong that his prodigious intellect is blocked off from poetry, into which he pours so much of his emotional self.

Sure enough, the rapt preference for retreat of his poetic years was by no means Coleridge's final intellectual stance. He had now identified his enemy in the new atheistical radicalism, the French Enlightenment tradition which meant in philosophy rationalism, empiricalism and materialism, and in politics levelling and innovation. During the first three decades of the nineteenth century Coleridge's task was to debate and to exemplify the part of the Christian intellectual in modern society, and he was no longer so fearful of system that he abjured argument as well. The first major production of his new career as a professed Christian apologist, his periodical *The Friend* (1809–10) announces an Object and Plan which are in their way boldly theoretical:

The Friend consists of a methodical series of essays, the principal purpose of which is to assist the mind in the formation for itself of sound, and therefore permanent and universal, principles in regard to the investigation, perception, and retention of truth, in whatever direction soever it may be pursued; but pre-eminently with reference to the three great relations in which we are placed in this world, – as citizens to the state, as men to our neighbours, and as creatures to our Creator, – in other words, to politics, to morals, and to religion.

The Coleridge myth is of a man who failed to fulfil his brilliant promise, through weakness of character and (if this is not the same thing) addiction to opium. Actually Coleridge's really significant or at least influential career was as a moulder of opinion, and it began with *The Friend* and continued with the *Lay Sermons* (1816–17), the *Biographia Literaria* (1817), the *Aids to Reflection* (1825) and *On the Constitution of the Church and State* (1830). Perhaps the most interesting part of this career falls between 1815 and 1818, years, significantly, of renewed public controversy. It is as though Coleridge was born despite himself to be a controversialist. His best years were those of universal political uproar, which were 1792–9, 1815–18, and 1829–32. The radical controversialist Peacock was similarly spurred to activity in the crises of 1815–18 and 1829–32, and quiet during the publicly quiescent years before and after.

The years 1815–18 marked the delayed end of the Napoleonic Wars and the establishment of a conservative peace. They saw the apparent defeat of the French Revolution; the restitution, all over Europe, of monarchies whose claims to legitimacy went back to feudal times; the restoration also of the Catholic Church and even the Spanish Inquisition. In England it was a period of national triumph followed immediately by hardship, unemployment, agrarian riots, machine-breaking, protest marches, and, by 1817, localized insurrection. After a wartime period of more or less consensus politics, clear and deep divisions emerged not only between the poor and the rich, but also between the landed gentry and the manufacturers. Coleridge in these circumstances felt a renewed call to address the public. He experienced or created a revival of interest in his earlier work: his hitherto unpublished poetry, including 'Christabel', came out in 1816 and 1817, and *The Friend* was published for the first time as a book in 1818. But the real core of what he wanted to say was new writing, and it made an interrelated series of themes for the times.

The creative period begins with a play, *Zapolya*, which the management of Drury Lane rejected in 1815, but which Coleridge published as a book in 1817. *Zapolya* adapts the plot of *The Winter's Tale*, turning it into a symbolic drama about the restoration of ancient, legitimate kings after the lapse of a generation, the forgiveness of selfish, erring subjects, and a universal or at least national experience of reconciliation. Such optimism was all very well for the year of European peace. Already by 1816 the stability of the British government looked more threatened than it had since in the 1790s, and Coleridge's reaction in the *Lay Sermons* became anxious. There were to have been three sermons, one each for the three social orders, but significantly Coleridge wrote only the two designed for the educated strata – the *Statesman's Manual*, 1816, 'Addressed to the Higher Classes of Society', and a year later a second Sermon, 'Addressed to the Higher and Middle Classes on the Existing Distresses and

Discontents'. It was evidently deliberate that these exclusive-sounding title-pages were matched by a text of consummate difficulty: Dorothy Wordsworth commented that the *Statesman's Manual* was 'ten times more obscure than the darkest parts of the *Friend*'.

Probably few people now read the *Lay Sermons*, but the second especially is a key document, in which the *Biographia Literaria* is indissolubly bound up. The *Biographia* is intended to convey in its first half the Christian culture Coleridge wants the educated Englishman to subscribe to; in its second half, to consider critically some of the subtler and better-intentioned deviations from that culture, like Wordsworth's. But the *Biographia* is inevitably, by its very strategy, a highly specialized book which demands a readership willing and able to tackle the most difficult contemporary philosophy and poetry. It is also cast, like so much of Coleridge's best work, in the introverted form of a personal apologia. The *Lay Sermons* were written to relate the personal experience to the national situation, and they create the context against which the Coleridgean life becomes not merely representative but exemplary.

The goal Coleridge sets himself in the *Lay Sermons* is to analyse what the current British ruling classes are like and what they might be like. Coleridge perceives the Constitution much as Burke did a generation earlier, as a mighty organism, slow-growing like a tree (pp.22-3), which merely needs stable conditions and continuity in order to continue to flourish. The first Sermon is a rather generalized discussion of the intellectual innovations which have caused the educated classes to swerve from the traditional concept of themselves as leaders. During the eighteenth century they were subverted by a new school of thought, headed by Hume, of materialists, sceptics, infidels, necessitarian historians and unitarians. Writing in the abstruse and lofty terms appropriate to his sense of an audience of hereditary leaders, Coleridge exhorts them to return to the religion, at once hierarchical and simple, learned and emotional, which ultimately sanctions both the Constitution and their privileged place in it.

In 1817, when the second *Lay Sermon* appeared, the political situation was uglier, so that the tone is more urgent. Instead of directing its attack on the intellectuals of the eighteenth century Enlightenment, it excoriates living misleaders of the people like Cobbett, the Hunt brothers and Hazlitt (pp.155-71). It is topical in its references to current issues, like unequal taxation (pp.171 ff.), and focuses far more closely than the first sermon on the real post-war state of society – 'we are ... a busy, enterprising and commercial nation' (p.216). It is indeed in the rise of the commercial spirit that Coleridge now sees the real danger to the Constitution. Traditionally there were counterweights to this acquisitiveness in the commitment of a more powerful and prestigious aristocracy to their landed estates, and in the moral advice handed out by a clerical or philosophical class which spoke with the authority of the national religion. But Coleridge sees the weakness both of the gentry and the philosophers in modern times, for both groups have lost their idealism and their understanding of their roles, which depended upon tradition – 'To the feudal system we owe the forms, to the Church the substance of our liberty' (p.248n.). In place of modern individualism Coleridge advocates a return to duty. He believes that the society which functions on truly social principles is the hierarchical one, which can be retrieved only when the present-day leaders become aware of their responsibilities:

> Our manufacturers must consent to regulations; our gentry must concern themselves in the education as well as in the instruction of their natural clients and dependents, must regard their estates as secured indeed from all human interference by every principle of law, and policy; but yet as offices of trust, with duties to be performed, in the sight of God and their country. Let us become a better people, and the reform of all the public (real or supposed) grievances, which we use as pegs whereon to hang our own errors and defects, will follow of itself.
>
> (pp.266–7)

As in 1797–8, Coleridge was both apposite and timely. His criticisms of the postwar gentry were shared by other conservative moralists, as the case of Jane Austen will illustrate. His fears for the stability of the constitution were common to the propertied classes throughout the country, so that for once his sermonizing strictures did not fall on deaf ears. Henceforth Coleridge, though never a best-seller, was listened to by that élite, and particularly the philosophical élite, which he designedly addressed. The *Sermons* – polemical, extreme, and frequently absurd – first provoked the hostility of young liberal intellectuals, and then more slowly helped to lay the foundation for Coleridge's influence on the next generation. By the 1820s, the religious revival for which Coleridge was calling had come, led as he wished by the upper orders. His *Aids to Reflection* (1825) found its readers in the Oxford Movement and among the Cambridge Apostles. His *Constitution of the Church and State* (1830) conveyed to the youthful future rulers a splendidly imaginative notion of British society as an aristocracy and a theocracy – even if it did so in the very era when two reforms, Catholic Emancipation in 1829 and the 1832 Reform Bill, removed the main features on which its constitutional analysis was based. To the end he was writing for a group, about membership of the group, that is about society, but out of a current experience of fragmentation.

Some of Coleridge's social observations were acute, but his claim to importance does not lie in his accuracy. Considered in absolute terms, as social criticism, theology and constitutional theory, his essays are always vulnerable. The same objections can be made to his selective, emotional approaches to philosophy and to literature. It could be argued that he gave intellectual justifications for shifting the emphasis from ratiocination to intuition and feeling, though his writing on abstract questions often deserves the rebuke that Kant administered to another subjective disciple, Jacobi. 'Philosophy', grumbled Kant, 'is fundamentally prosaic.' In fact the objection is irrelevant, since Coleridge was no academic, in quest of unknown solutions and unbiased about what these would turn out to be. He wrote as an active participant, a Christian apologist, and thus he was always in the last resort didactic.

It is all too easy to exaggerate the influence of a single thinker or writer. The religious revival of the 1820s was a European phenomenon and its powerful impact in England was certainly not worked by Coleridge. It is however surely reasonable to attribute to Coleridge some influence over who was touched by religion, and in precisely what form. No other writer so habitually interwove literary and philosophical questions not merely with theology, but with active, practical Christianity. His great intellectual range was put to the service of religion, so that over and again, in every sphere of knowledge he touched, he made the religious aspect unavoidable.

The polemicist must be, to use the older word, a rhetorician; a newer word is a publicist. Coleridge in his later career learnt what he had not known in the 1790s, the art of persuasion. The density of his style when he writes of German philosophy may be justified on the grounds that it is appropriate; a better defence is that it is effective. Coleridge meant to use his writings to find out an élite, and to help remould it in better accordance with his ideal. The style of his writing helped him to his audience, since the strangely specialized tone made a kind of compact with the reader, flatteringly promoting him to membership among the elect. It is frequently the function of an intellectual jargon that those who have once learnt the tone and language remain of the party. Coleridge is surely the first example, in England at least, of the sage who turns himself into a cult-figure for the next student-generation. It can hardly be called an accident when it was the very essence of his literary strategy. All along, his work internalizes: it moves the sphere of significant action from the world of event to the world of thought, from system to experience, from the literal and scientific to the imaginative and moral. With all its incidental weaknesses, Coleridge's œuvre succeeds impressionistically in validating the experience of the individual intellectual, and in refuting the notion that the isolated, alienated thinker is either worthless or without influence. However unmethodical, his thinking is directed towards emotional solutions for the loneliness of his type. He finds comfort in personal religion and (unlike the German Romantic) in the more social concept of membership of an ideal community. Pantisocrasy is a lost dream of his youth, the tight-knit circle of family and friends is dissolved, but he replaces them with the 'clerisy', the State and the Church. Not surprisingly, twentieth-century intellectuals of both the Left and the Right, the socialist and the churchman, have continued to find value in his writing. The emotional appeal has outlasted the immediate situation, and also outweighed flaws in the argument.

Above all, among his persuader's armoury of weapons Coleridge had himself. It is difficult to say how consciously he learnt to exploit his own personality. He had no terminology to define what he was doing, and no doubt his self-characterization in his writing is largely intuitive. As in the poems and letters, so in *The Friend*, the *Lay Sermons* and the *Biographia Literaria*, he appears vulnerable, victimized, yet always, in his happier moments, capable of the barely controlled, inspirational flight. Constantly in his appearances before the public he is the poet-figure of 'Kubla Khan', magical and extraordinary, drunk upon the milk of Paradise. In the last resort he probably matters more for what he is than for what he writes. To put it another way, the writing seems not to originate in a literary theory, a deliberate poetic original to Coleridge or borrowed from Germany, but in a state of self and group consciousness. Coleridge wrote as he did because he was a certain kind of man – who for historical reasons had many counterparts among his fellow intellectuals. His own life – beginning with drastic disillusionment with ideas in the 1790s, continuing with a quest for solutions that are far more meaningful in the world of thought than in the world of action – the life and its refraction in the writing make up the achievement.

M. H. Abrams begins his celebrated study *The Mirror and the Lamp* by arguing that Romantic literary theory centres upon the poet, but he finds it hard to show that a coherent theory of the poet or of the poetic imagination was widely disseminated, let alone accepted, in England much before 1830. What does emerge earlier, most brilliantly with and through Coleridge, is a new recognition of the distinctiveness of the poet as a type. It was Coleridge who in the second decade of the century, that Restoration era when so many German and French painters were creating soulful, alienated portraits of themselves and one another, produced his English writerly equivalent, the *Biographia Literaria*. At the same time he exerted a curiously hypnotic spell upon younger writers. Byron, Shelley and Keats not only admired his poetry but were profoundly aware of him as a man. It is no accident that so much of the response to Coleridge in the 1820s was personal, and that (for example in the remarks of Hazlitt,

De Quincey and Carlyle) it contained so acute a sense of Coleridge as a personal failure. That sense of frustration and of despair was as necessary for his hold on the sympathy of his fellow-intellectuals as was the inspiration proffered by his self-generated solution. Coleridge represents our idea of the artist in its modern variant, and it appears to be necessary that he should be tragic: neurotic, displaced, the Hamlet of our times, an appropriate culture-hero for the nineteenth and twentieth centuries. In 'The Ancient Mariner' and 'Dejection: an Ode' Coleridge gives poetic form to the concept, but it is no less expressive that he lived it.

4 Novels for the gentry: Austen and Scott

The end of the eighteenth century might have been a period of technical take-off for the novel, had the generation to come been one that favoured innovation. Writers of less than first-class rank nevertheless made interesting headway in promising new directions. The sentimental tradition detached itself from socially specific settings in order to concentrate more fully on the apprehensions of the central character, and the talented Ann Radcliffe developed a particularly significant technique of subjective, internalized narration. Wholly different experiments meanwhile emerged from scientific and humanist Dissenting circles, based on precise documentation of real-life manners and language and (since the intention was often pragmatically educational) on the thought-processes of children. Here another woman, Maria Edgeworth, was the most important pioneer. In the short era of revolutionary enthusiasm in the early 1790s, new political and social ideas were conveyed into the novel by a group of polemicists, of whom the most capable were William Godwin, Elizabeth Inchbald, Thomas Holcroft and Robert Bage. Charlotte Smith, probably the ablest exponent in this decade of the standard popular social novel, was a liberal sympathizer and so frequently echoed the same causes. Most striking, though not most significant aesthetically, the feminists Mary Wollstonecraft (*Mary*, 1788, and *Maria or the Wrongs of Woman*, 1798) and Mary Hays (*The Memoirs of Emma Courtney*, 1796) also seized upon the novel as a vehicle for the dissemination of their ideas.

All these innovators were affected by the turning tide of taste, from liberalism to reaction, in the first half of the 1790s. With the elevation of the close-knit family unit to symbolic status, as the corner-stone of the social edifice, the very topic of feminine independence and the merest hint of female sexual incontinence became virtually taboo. Godwin's frank *Memoirs of the author of a Vindication of the Rights of Woman* (1798), which detailed the love affairs of his dead wife, Mary Wollstonecraft, and her attempted suicide, caused a considerable *frisson*, and contributed to a situation in which, for at least two generations, it was hard for women to articulate the feminist case. Maria Edgeworth prudently inserted a grotesque caricature of a feminist, Harriot Freke, into her mildly liberal novel *Belinda* (1801), in order to ward off any suspicion of her own principles. Already by 1794, with *The Mysteries of Udolpho*, Ann Radcliffe was carefully including warnings against sentiment in a quintessentially sentimental text, but these could not save the genre. Public suspicion of its unsoundness was clinched by the advent on the scene of M. G. Lewis's shocker, *The Monk* (1795), in which a pillar of the Church is revealed as a fornicator, a sadistic rapist and a murderer, and a convent, along with its abbess, is torn in pieces by an outraged mob, in a scene all too reminiscent of recent events in Paris. After one attempt, *The Italian* (1797), to accommodate Lewis's manner to her own apparently safer one, Ann Radcliffe fell silent.

It was thus not merely professedly radical writing which suffered a rebuff in the reactionary atmosphere of the times. Other more subtle innovations – including women's writing less polemical than Mary Wollstonecraft's – also became compromised, or altogether frustrated. Ann Radcliffe's novels do not canvass for specific rights nor dwell, too pleasurably, upon extreme visions of disorder, but they do focus with such sensitivity and naturalness upon the psyche of the central character that they convey what may have been in the context of the hour a suspect attitude to human nature. The Radcliffe novel is to an unusual degree subjective and relativist. Its concern is not with what the heroine sees but with what she thinks she sees; its ghastly secrets are not literal acts of violence but long-buried psychic wounds. Later critics laughed at Ann Radcliffe for not using real horrors in her novels. They failed to see that her preference for her heroine's consciousness was daring in a perhaps more intelligent vein. In *The Sicilian Romance* (1790), *The Romance of the Forest* (1791) and *Udolpho*, experience itself, the flow of consciousness, interests for its own sake, and the acutely sensitive heroines interest too, for their capacity to register and respond. The feminine experience, passive intelligence, impotent receptivity, is portrayed though not analysed. While not supporting nor presumably consciously sharing the feminist ideological position, Ann Radcliffe pushes further than anyone yet the novel's technique for seeing the world through explicitly female eyes.

Maria Edgeworth is an equally interesting example of the woman writer who experienced the pressure of the times. She was emotionally and intellectually under the influence of her father, Richard Lovell Edgeworth, an Anglo-Irish gentleman with social and intellectual tastes which led him to associate with Midlands entrepreneurs and industrialists. Like the others, Edgeworth was a political liberal, who supported the causes of parliamentary reform and popular education in Ireland. He was also in his own right an able and enlightened educator, who believed in letting children learn by experiment, at a curriculum that put more weight on applied science than on the traditional classics. His *Practical Education* of 1798, on which his daughter Maria collaborated, left out feminine accomplishments, and let girls learn mechanics and chemistry. It also omitted religion. The failure to bring in religion made Edgeworth notorious to Tory journalists like William Gifford and John Wilson Croker, who indeed remembered the offence for a whole generation, and brought it up in the *Quarterly Review* of 1820 in a vicious attack on Edgeworth's posthumous *Memoirs*.

Her background ensured that Maria Edgeworth began her writing life in 1795 as an enlightened woman and a moderate feminist. Her early stories (like the children's series *The Parent's Assistant* (1796) and the novel *Belinda*) feature very sensible protagonists, often girls, who learn an unconventional degree of independence, and come to rely upon themselves instead of society. Later she developed the genre for which she is best remembered, naturalistically observed stories set among the Irish peasantry. Both types of story are didactic, in the grave public-spirited manner of the Enlightenment. The Irish tales, for example, are designed to make the English better disposed towards their neighbours by bringing out the warmth and humour of the peasantry; they are also a semi-documentary record of Irish manners, phrases and customs. The precision of this way of writing and its utilization of documentary detail again made a contribution, and a significant one, to the nineteenth-century novel of provincial and low life. In her novels of manners, on the face of it less original, she continued to depict women as intelligent and often masterful individuals, rather than the stereotyped, willing domestic creatures so common in the fiction of the counter-revolutionary period. But there is apparently a puzzle here. Why did Ann Radcliffe fall silent while Maria Edgeworth, the identifiable liberal, was able to continue and indeed to develop her techniques throughout the sensitive war period?

Maria Edgeworth's heyday, from 1795 to 1817, coincides more or less exactly (as does Jane Austen's) with the alarmist years. Within this period she was remarkably successful. Francis Jeffrey, Walter Scott and Jane Austen were among her admirers, and for one novel, *Patronage* (1814), she was paid £2,000, compared with the top price Jane Austen got – for *Emma* in 1816 – of £300. After 1817 the tide of taste began to turn against her, partly because the religious revival made the secular and scientific premisses of the Edgeworthian education system suspect. One has the impression that she was not much read after the 1830s, except by the children of parents of agnostic leanings, as a welcome alternative to the hellfire and deathbed repentances of the juvenile school of Mrs

Sherwood, author of *The Fairchild Family* (1818). But it seems interesting that the decided vogue for this daughter of the Enlightenment lasted so long, and virtually through the productive periods of all six major 'Romantic' poets.

The phenomenon is less baffling if we recall the flexibility and absorptive genius of the English gentry and aristocracy in this expansive era. Just as classicism remained a dominant influence over taste throughout the Napoleonic Wars, so did utility, despite the distinct radical associations of both. With the Continent closed to their sons, the English aristocracy sent them to finish their education in Edinburgh and even Glasgow, home of the 'dismal science' of political economy inaugurated by Adam Smith. Bowood, the country house of the liberal Whig Lord Lansdowne, functioned during the war period as an intellectual centre of the new economics and of a liberal, reformist political philosophy. The Genevese Etienne Dumont, formerly the aide of the French revolutionary Mirabeau, now the amanuensis of the radical English reformer Jeremy Bentham, lived intermittently at Bowood on a kind of informal research fellowship, as Joseph Priestley had been supported for a time in the 1780s by the previous Lord Landsowne. Maria Edgeworth corresponded with Dumont about education and penology, and from 1813 was an occasional visitor at Bowood. Thus, though she was probably the most liberal of successful writers in the period before Byron rose to fame in 1812, her kind of liberalism remained acceptable because it was the practical wealth-getting creed of an increasingly large and influential section of the propertied classes. Besides, unlike her father, Maria Edgeworth was no controversialist. Deferential herself, tactfully feminine, she preached in her books social harmony and enlightened progressiveness within the present order of things. Therefore she prospered, and the fact that her novels eclipsed Jane Austen's in celebrity at the time of publication is an indication of the survival in England of a prudently modified Enlightenment taste during the first two decades of the nineteenth century.

Maria Edgeworth was optimistic about man and woman; wrote about, and even for, all classes of society; addressed herself on general issues to the public at large. Jane Austen did none of these things. The tendency of her fiction is to rebuke individual self-assertion. The six Austen novels are about the gentry, and addressed to the gentry, in a style clearly influenced by public opinion in the 1790s. Jane Austen was of an age, as Coleridge was, to be peculiarly susceptible to the extremes of the counter-revolution, the hysterical reaction of 1796–8. Once a writer has arrived at maturity and his cast of mind is formed, outside events or movements may influence such opinions, but are hardly likely to be formative. Maria Edgeworth arrived at the age of twenty-one in 1789; Wordsworth in 1791; Scott also in 1791 or perhaps 1792; Coleridge in 1793, and Jane Austen in 1796. Her age is one reason why her novels have the stamp of those years of strong reaction, years when the English cultural habit moved from internationalism to Francophobia, and deep-rooted popular modern English Toryism was born. Among other things, Jane Austen's Toryism made it hard for her to countenance, even as much as Maria Edgeworth did, Enlightenment criticism of social constraints upon women. The woman novelist of the era of reaction, the late 1790s, was inclined on the contrary to idealize 'feminine' traits in female characters, such as humility, contentment with a domestic role, and absence of sexuality. Jane Austen retained quite enough of the eighteenth century and quite enough respect for her own intelligence to give her heroines character and rationality. Yet the distinctive turns of her plots, unlike those of Maria Edgeworth, rebuke individualistic female initiatives, and imply that the consummation of a woman's life lies in marriage to a commanding man.

It has not been the received view that Jane Austen is a child of her time. Victorians and Edwardians used to remark on her failure to mention the French Revolution or the Napoleonic Wars, and twentieth-century critics brought the complaint (if it was one) up to date by regretting the omission of the Industrial Revolution. Jane Austen might have introduced overt discussion of politics, as many of her contemporaries did: her decision not to is positive evidence of her literary tact, or of her genteel acceptance that ladies do not interfere in the masculine sphere. She could not have mentioned 'the industrial revolution', if by this is meant its obvious outward manifestation, the growth of slums around steam-driven factories in the manufacturing towns. Urban industrialization was a phenomenon of the 1820s, when the general change from water-power to steam-power occurred, enabling manufacturers to take their factories to the already populous towns. It was not till about that time that painters began to express the characteristic early Victorian recoil against the human misery and visual horror of the cities. Before then, water-powered factories were situated among hills or mountains in the pleasant places of the earth; and though some writers – including Wordsworth, Southey, Godwin, Coleridge and Peacock – voice their distaste for the lives led by the workers, especially the children, this is nothing like the hell on earth, or megalopolis, that broods over the literary imagination of the early Victorians.

Jane Austen did not introduce the war and still less industry as public issues, but at a subtler and profounder level she was engaged in the controversies of her class and generation. Unusually for a writer, she was of a secure, old-established family of minor gentry. She had 'good connections': her niece married the nephew of Sir Samuel Egerton Brydges – whose boast about the derivation of his name from the Norman 'Bourgh' amused her – and her brother Edward inherited a landed estate, after which he changed his name to Knight. She adapted these two surnames of her own family for two of her upper-class landed characters, Lady Catherine de Burgh and Mr Knightley. Her own immediate family was much less well off, for her father was a country clergyman with only a small private income. The generally successful careers of the Austen brothers – in the Navy, the law, the Church – illustrate the relative mobility of the English class system, and the steady tide of prosperity which made it relatively common at the end of the eighteenth century for young men to better themselves. Had times been less prosperous for the gentry, Jane Austen might have written less sanguinely about the role of the individual within society. Had they been more prosperous for her, she might not have seen so clearly the effect on her class of its increasing wealth.

She is the gentry's greatest artist, and she arises at a time when they seem to be still at the height of their power, influence and prestige. We have seen how their leaders controlled Parliament and all the patronage and public office that flowed from it. Locally, in the shires, the small towns and country villages, the completeness of the dominance was inescapable. In England, the gentry had steadily over the centuries acquired complete legal ownership of the land. It was theirs, neither the state's nor the king's, as in the feudal system which still prevailed to some degree or other on the continent of Europe. Consequently England had no peasantry: only tenant-farmers and agricultural labourers, who had the civic advantage of not being legally directly subordinate to the gentleman, and the disadvantage of having no rights whatever to the land. On his own estate and in his village the English gentleman enjoyed a position of unique autonomy.

This does not mean that life for the gentry felt stable or unchanging when Jane Austen arrived at her maturity, as so many of her admirers have supposed, for by the mid-1790s the present order seemed threatened from within and from without. The very idea of aristocratic government was challenged by the régime across the Channel, which was based on the principle of the sovereignty of the people. At the same time, new social conditions at home, created in large measure by the landed class's own dynamism, were beginning to change the whole basis of England's old system, largely because they changed the role of the aristocracy itself.

It now seems obvious that the English government and upper classes exaggerated the danger of violent overthrow in the 1790s. It is not so certain that the gentry scattered among the villages could reasonably have known this, at a period when the news was of French victories abroad and the need for repressive legislation against radicals at home; when newspapers and journals were full of loyalist sentiment, and sermons, pamphlets, novels, and satirical verse fervently preached the old-fashioned anti-revolutionary values of piety and patriotism. Novels in particular found their way into the Austen household, and in the later 1790s novel after novel – by largely forgotten figures like Mrs Jane West, Charles Walker and Isaac D'Israeli – adapted their conventional plots and situations in order to convey the new counter-revolutionary fears. Their youthful heroes and, more often, heroines were shown suffering from the dangerous vice of individualism. Through undue reliance on their own judgement and their own emotions, in plot after plot they succumbed to temptation from the wrong suitor. The commonest anti-jacobin story features a modern-minded stranger, often in this period of anti-intellectualism a philosopher, who arrives in a small country community and has soon subverted at least one rising member of the gentry from ancient ways. Jane Austen employs a much-naturalized version of this anti-jacobin fable in the first two (completed) novels she began: *Sense and Sensibility* (begun in 1795), in which Marianne succumbs to the dangerous charm of Willoughby, and *Pride and Prejudice* (begun in 1796), where the over-confident Elizabeth is taken in by Wickham.

Yet, as Jane Austen also from the beginning evidently sensed, the landed classes were much more likely to undo the old system for themselves than to have it overthrown by enemies. Their own dynamism had been one of the most important instruments in bringing the country to the threshold of a new order. England in the late eighteenth century, and by the 1790s very palpably, had arrived at the point of take-off into self-sustaining economic growth. In part the country was reaping the commercial advantage of victory in the Seven Years War, back in the 1760s, which gave England mastery of the seas and a crucial lead in overseas trade. But the new wealth also owed much to an aristocracy so untrammelled by law and custom, so effortlessly superior, that it was able to take the economic opportunity when it came. The landowners went into mining, roads, canals, the building of towns. They also revolutionized agriculture with new machinery and methods and en-closed the common land, a steady and often ruthless agrarian revolution that made England one country that could feed its new surplus population.

These new economic activities, so different from the traditional role of the local landowner, gradually made inroads into the gentleman's self-image. The old system was pyramidal, a tight-knit local community with the landed gentleman at its head. In effect, he had accepted responsibilities in return for his power. His duties were symbolized by the centuries-old Poor Laws. Parishes accepted responsibility for their own poor, so that no one should starve; the payment for this came out of the pockets of the richest members of the local community. Notionally JPs might fix local wages and prices, which meant in hard times ensuring that wages were above starvation level. In fact, in the prosperous eighteenth century these minimal safeguards for the poor had fallen out of use. Then came the bread shortage and high prices of 1795, and practically in the counties and explicitly on the floor of the House of Commons it was clear that the attitudes of the landlords had changed. 'Trade, industry and barter would always find their own level,' said Pitt, 'and be impeded by regulations which violated their natural operation.' But in 1799 and 1800 his government put through the Combination Laws, thus maintaining their traditional paternalist denial of the right (or need) of workers to barter from strength.

It is clearly of the greatest importance to the study of Jane Austen as a writer of the gentry that it was in her adult years, between 1795 and 1817, that the older obligations of the gentry towards the poor were one by one disclaimed. In turn during this period the gentry's leaders and representatives affronted both the more traditionally minded and the spokesmen for the poor (who were often traditionally minded too) over three major issues. In 1795 the House of Commons refused to regulate wages. In 1815 it passed a new Corn Law which kept out cheap imports and so kept up the price of wheat and the price of bread the poor had to buy. Throughout the period, a campaign was waged in Parliament and outside to do away with the old protective poor laws. Though the terminology with which gentlemen learned to argue their case was that of the new science of political economy, it was a very selective version of Adam Smith's doctrine that went into circulation. Gentlemen quoted Smith when the principle of competition in a free market suited them – as it did over wages – and ignored him when it did not, as over the price of corn. What seems significant is that once again it is the upper classes, not some new men from the middle classes, who led the way. Ruthless competition, the doctrine of the survival of the fittest, the challenge to an old and admittedly very unequal notion of communal interdependence, was not a doctrine introduced into national life by the factory owners, the new entrepreneurial class; it was voluntarily conceded by the gentry themselves. The most splendid apologist for the gentry in the Enlightenment period, Edmund Burke, wrote a tract in 1795, *Thoughts and Details on*

Scarcity (published 1800), which opposed government interference in the economy. Pitt, Addington, Liverpool, Canning, Wellington – the parliamentary leaders of the gentry – steadily maintained the same doctrine throughout the next generation. It was a widespread, voluntary change in attitude, an assumption of selfishness, that led to resentment on the part of the other classes, and a sense of the separation of class interests, which by the end of the Napoleonic Wars was being clearly articulated. 'An abdication on the part of the governors', Carlyle called it, the landed class's voluntary abandonment of the old notions by which they had ruled.

A class does not voluntarily commit suicide. The English aristocracy have been lauded for their flexibility and practicality. Through their enterprise stability was maintained, the population fed, the conditions created for further wealth. It is no easy matter to falsify the argument of the political economists, that the self-interest actually was enlightened, and operated to the greater good of the greatest number. Britain's real national income per head quadrupled in the course of the nineteenth century.

This kind of theoretical, long-term economic wisdom was not, however, in Jane Austen's line of thinking. As a clergyman's daughter, belonging to a landless family, Jane Austen, like her sister and her widowed mother, had not shared in the aggrandizement of their class. Her reading, in sermons and conduct-books, must have given her old-fashioned notions of social cohesion and obligation, such as were still invoked, when it suited them, by conservative propagandists like Burke. In her own county of Hampshire, she could see the grounds for criticizing her class. Though on the whole the population was better off in 1850 than in 1790, the rise in real income was unevenly distributed. Landowners and large farmers did relatively well early, and over the main period of enclosures, from the 1780s to the 1820s, rents and farming profits nearly doubled. The new money went into the new consumer-goods – carriages, muslins, Wedgwood china – domestic improvements, but also conspicuous status-symbols. During the same period, real wages for the farm labourer declined, at least in the South of England, where he fared badly. In the Midlands and North, proximity to the new manufacturing industries kept farm wages up; in the rural South, where there was no alternative employment, they often fell below subsistence level.

As if the widening gap between rich and poor were not enough, Jane Austen could also see physical signs that the traditional relationship between the orders was changing, and the old cohesive village breaking up. Enclosing common land and marginal land meant more food, but also made it harder for the poor to keep the cow or pigs of their forefathers. Instead of farming their strips in the community fields round the villages, they now found the land reapportioned in coherent, manageable blocks, and given to the large landowners or middling yeomen. The poor became hired workers, largely or wholly dependent on a wage; more numerous than ever before, and more of a problem, as parishes haggled over how to feed them. The lucky middle-sized men who got land moved out on to it, and built new farmhouses there, on a quite different system from the old farmhouses, which had been the home not only of the immediate family but of a larger miscellaneous group of cowherds and dairymaids. In short, the Hampshire village, in Jane Austen's lifetime, was in a centrifugal phase as a community: the classes grew wider apart in wealth and physically moved away from one another. The fact that the old paternalistic system was ceasing to exist was made public not only through parliamentary speeches, which few might read, but visibly in the countryside as the better-off villagers moved upwards and out. The plight of the labourer in the South of England, the dereliction of duty by the gentry or even the successful yeoman, was a matter for public comment. William Cobbett, who bought a farm at Botley in Hampshire in 1804, for the rest of Jane Austen's lifetime and long after thundered away in his *Political Register* about the exploitation of the rural poor and about the modern falling-away from old communal values. Jane Austen would have hated Cobbett's radical politics, but the facts on which he based them were within her daily view around Steventon and Chawton.

Three of Jane Austen's six novels, *Sense and Sensibility*, *Pride and Prejudice* and *Northanger Abbey*, were first drafted in the period of most violent counter-revolution, 1795–8. Part of the logic behind their structures is the defence of the old system. In *Sense and Sensibility*, for example, Jane Austen picks up a plot already much in use by conservative, Christian novelists, especially women, who for obvious reasons tended to write about a heroine and to use a domestic setting. We have seen that, as it affects Marianne, the plot is the popular myth of subversion: new, individualistic ideas (sensibility) encouraged by a specious rootless stranger, Willoughby, bring her not to seduction – the subverted heroine's usual fate – but to the verge of death.

Why is sensibility such a danger? Believed in by an affectionate girl like Marianne, it nevertheless becomes an excuse for anti-social and actually unkind behaviour. Marianne is unfair to her mother and sister, as well as rude to Lady Middleton, Mrs Jennings and Mrs Ferrars. To trust as she does in her own heart is too individualistic a philosophy for society, and too individualistic even for Marianne's own good, for she cannot really depend on her intuitions. Sensibility, one of the typically human-centred concerns of the previous expansive era, is now in the reactionary period identified as egotistical, solipsistic and potentially anarchic.

But Jane Austen shows her clear adherence specifically to the *gentry* by making sensibility also the cult of characters much less fundamentally well-meaning than Marianne. The other two female characters who profess it are Lucy Steele and Fanny Dashwood, both in reality cold, ambitious hypocrites. They each originate in a class below the gentry; both are on the make. Of course they do not really possess hearts or delicate nerves at all, though when it is to their advantage they talk about their love of children or have the vapours. It is nevertheless appropriate that they should adopt the language of sensibility as a fashion, because it is a true correlative to their real philosophy – egotism, ignorance of the inherited culture and religion and responsibility that is passed down within a hereditary aristocracy.

Contrasted with this middle-class self-centredness and personal ambition is the positive creed represented by Elinor. Elinor is placed throughout in situations carefully made comparable with Marianne's, and we are meant to feel that as an emotion her grief is of the same order as her sister's. But her creed is a different one. In this period Jane Austen does not need to spell out that Elinor's attitudes connect her with a more traditional kind of Christianity. She believes human nature to be fallible, and she therefore trusts neither herself nor Edward Ferrars too completely. But the main impulse behind her behaviour is always to protect others, especially her mother and sister, but also, on a more social level, Colonel Brandon, Mrs Jennings, the Middleton and Ferrars circles. This social credo is always associated in Jane Austen's mind with the gentry: *noblesse oblige*. Visible egocentricity, whether in Robert Ferrars or Mrs Elton, is an infallible symptom of vulgarity.

In all Jane Austen's novels, characters are judged by their manners. But one is not born with manners, nor can one easily pick them up; one is taught them as a child, by parents who had them. The issue of manners is raised more explicitly in German literature of Jane Austen's period than in English. In that country of legalized class distinctions, burger writers could not rise socially; they had to use their inner resources, and make a self-justifying system out of solipsism – Romanticism is such a system – because their manners, or lack of them, would always exclude them from the charmed circle of the hereditary aristocracy. For Jane Austen, the writer who expresses the ethos of the landed gentry, manners are indeed the passport. But true to her function at its highest, she idealizes manners and endows them with all their theoretical value. Manners like Elinor's are not merely the device of a caste to exclude a Lucy Steele. They proclaim that the old style of social responsibility is accepted, *duty* (the idealized reading of upper-class motivation) put before the new individualism.

All Jane Austen's novels are fables which act out traditional concepts of the qualities and the role of the gentry, though this is not to say that they are nothing else. Her principal characters always belong to the gentry, though in the three works begun in the 1790s a wider, more heterogeneous range of characters from other classes appears. The greater exclusivity of the worlds of *Mansfield Park*, *Emma* and *Persuasion* reflects the clearer demarcation of the upper classes into horizontal strata by the second decade of the nineteenth century. Above all, the central plot is always a pointed adaptation of the Cinderella myth, which is also the *Pamela*, *Grandison* or *Evelina* myth. According to this convention, the heroine must find the best gentleman to marry: but Jane Austen has a new definition of excellence. The heroines of her first five novels all marry country clergymen, or a landed gentleman living on his land. The sixth, *Persuasion*, is not, as we shall see, a complete break from this pattern, even though Anne Elliot marries a sailor. The point in each case is that the village community's leader is being sought, the true hereditary gentleman. It is this *social* concern which is new with Jane Austen, the product of her uneasy times. Richardson and Burney put by comparison very little emphasis on the claims which the community has the right to exact from its leaders.

Ultimately Jane Austen's outlook profoundly favours the gentry, but this does not mean that she flatters them at a more superficial level. On the contrary, she is as critical of the current practice of her class as she is admiring of the ethical theory that sustains it. She never has any time for members of the gentry who expect adulation for their rank and give nothing in return. The haughty Lady Catherine de Burgh and her clerical toady Mr Collins might almost have come out of Robert Bage's anti-aristocratic satire *Hermsprong* (1796), with its tyrannous Lord Grondale and his acolyte the Revd. Mr Blick. *Hermsprong* came out in the year *Pride and Prejudice* was begun, and Jane Austen owned a copy, but in its final form her novel is not an anti-aristocratic satire in the same mould. Mr Darcy is the most socially elevated of all the Austen heroes, and he is proved to be a model paternalist, a fact which influences Elizabeth profoundly in his favour. Despite Lady Catherine's objections, Elizabeth is justified in asserting that Darcy has not offended against the class system in proposing to her, since birth and not riches is the true (old-style) determinant of class. 'I am a gentleman's daughter. Thus far we are equal.'

But, though criticism is always accommodated within an idealizing fable, it is also evident that Jane Austen becomes more severe about the faults of the gentry in the later novels. While her art and her perceptions are maturing, the real-life political danger recedes. Her last three novels – written between 1813 and 1816, the years of England's final victory against France – are not only more concentrated, through being virtually restricted to a well-defined circle of gentry; they also contain a far more specific critique of the gentry in its performance of its function.

The key characters in this respect are the middle-aged, who are (or ought to be) the leaders of society in the present day. Even the earlier novels have ineffective parents or parent-substitutes, such as Mrs Allen in *Northanger Abbey*, Mrs Dashwood in *Sense and Sensibility*, and Mr and Mrs Bennet in *Pride and Prejudice*. But on the whole at this stage the device is used to give the younger generation a chance to make their own mistakes – and ultimately, in the case of the leading characters, to do better. The later novels set Sir Thomas Bertram, Mr Rushworth and Sir Walter Elliot far more richly in the context of their homes and their estates, so that the social part they play is more clearly in focus. And in doing so they surely reflect not only the growing awareness of class difference in the second decade of the new century, but a greater sensitivity to upper-class responsibilities such as is also expressed by conservative writers like Wordsworth (*The Excursion*) and Coleridge (the *Lay Sermons*).

Jane Austen's later sequence of portraits of failed paternalists is 'anticipated' by only one character in the first three novels, General Tilney of *Northanger Abbey*. It may be that the creation of this character-sketch dates at least in part from the post-war period. Although the novel was begun in 1797–8 and as *Susan* sent to a publisher in 1803, it remained unpublished until 1818; a likely time for Jane Austen to have revised it was after she completed *Persuasion* in June 1816 and before she began *Sanditon* in January 1817. One detail, Henry Tilney's reference to a riotous mob attempting to seize the Tower (p.113), has a topical ring, and may have been partly suggested by the Spa Fields riot of 2 December 1816. Others, relating to General Tilney, more amply reflect the national concerns of the second half of 1816. As a rich man, a father and a landowner, General Tilney should behave like a responsible patriarch, but of course he does not; he merely competes with his neighbours in the acquisition of china breakfast-services, kitchen gadgets and greenhouses. If Jane Austen had been writing or revising only a little later, in the 1820s, she would probably have coincided with Coleridge and Cobbett in developing more fully the historical function of the abbey, both as the spiritual centre of the community and as a source of paternalistic charity.

There is surely already a sidelong allusion to this theme in the observation about the General's kitchen fittings: 'His endowments of this spot alone might at any time have placed him high among the benefactors of the convent' (p.183).

The developed critique of General Tilney as a specimen of his class is so out of place in *Northanger Abbey*, where there is no sense of community to support it, that the message hardly gets across. *Mansfield Park*, a wholehearted study of gentry values, is a far more effective context for a vignette like the Rushworths of Sotherton. Mrs Rushworth 'had been at great pains to learn all that the housekeeper could teach, and was now almost equally well qualified to shew the house' (p.85). She does indeed show it, in the manner that Maria Bertram is already viewing it – as a splendid material possession. The chapel should, of course, have been the symbol not only of the Christian principles of the family and household, but of the theoretical basis of the constitution, the alliance between aristocracy and Church, the throne and the altar. Mrs Rushworth's leading observations are about the re-fitting '"in James the Second's time. Before that period, as I understand, the pews were only wainscot; and there is some reason to think that the linings and cushions of the pulpit and family-seats were only purple cloth"' (p.86). The pattern – of giving over a serious place to frivolous use – afterwards repeats itself at Mansfield. Sir Thomas's sanctum is violated by the staging of an anarchic play. The room that has an even better claim to be the heart of the house, the old schoolroom, is now chill and neglected except by Fanny.

Similar points are made in *Emma*, where only Mr Knightley among the principal characters upholds paternalistic ideas. Emma's self-reliance, and her patchiness or downright laziness in relation to her social duty, introduce into Jane Austen's most sustained portrait of a village precisely that centrifugal tendency which she could observe in life. Though Mr Knightley sends apples to the Bateses, his social instincts are in a state of atrophy. Only the meretricious newcomers, Frank Churchill and Mrs Elton, actually cultivate sociability – and so act as a rebuke and an irritant to the residents whose role they usurp.

Perhaps the severest portrait of an unworthy paternalist appears in *Persuasion*. Sir Walter Elliot is vain of his appearance and of his rank, but only for the status it gives him. He has been a selfish, self-indulgent landlord. Giving up Kellynch causes him no wrench, provided he can find means of flattering his social self-esteem at Bath. There, his circle is narrow, cold and stupid, rank being the only principle used in selecting it. Sir Walter is at the mercy of cunning adventurers who know how to play on his personal weaknesses, like William Walter Elliot and Mrs

Clay. But elsewhere in the world of *Persuasion* the gentry are not much less frivolous, nor more mindful of their traditional role on the land. The older Musgroves are passing in a generation from an old style of gentry to a new, as their half-modernized drawing-room indicates; their son Charles and his wife Mary are engaged in converting a working farmhouse to a non-functional 'cottage' with French windows. Lady Russell, Anne's substitute mother, is well-meaning but a snob, hidebound and therefore superficial in judgement. Jane Austen's point is not, however, the radical one, that the gentry are no longer fit to rule. She puts her sailors Captain Wentworth and Admiral Croft into the novel to make an entirely moral point, that the old system absolutely depended upon its belief in the gentleman as a leader. By the last year of her life, when the gentry successfully got a new Corn Law through Parliament, they were no longer representing themselves as heads of the local community, and as custodians for all its members; they were openly pursuing their own material interests, as individuals or as a class. It is the abdication of the governors that Jane Austen depicts in her final years as a writer. Sir Walter Elliot is followed by Mr Parker of the last fragment, *Sanditon*, who has left his old house in order to pursue a fashionable fad and an entrepreneurial gamble, the creation of a resort for the idle rich.

Jane Austen's satirical sketches of gentry beginning to think like new men are so sharp and so *à propos* that it is tempting at first sight to see in her a critic of the old system, and perhaps in modern terminology a progressive. This would be to get her emphasis quite wrong. From the beginning, when she takes up a typically conservative plot, she is writing defensively – fearing subversion, advocating the values which in times past justified the rule of the gentry. She never allows us to contemplate any other ideology. The very real sufferings of the agricultural poor, on which Cobbett based his more radical opinions, are not allowed to appear, except once, very allusively, in *Emma*; and it is significant that caring for the really poor is the one social duty Jane Austen does not allow the backsliding Emma to neglect. As the defender of the old role of the gentry, she dare not. Conversely, a Cobbett or a Bage would have made much more positive use of the honest worth of a middle-class figure destined to succeed by his own efforts, like Fanny's sailor brother, William Price. But by the time she has come, in *Persuasion*, to see the value of using such types as alternatives to a supine or selfish gentry, Jane Austen has also given them (especially in Wentworth's case) the *manners* of gentlemen. By his verbal fluency and poise, by his chivalrous behaviour – when, for example, he takes the rowdy child off Anne's back – Wentworth proves his right to a place in a drawing-room. He is like most of the heroines: of the gentry, yet a champion of its traditions and its ideals rather than a present possessor of land. Such principals are well placed to see and to point out for the reader the shortcomings and moral deviations of representative characters who are no more than their social equals. At the same time they are sufficiently detached from the current vices of modernization, commercialism, individualism, to uphold Jane Austen's own old-fashioned ideology of the gentry. As in the final chapters they marry, they point the model way, towards responsible paternalism and effective leadership in an imagined future which is a mirror-image of the idealized past.

Although an avowed Tory in real-life politics, Scott in his writing is less clearly sectarian. Three factors contribute to a striking moderateness of tone. One, that his education, which pre-dated the execution of Louis XVI, was a thorough grounding in the precepts, methods and topics of the Scottish Enlightenment. Two, that Scotland had a much smaller, less wealthy upper class: Scott's Toryism is more a matter of old customs and general social continuity than a system based, like Jane Austen's English ideas, on veneration for property. Three, Scott did not begin to publish novels until 1814, when the threat from outside to national security was virtually over. This makes him less defensive than Jane Austen, less bent on maintaining the old system, and proportionately more ready, with the peace, to turn his mind to reconstruction and compromise.

In some ways, Scott's novels read like those of an out-and-out liberal, but he is actually a man of the Enlightenment, not necessarily quite the same thing. He shares with Maria Edgeworth, and indeed with many of his educated type and generation, a scientific passion for observing and recording social reality, the thing as it is. But, and this is equally typical of the late eighteenth century, he shows a strong sympathy with the individuals at the centre of his world. Technically his novels have points in common with both Maria Edgeworth's and Ann Radcliffe's. Scott's heroes are not vividly characterized, and this is deliberate. They are slightly simplified, in order to be representative. They are also passive rather than active, played on by events rather than mastering them, because once the old pre-Revolutionary optimism faded, it was a matter of observation that they should be so. The emotional heart of Scott's novels, and the reason why they strike us as true not only as documentaries, but as accounts of the human condition, is the helplessness, the perennial frustration of his heroes, whose plight as society's unwilling, passive victims is presented with the most active Enlightenment pity and concern. 'From childhood's earliest hour', Scott reflected in his mid-fifties (*Journal*, 22 June 1826) 'my heart rebelled against the influences of external circumstances in myself and others.' Where Jane Austen rebukes individual aspirations, Scott pities them, and feels the pain of their frustration.

Scott surely did preach to his age, no less than Jane Austen, but as times had changed, the message changed with them. Scott's underlying didactic aim is clearly the cause of social harmony. All his great early novels, from *Waverley* in 1814 to *The Bride of Lammermoor* in 1819, are set in times of revolution. *Old Mortality* has as its background the rebellion of the Scottish Covenanters in the 1670s; *Rob Roy*, the first Jacobite rising of 1715; *The Heart of Midlothian*, the Porteous riots, 1736; *Waverley*, the Jacobite Rebellion of 1745; *The Antiquary*, the recent French war, at a time when invasion threatened. The generation of nineteenth-century historians now growing up, Carlyle, Macaulay, de Tocqueville, were also to take the revolutions of their respective countries over the last two centuries as their prime historical subject. It has not been adequately noticed that Scott anticipated them, for revolution is more genuinely his subject than Scotland is.

His important characters have been brought up with certain sectarian ideals. Of these, the most common is Burke's generalized term for the characteristic of the old European nobility – chivalry, a notion of personal honour which is originally derived from martial prowess, and still entails leadership. Scott also recognizes a more middle-class inheritance, the unbending Calvinism of John Balfour of Burley in *Old Mortality*, or of David Deans in *The Heart of Midlothian*. But Scott's point, different indeed from Jane Austen's, is that a stiff-necked adherence to the ideals of the past, deriving as they do from a more primitive society, becomes a deadly self-indulgence, anachronistic, and as pointless as it is cruel. Scott's heroes learn precisely *not* to follow the type who can be identified as a traditional leader. Waverley weans himself of his immature attachment to the Jacobite clan chief, Fergus MacIvor. Henry Morton of *Old Mortality* renounces fanatics of both sides in Burley and in the equally inhumane Royalist, Claverhouse. In a later novel, Darsie Latimer declines to take up his family's Jacobitism when urged to do so by his uncle, Redgauntlet. For all these heroes, the very notion of personal leadership is outmoded. They end up in precisely the opposite vein from Jane Austen's, opting to be private citizens in a society which has chosen peace and commerce; a new, tolerant middle-class world where nobody leads.

Nothing indeed is more significant in Scott than his sense of the interdependence of the classes. The old aristocracy are pitiful and even a little ridiculous when they start asserting their traditional claims as chieftains. Coleridge romanticized this feudal notion, in terms which by 1817 were decidedly farfetched, when in his second *Lay Sermon* he longed to see again a healthy, loyal English tenantry, 'ready to march off at the first call of their country with a Son of the House at their head' (p.252). Scott develops a more realistic and egalitarian account of the relationship between the classes in, for example, *The Antiquary*, 1816, which is a study of the pretensions to antiquity, to rank and to houses of three Scottish gentlemen. Their stories are interwoven with those of the fisherfolk who live, work and die at the foot of the cliffs on which the great houses stand. A choric character, the beggar Edie Ochiltree, moves between the families, satirizing and in effect levelling their pretensions. In a violent storm, Edie and the baronet Sir Arthur Wardour are caught on the shore by the incoming sea:

'Good man,' said Sir Arthur, 'can you think of nothing? – of no help? – I'll make you rich – I'll give you a farm – I'll –' 'Our riches will soon be equal', said the beggar, looking out upon the strife of the waters – 'they are sae already; for I hae nae land, and you would give your fair lands and barony for a square yard of rock that would be dry for twal hours.'

(chapter vii)

Gentry and peasantry are, in the last resort, mere mortals. Distinctions of rank, as of interests and ideology, are folly in times of peace, and dangerous delusions in times of social disintegration.

Scott is the first novelist to place his characters convincingly within a recognizable portrait of a complex society. His rendering of a stratified, mobile, interacting national community derives from the sociology, economic history, and law of the late Enlightenment. His sympathy with man and his respect for man's emotions and idealism are typical of the same era. But we can also see, in the hints of anxiety and pessimism, the awareness of potential tragedy, that Scott has lived through a Revolution. His happy endings feel more precarious than Jane Austen's. Lives, as well as youthful aspirations, have been lost along the way. Scott is a great writer, subtle, sane, very original in the fable he devises for his time. His novels are formally much more original than Jane Austen's, and for a number of reasons the mode he developed proved more useful to his successors. He devised a vehicle that could convey a portrait of contemporary society, and at the same time represent as central the plight of individuals whose lives were caught up in an impersonal mechanism. Dickens, Thackeray, George Eliot all adapt Scott's form, as do the novelists of most of the important European traditions. But, in addition, his theme was less sectarian than Jane Austen, and seemed less bound to date. He preached the right lesson for Europe in the years of restoration and reconstruction after 1815. In preaching it he meant to help the gentry to survive, but to do so by wisdom and accommodation and by accepting the irreversibility of history.

This is not to deny that a sense of Jane Austen's greatness was to come, but her stature did not rank with Scott's until the second half of the nineteenth century. By then the Old System which she defended was defunct, so much so that allusions to it could not even be recognized. For latterday readers a somewhat different type of conservatism – less specific and timely, and more certainly altruistic – has bestowed an unpolemical charm upon her moral fable.

5 The Cult of the South: the Shelley circle, its creed and its influence

There is a watershed in European art at or near the year 1800, when Enlightenment confidence and universalism retreats into an irrational and generally gloomy introversion. But that is the general picture, and in England it has some distinctive features, local factors affecting the educated classes and hence the art which, more or less literally, they commissioned. Of pre-eminent importance was the break in widespread middle-class sympathy with the native tradition of liberal individualism, which culminated in the late 1780s in the Dissenters' campaign to persuade Parliament to grant them equal civil rights. This campaign attracted support well outside the ranks of Dissent proper, as the parliamentary votes show; it was all the greater in certain provincial centres, where many wealthy members of society were Dissenters. Some of the leading English writers who were either already writing or intellectually maturing around 1790 were either active Dissenters or from Dissenting families, including Blake, Godwin, Paine, Priestley, Wollstonecraft and Hazlitt. Others had strong social contacts with Dissenters, and showed clear intellectual sympathy with the Dissenting position over reform, based as it was on rationalism and individualism. The latter group included Wordsworth, Coleridge, Erasmus Darwin, and R. L. and Maria Edgeworth.

Far fewer British citizens felt radical sympathies in 1800 than in 1790, and far fewer writers. But it is also significant that a schism had opened between intellectuals and Dissent: whether or not they retained reformist inclinations, few of the writers mentioned as having close contacts with Dissent around 1790 were of the same sympathy in 1800. Dissent had been a homely English social phenomenon, with long and deep roots down into the population, and for this reason writers associated with the Dissent-dominated radical movement of around 1790 had access to – or thought they had access to – a range of readers which was sociologically unusual, certainly in terms of what one supposes the early eighteenth-century audience for poetry to have been. Wordsworth, Cowper, Burns and the young Coleridge and Southey write as though they are responding to the same events that other citizens experience; they do it with less rather than more literary artifice, partly because literariness separates them from their notional readers. Already in 1798 the twenty-three-year-old republican Walter Savage Landor was publishing a quite different kind of 'advanced' poetry, his difficult Miltonic epic *Gebir*; while writers younger still, Byron, Peacock and Shelley, were classical and French trained, more avowedly aristocratic than their elders, and generally more consciously cultured. Their readiness to range abroad or backwards in time into esoteric cultures contrasts with the parochial settings of the poetry of Wordsworth and Coleridge or the tales of Maria Edgeworth; they are also much less homely in idiom than Burns, Cowper or Blake. But in one respect the younger writers are narrower: they posit a reader drawn from a narrower band at the top of the social hierarchy. Writing which was earlier intended for mankind or for the nation was, however radical, now addressed to an élite, to what Shelley in the Preface to *Prometheus Unbound* called 'the more select classes of poetical readers'.

The emergence of a sense of class was a large phenomenon in which urbanization, industrialization, the growth and movement of the population out of the relatively cohesive rural pattern all played a part. More specifically in England, the uneven bearing of the war against France on different sections of the population must have been significant too. Naturally all individuals within a certain class did not think alike; even if the interests of an entire class can be supposed to be really identical, they will not be perceived as identical by everyone. Some liberals of the upper and middle classes continued to oppose the war, though they did so after about 1796 more consciously as a minority among their own kind. Pitt's war policy on the whole had the support of commerce, not necessarily because England was fighting democracy, but because she was competing against the old enemy France in a much longer-term struggle for Continental and overseas markets. Even though the war impeded Continental trade, and so hurt some manufacturers, it contributed to the making of fortunes among others – those engaged for example in making armaments, shipbuilding, or in clothing the troops – and among landowners and larger farmers. The demand for munitions encouraged a greatly increased output of iron and steel, and so gave a general boost to the economy. Much more uncertainly, careers in the Navy in particular enabled the younger sons of the gentry (Jane Austen's brothers, Byron's friend Edward Trelawny) to make good or at least find occupation.

But the war hit the masses hard. Vicissitudes of trade caused by the sudden closing of markets, which were temporary setbacks for their employers, could be a matter of life and death to them. Particularly severe recessions were experienced in 1795–7, 1806–9 and 1810–12. In addition it was the people and not their social superiors who actually fought. Repeated recruiting drives for both army and navy scoured the countryside, until in 1809 one man in six was probably serving. Losses were prodigious, from disease even more than injury. It has been calculated that the Napoleonic Wars may have cost more lives in proportion to the British population than the 1914–18 war. The almost complete failure of literature to reflect the holocaust is socially highly significant; it is in total contrast with the First World War, in which the young officers both wrote and gave their lives. In these circumstances the fact that Jane Austen barely mentions the Napoleonic Wars fits into the altered perspective. To do so was no natural part of her experience, any more than it was a topic which necessarily forced itself upon Wordsworth and Coleridge at the height of their powers. Yet earlier these last two, like Southey, Blake and Burns, thought it their duty to imagine what war meant to the poorer classes. When after 1800 such questions largely cease to be asked, it is a commentary on the selective effects of the war, on the growing insularity of different classes, and on the growing stratification of literature, too, as it becomes more consciously directed at the classes likely to read it.

The intellectual life of the capital contracted noticeably during the war years. There was an unmistakable gentlemanly consensus whereby the extremisms of the last half-century, in style as in politics, were driven from the scene. For about a decade from 1802, no translations from German were published in English, and even the importation or translation of books from France, which had before been a flood, was reduced to a trickle. Though communication with the Continent was maintained during the war in ideologically neutral subjects like the sciences, the arts were more sensitive. The easy international culture of the Enlightenment gave way in some parts of Europe, such as Germany, to cultural nationalism. In England, as we have seen, experiments like the *Lyrical Ballads* in a purely native tradition came to smell of populism, and so were frowned upon. The successful poetry of the next decade was Scott's – first his collection of the *Minstrelsy of the Scottish Border* (1802), popular ballads accompanied by a wealth of specific historical documentation, and then his own poetry, the flavour of which was more antiquarian than primitive. In criticism too the Enlightenment appeal to universals was insistently rebuked by an emphatic traditionalism, a fussy insistence upon the rules of grammar and metre, and knowledge of the classics. In its motivation the appeal to standards of correctness was not as superficial as it afterwards tends to look, since it proclaimed that cultural authority was vested in those with a genteel and clerical education. The task of imposing a safe discipline upon the arts and intellectual life was made simpler by a development which centralized opinion to a probably unprecedented and unrepeated degree – the ascendancy of two journals, the *Edinburgh* and the *Quarterly*.

The large part played by Scotsmen in founding these was not fortuitous, since, with the Continent closed, the Scottish cities became intellectual centres for the whole of Britain. Despite the prevailing Toryism of Scotland's actual politics, the influence of its academics, men like Dugald Stewart and John Millar, was still that of the Enlightenment, politically progressive, rational and empirical. But the young men who flourished in such an atmosphere, many of them lawyers, found ideas an impediment to promotion in a profession dominated by the Tory political establishment. They and others like them were given an outlet with the founding of the *Edinburgh Review* in 1802 and its Tory offshoot, the *Quarterly*, in 1809.

Political opponents at the time considered each journal distinctly partisan, and indeed the *Quarterly* would not have been founded had not a number of the *Edinburgh's* Tory contributors objected to its Whig bias. But in a sense the real significance of these two wartime journals is that they reflect the large degree of consensus of a period which is not only post-revolutionary but in flight from the excesses of the counter-revolution as well. Anti-intellectualism might remain evident elsewhere in national life; there might be much didactic emphasis, especially in works meant for the young of all classes, on the virtues of piety, humility and sober hard work; the two reviews, with their coverage of books on science, politics, economics and the arts, established large areas on which it was possible for grown men to meet in rational and on the whole temperate discussion. They were able to do so by a constant reaffirmation of their political moderation and their sound patriotism. The *Edinburgh's* literary reviewing, dominated as it was by the editor, Francis Jeffrey, was always responsibly aware of its duty to detect subversion (as it did in the *Lyrical Ballads*). It was not until the military danger from the war appeared to be receding, in 1809, that Jeffrey felt the government at home represented a greater threat to liberty than Napoleon, and thus conceived it proper to launch one of his principled attacks on the Tory administration.

Some of the less obvious consequences of this policy of mutual restraint, or conspiracy of silence, are among the most interesting. In their heyday, about 1812–14, the two great reviews each sold upwards of 12,000 copies an issue, which they calculated gave them a readership three or four times that number; it has indeed been estimated that they were read by 100,000 people. Burke's guess, that only 80,000 of the population could read in 1790, must be far too low. Even so, the proportion of the leisured public with access to or an interest in new books which these two journals reached must have been by any modern standard of comparison phenomenal. They maintained a forum for the dissemination of ideas; they were the medium by which books which might not themselves be read nevertheless contributed to public discourse. The reviewers determined the manner in which such works, including novels and poetry, were discussed, and it was essentially as a contribution to 'opinion'.

If the individual artist had lost the security of knowing his patron, he might find his ideas clarified by the clear image the reviews offered of his public – a group of beings devoted to ideas (even to the exclusion of more technical or aesthetic considerations), but nervous of ideas that might threaten the present order of things. It may well be in part to the presence of the reviews that we owe the dialectical habits of writers in the first decades of the nineteenth century, their inclination to take up positions as broadly simple and tailored for public recognition as the statements of politicians in a two-party state. In 1818 Peacock and in 1824 James Mill would fulminate against the political and intellectual cowardice of the *Edinburgh*, declaring that it had operated to flatter the rich and powerful, and to distract everyone else. It could on the other hand be argued that the *Edinburgh* and *Quarterly* maintained a modicum of rationality when irrationality was particularly tempting to France's enemies, and that their fidelity to the tastes and values of the Enlightenment made possible the distinctive and remarkable late flowering of Neoclassicism in England in the second decade of the century.

Nothing better epitomizes the superficial consensus of the later war years than the common cultured sympathy with the peoples of the Mediterranean. Even political animosities were stilled when citizens of the ancient centres of civilization spoke out in the name of their liberties. The special appeal of such patriots to British public opinion is well illustrated by the popular outcry against the Convention of Cintra in 1809. When the British army signed a truce with Napoleon's army in the Peninsula, they in effect sacrificed the interests of their allies, the Spanish resistance. There were a number of wholly different reasons for the British public to dislike the deal. For Tories it suggested an accommodation with Napoleon, something less than war to the death. For the more liberal, it abrogated the rights of the Spaniards, both hereditary government and people. The conservatives Wordsworth and Coleridge both wrote indignant pamphlets, Coleridge rejoicing that he could do so in the terminology of his youthful Good Old Cause, the English revolution of 1688:

It was the noble efforts of Spanish patriotism, that first restored us, without distinction of party, to our characteristic enthusiasm for *liberty*; and presenting it in its genuine form, incapable of being confounded with its French counterfeit, enabled us once more to utter the names of our Hampdens, Sidneys, and Russels, without hazard of alarming the quiet subject, or of offending the zealous loyalist.

(Essays on his Times, ii.38)

In December 1809 it was premature to suppose that the age of doctrinaire politics was over. In fact, enthusiasm for Spanish independence did not long remain a general battle-cry of English conservatism. Ferdinand of Spain had legally transferred his sovereignty to Joseph Bonaparte: resistance to the French implied accepting the doctrine that sovereignty lay not in the crown but in the nation. Nevertheless, the immediate emotional appeal of the Spaniards to the English public was significant, and was to find an echo in a number of similar bi-partisan enthusiasms during the next few years.

Some three years later, in 1812, Lord Byron made his name with a poem which begins in Spain, and celebrates the efforts of the freedom fighters, *Childe Harold*. The setting of the second canto is transferred to the Eastern Mediterranean, to Albania and Greece, where Byron had recently been. Again, the topic is a struggle for national independence, this time against the Turk. In fact the change of setting changes the emphasis where the issue of liberty is concerned. Merely by adding a second theatre of war, Byron implies that liberty itself is a universal ideal. The enemy is not Napoleon, who is England's enemy; it is tyranny.

Byron now succeeded Scott as the most fashionable author of the day, and he did so because his appeal, which was superficially rebellious and hence exciting, remained at a deeper level bi-partisan. In *Childe Harold, The Giaour, The Bride of Abydos, The Corsair* and *Lara* he developed the Byronic hero from prototypes such as Schiller's Karl Moor and Scott's Marmion. Masterful, moody outlaws, haunted by some secret consciousness of guilt, these heroes act as a focus for contemporary fantasies. Not the least element of guilty complicity about them is that they echo the French cult of Napoleon: they are fictional equivalents of David's handsome idealized portrait of the French emperor on a white charger surmounting the Alps. By this daring hint, and by translating his hero from Scott's historical setting to a present-day theatre of war, Byron implies the possibility of effective action in the real world. Even so, his rebellious Corsair is sanitized, as far as the English public is concerned, by wielding his sword well away from the French proponents of liberty and equality, and still further from the machine-breakers and petitioners of the English provinces. Nor has his rebellion any hint of a philosophic dimension. It is drained of ideological content, to a degree actually remarkable in the literature of the period. An image potentially of revolution is presented in terms sufficiently unintellectual to allay the fears of the propertied public.

The paradox is that Byron was also always felt to be sailing near the wind. To other young liberal writers, like Leigh Hunt, Shelley and Peacock, he was unmistakably one of themselves, and his example pointed the way to a radical vein of poetry: Shelley's revolutionary poem in an Eastern Mediterranean setting, *The Revolt of Islam* (1817), seems to make a point of being Byronic rather than Wordsworthian. Moreover, even though he was the darling of the drawing-rooms from 1812 to 1815, and all things to all men, Byron's ambivalent reputation contributed to his fall from favour in the political panic of 1816. In that year his marriage failed, amid rumours of unnatural practices inflicted on his bride and even the possibility of incest with his half-sister. The scandal brought to the attention of the public his other unconventionalities, all of which became symptomatic in a year when the stability of society seemed in question. Journalistic references to Byron at the time of his departure are marked by a clear political animus. Nevertheless the acceptability of Byron's cautious liberal internationalism in the later years of the war is not surprising, for it is supported by other symptoms of a tolerant public taste.

After the long moratorium on significant Continental books, two important translations from the French appeared in 1812 and 1813. The first was by the Swiss J. L. Sismondi, historian, economist, *philosophe*, and friend of Madame de Staël. His was a major study of Italian history, *The Rise of the Italian Republics*, a survey of late medieval and Renaissance history that repeated a familiar eighteenth-century myth and seemed to pick up where Gibbon had left off. It explained how after the long, feudal, king- and priest-ridden medieval night, the Italian republics, notably Florence, burst forth, in a new morning of personal and civic liberty and glorious expression in art. Sismondi saw the Florentine republic as a revival of ancient Athens; he depicted Dante, a patriot as well as a poet, as the type of the responsible, individualistic citizen-artist. *The Italian Republics* was very favourably reviewed in England, even more favourably in the *Quarterly* than in the *Edinburgh*. Admittedly the passages which seemed to give particular pleasure to the *Quarterly's* reviewer, probably J. H. Merivale, were the ones where tyranny (which could be linked with Napoleon's) was censured. Nevertheless Merivale's nerves seemed proof against the fact that his quotations were also libertarian and republican, and couched in some phrases that read like a throwback to the enthusiastic social generalizations of the pre-revolutionary era.

Madame de Staël's *De l'Allemagne* (1810; first translated into English, 1813) was another work of Enlightenment cultural history adapted as a rallying-point for opposition to Napoleon. Here the German nation received the sympathetic treatment Sismondi had given to the Italian republics. According to Madame de Staël, Europe had two dominant cultural traditions: the classical, Mediterranean inheritance, perfectly expressed in comedy, and culminating in predominantly French modern classicism; and the Northern or Germanic alternative. A wholly different historical experience accounted for the sharply differentiated tone of the literature of the North. The Germanic races did not organize themselves in large states. Man was isolated in very small communities, effectively on his own and dwarfed among the vast, oppressive, unmastered phenomena of Nature. He was obliged to look inwards for inspiration, or upwards to the mountains or to God. The literature of the North accordingly became introspective, pessimistic and essentially religious. Its religion was not social but individual, an intense unfulfilled aspiration which was perfectly expressed in Gothic architecture, or in the passionate irregularity of Shakespearean tragedy. The Northern or Romantic tradition (which as Madame de Staël makes plain is the unified culture of the Germans and the English, Napoleon's leading enemies) has become the most vital and imaginative intellectual force of the present day.

The respected liberal Whig Sir James Mackintosh, who had read some German philosophy, received Madame de Staël's book coolly in the *Edinburgh*. He recognized its affinities with the modern polemical school of German criticism, headed by the Schlegel brothers; he pronounced the political tendency of the movement unenlightened, and suspected that religious bigotry was a motivating force. The *Quarterly* likewise indicated its lack of sympathy by lavishing more attention on Sismondi. A mystical reactionary Catholicism might have established itself in Germany, where it had strong native roots. It might appeal, as in the event it did, in those Catholic countries where medieval monarchies and the Church were restored after Napoleon's fall in 1814–15. In England it was for the time being still alien.

Over the next five years, however, the typical wartime consensus gradually broke up. Coleridge took up Madame de Staël's role as a mediator for contemporary German ideas, and made some seem more relevant to English conditions, others intellectually more exciting. In his *Lay Sermons* (1816–17) and his *Biographia Literaria* (1817) he too retained the polemical edge given to Germanic writing by its opposition to the atheistical and French. No disinterested exegesis of contemporary German literature or philosophy – nothing that separated Kant, the Schlegels and Schelling from the now triumphant cause of the extreme

Right – was available in England while the younger so-called Romantics were beginning to write; a fact which closed new German intellectual insights to them far more effectively than the language barrier. Nevertheless such simplifications as Madame de Staël dealt in had their uses, for they were both provocative and easily communicable. The battle in defence of the classical and Mediterranean South was stoutly fought for a decade from 1812 by a generation of liberal English writers who believed they were fighting for their political principles. After them the religious revival prevailed, the Goths of the North swept in, and a change occurred in the spirit as well as the style of the arts far more absolute than the variations of nuance between Grecian and Gothic in the eighteenth century.

Probably the post-war right-wing cult of the Germanic did not so much induce as help to crystallize a left-wing cult for the classical, which was already flourishing before *De l'Allemagne* appeared in English. Well before the end of the war the most avant-garde of young writers, Percy Bysshe Shelley, was developing the partisan, inconoclastic tastes which wartime decorum tried to avoid. He had put himself through a course of reading in the eighteenth-century progressives, and his poem *Queen Mab* (1813) reveals a tendentious enthusiasm for materialists like Holbach and atheists like Hume and Godwin. Shelley's friend Thomas Love Peacock, who had been brought up by his mother to admire the notoriously anticlerical Gibbon, further urged Shelley into esoteric fields with controversial implications. Together the two seem to have read the comparative religionist Sir William Drummond, who in 1811 and 1812 was reviving the anti-Christian mythological enquiries of some two decades earlier. At least one other member of Shelley's circle, J. F. Newton, was immersed in Zoroastrianism, one of the ancient religions popular with sceptics because it provided disquieting parallels with and precedents for Judaism. Peacock used Newton's type as a target for satire, but took more seriously the field of interest, which was none other than the progressive, agnostic vein of Bible criticism found in Volney. The traces of that writer's *Ruins* are clear in *Queen Mab*, and Zoroastrian mythology provides a framework for Peacock's epic fragment *Ahrimanes*, which probably also dates from 1813. Though both these works are immature, they already display a kind of orientalism with more complex potential than Byron's. In the tradition of learned polemic absorbed by Shelley and Peacock, the classic tale was not poetic fancy but religious myth, a means of conveying a universal truth through allegory. Imitation of a mythological antecedent inhibited introspection by the individual author, or the boyish, adventurous fantasy of Byron's eastern tales. Instead it dramatized and objectified a truth, and so allowed for an intellectuality which Byron's vehicle did not. After his disgrace in 1816, Byron extended his range, and played the key part in leading literary fashion into some curious, even contradictory, paths. His *Childe Harold*, Canto III (November 1816), described his travels through parts of Europe with Germanic associations, and was gloomy. It was followed the next year by *Manfred*, with a Northern setting among the Swiss Alps and a German model, Goethe's *Faust*. Yet the second act of *Manfred*, set in the spirit kingdom, contains some surprises. When Manfred calls his dead love Astarte from the shades, he sounds like Orpheus summoning Eurydice, while the shadow-kingdom is ruled over by Arimanes, the evil deity of the ancient Persian religion. Byron, too, like Peacock and Shelley, was toying with esoteric kinds of paganism, though, being Byron, he seemed to appropriate his myths to an immensely potent cult of self. The idea of the mortal's love for an immortal or spirit bride was to prove exceptionally haunting and influential over the next few years. Byron himself produced an eloquent short study of the topic: in a sequence in Canto IV of *Childe Harold* (1818), beginning at stanza 115, he beautifully alludes to the love of the early Roman philosopher-king Numa for the nymph Egeria. Here love for the supernatural being symbolizes the human worship of the ideal and the artist's love of his creation. It is a model for a host of literary encounters between mortals, often identified with the poet, and nymphs or goddesses, often identified with the poet's Muse. The mythopœic love-story came to support introverted literary meanings, but not invariably and not at once, for its connections with controversial modern paganism were to be kept in view by the major poets.

The very remote ancients remained a specialized terrain; especially after Sismondi the early Italian Renaissance was a much more popular source of material. It may have been all the better that the German critics, like most English eighteenth-century critics, made no division between the Middle Ages and the fifteenth or sixteenth centuries: thus each party claimed Dante, Petrarch, Spenser and Shakespeare as peculiarly their own. Coleridge for example in the *Biographia Literaria* enthusiastically grouped together Italian and English writers, from the age of Chaucer to that of Spenser – 'the youth and early manhood of Christian Europe, in the vales of Arno, and the groves of Isis and of Cam' (ii.24). The liberals used a longer perspective and like Sismondi represented culture as rather more of a sandwich. The Greeks, republican and hence free in body and spirit, gave place eventually to the tyranny of imperial Rome and the Dark Ages; then republicanism and individualistic literature re-emerged together, and modern libertarians could claim as precursors Dante, Boccaccio, Spenser, Shakespeare, Boiardo, Ariosto and Tasso, and above all Milton.

A Renaissance and particularly an Italianate fashion flowered in England, which logically could have been politically neutral, but in practice became more distinctly associated with the more fertile and younger group of writers. In 1816 Leigh Hunt published his *Story of Rimini*, a joyous, approving description of the loves of Paolo and Francesca, which he had found – viewed more repressively – in Dante's *Inferno*. Keats was writing in the same vein with *Isabella*: he and his friend John Hamilton Reynolds planned a volume of narrative poems based on Boccaccio. Early in 1817 Peacock published *Melincourt*, a prose satire on contemporary events from a strongly radical point of view, which is nevertheless lightly based on romance epic and rich in allusions to Spenser and to Tasso. From this year Shelley switched from eighteenth-century to preponderantly classic and Mediterranean models. His major work in 1817 was *The Revolt of Islam*, a Spenserian epic set in Greece. Thereafter he drew eclectically on the classic tradition, on the dramas of Aeschylus and Calderón, the Homeric hymns, the Dantesque allegorical vision, the Miltonic elegy. Indeed, for about five years after 1817 the whole thrust of writing by the younger English generation came from the South. The style of Keats and the mature style of Shelley coincide, after all, with the apparently inexplicable volte-face in Byron, who went from the gloom of the third canto of *Childe Harold* (1816) and the Germanism of *Manfred* (1817) to the sprightly *Beppo* (1818), which was based on the manner of the fifteenth-century Florentine Pulci; and thence to his masterpiece, the one assured epic of the cult of the South, *Don Juan*.

Viewed in the light of their revived and conscious classicism, the so-called 'younger Romantics' – Byron, Shelley and Keats – make, together with their friends Peacock, Hunt and Hazlitt, a clearly defined literary group. They have no journal like the German *Athenaeum* to articulate their position – Hunt's *Examiner* does not rise to that. Though labelled 'the Cockney school' in 1817 by their political opponents in *Blackwood's Magazine*, the liberal poets are hardly so beholden to the Londoner Hunt. They do not issue anything like the Pre-Raphaelite manifesto. The most theoretical among the six, Peacock and Shelley, debate many of the issues, but often in essentially private terms meant for one another, and hard now to unriddle. Nevertheless their movement defines itself by what it is not. It is not the literature of the North – German Romanticism, in Madame de Staël's account of it, which is introspective and Christian. It is not like Wordsworth's *Excursion*, reflective, autobiographical, exalting privacy and withdrawal from society. Nor is it like the ideal of art which Coleridge sketches in the *Lay Sermons* and especially in the *Biographia Literaria* – religious, medievalist and professedly exclusive. The English liberal writers of the post-war period are extrovert not introvert, and pagan not Christian. They prefer objective forms, such as narrative and drama, to the confessional forms like autobiography. In keeping with their formal sense and their inclination to objectivity, they use traditional genres – elegy, ode, drama, verse epistle – more consistently and consciously than their elders. Moreover their poems are deliberately structured, often along dialectical lines that suggest the rational play of mind.

Meanwhile the self-acknowledged Romantic, the kind of writer who after the end of the war increasingly appears throughout Europe, tends to project an imaginative world which is clearly distinct from the actual world. The German writer of novellas, E. T. A. Hoffmann, evokes a mysterious universe, in which events are inexplicable, unwilled by man; if the world is ultimately coherent, its ordering is divine and not human. The narrative poetry of Byron, Shelley and Keats cannot be said to create a dream-world resembling Hoffmann's, even though two of the three, like almost all their contemporaries, use dreams. The three leading young English writers present the external world non-religiously. Their manner of perception is hardly mundane or prosaic, but nor is it deliberately distinct from that of the scientist. Byron's world in *Childe Harold* and *Don Juan* is avowedly this world, Europe in the period of the French Revolution, and not some other. Keats avoids an urban contemporary setting, but he brings circumstantial detail vividly to bear to realize the household in 'The Eve of St. Agnes', and the garden in the 'Ode to a Nightingale', and the countryside in the 'Ode to Autumn': he is anything but immaterial. The apparently more ethereal Shelley in fact projects what precisely is the scientist's universe: atomistic and fluid, driven by natural forces of wind and tide, electricity and volcanic eruptions. It is always evolving, not randomly but according to physical laws that man can comprehend, even if he cannot much influence them. Shelley's universe is governed by historical necessity, an order that is natural and not divine. As the most intellectual and articulate of the three poets, Shelley goes out of his way to deny essential tenets of religious belief – miraculous intervention, the immortality of the soul – in *Queen Mab*, 'Mont Blanc', *Prometheus Unbound* and *Adonais*. It is significant that he, like Keats more intermittently, is given to allegory, that most explicitly intellectual of literary devices, while the preference which Coleridge and the Germans were developing for symbol seems religiously determined: symbols can be made to imply that meaning or 'reality', if it can be apprehended at all, resides in a world elsewhere.

Time does not stand still. There is no such thing as a genuine literary movement that is essentially antiquarian or revivalist. Eighteenth-century classicism was not at its best concerned with copying the classics.

Shelley's group can in no sense be thought of as copyists, for they neither seek to reproduce the classics nor the recent art of the Enlightenment. While proclaiming their continuity with the eighteenth century, they also mark a development, distinctive in its emphasis and effect.

In tone the post-war liberals seem much less optimistic than their pre-war precursors: Shelley is given to despondency, Byron to cynicism. Symptomatic of their difficulty in believing in man's power to change things is their positioning of their heroes in relation to an action. Both in early works incline towards activist-heroes who achieve great deeds on a scale of fantasy (the Giaour and Lara, Laon and Prometheus); later both cast most of their heroes as bystanders. In fact the art of the post-war liberals, though staunchly humanist, is much less human-centred than it might have been. A generation earlier the visual arts and poetry – say the paintings of Blake or the poetry of Burns – typically focus on a large human figure, centrally placed. The reader of the most successful new poems of about 1820, perhaps *The Vision of Judgment*, 'The Grecian Urn' or *The Triumph of Life*, is probably more aware of a scene or setting than of the actor in it or the poet-persona who contemplates it.

During the period there is a movement, affecting both poetry and the novel, in the direction of sustained self-sufficient narrative. Eighteenth-century narrative action seems typically to depend upon the central character: that is, the specified, individualized, naturalistically perceived man or woman is made to seem the agent capable of determining the action in which he or she appears. In the novels of Scott – which belong precisely to the post-war years – the protagonists are not free. The effective agent is society, which has the impersonal momentum of the historical process. Even among authors less conscious of history than Scott, one notices in the narratives of the second decade of the nineteenth century a new emphasis on a flowing story which appears to set up a dynamism independent of any character. Fluidity is one of the main characteristics that distinguishes nineteenth-century narrative art from eighteenth, and dates earlier tales, even more than novels, for the modern reader.

This new sense of movement, observable in works as different as *The Heart of Midlothian*, *The Corsair* and 'The Eve of St. Agnes', is part of the sea-change that occurs in the arts around 1800, and can only be a general historical phenomenon. Since art is a group activity, involving maker and audience, the most fundamental forces shaping it lie within the ambit of the group. At one intellectual level group-consciousness expresses itself in ideology, a system of beliefs and values, often considered by the holders to be objective, which in fact helps to maintain the group's cohesion and presents it in an ideal light. Ideology is not bound to art in any simple way, but the ties are nevertheless inextricable; the images and the implicit ideals echo one another, for the consumers and thus ultimately the makers are the same. So the saliency of the hero in the later eighteenth century was not an observation of external 'reality' so much as a reflection of what the artist and his audience needed or wished to think. That style originated with a confident, expanding upper class, and its emphasis on human centrality and free will reflected the optimism of its consumers. Its *fictional* quality, even at the time of its production, can easily be demonstrated. Outside the arts, writing science and history, the men of the Enlightenment did not attribute to individuals that kind of importance. The vast Newtonian cosmos, the large-scale, impersonal historical movements depicted in historians like Hume, Gibbon and Robertson, the sophisticated portraits of entire societies in Ferguson, Smith and the French *philosophes* – all these specifically contradict the fantasy-portrait of man at the centre of the universe which we see in art-products as diverse as Blake's prints and Jane Austen's novels.

It could not therefore be a new intellectual discovery, still less a mere change in fashion, that would account for art's shift in tone and emphasis about the turn of the century. No doubt contributions were made in the fields of study that always nourish the arts. The Enlightenment's tendency to produce vast schema for society on a universal and historical scale produced its backlash during the revolutionary aftermath: the known and local were all emotionally much more reassuring. Besides, the spectacle of a contagious revolutionary movement, spreading like a plague or fire across Europe, must have seemed to many a corrective to the notion that Nature or history acted benignly and to the notion that individual man commanded his own destiny. Though conservatives might exclaim, as Burke did, against the de-humanized revolutionary, it was not the image of a dignified whole Renaissance man that they sought to restore. The ethos of the counter-revolution discouraged individualism, and conditioned the loyalist to believe that organic life and power resides in the nation, the whole rather than the part. In addition to the danger from the mob, it may have been the insecurities experienced within the old societies in a period of expansion and population-growth that forced attention on to a harsh environment, and kept it there. At any rate a sharp change of tone, a loss of confidence and assertiveness, affects the arts shortly before the turn of the century, and affects them regardless of the political persuasion of the individual author.

The 'Romantic' personality acts out in life his neurotic gloom; he is frustrated and alienated from society; in his art he proposes an alternative world as a surrogate. The early nineteenth-century Neoclassical artist has not on the willed and rational level given up the cause of mankind, yet his perception of how the world looks has much in common with the viewpoint of his Romantic contemporary. His portrayal of the world of historical necessity is grim and disenchanted. In the long run men may achieve a juster society, but in the short run man – the poet himself – has to face a life of pain and difficulty, and moreover has to face death without the comforts of religion. The English post-war writers – Shelley, Keats, the ambivalent Scott – reject any fantasy-world as immature and preach acceptance of reality, but do so in a mood of grim stoicism. Their humanism is more a matter of generalized faith than of much hope; and it is disconcertingly abstract since, if individual character determines nothing, there is not much point in refining on character. It could almost be argued that, though he rejects the Romantics' supernaturalism, the new classicist has also taken a decisive step away from the old literature of man. Nature, scientific necessity or historical determinism are no more comfortable as protagonists than a mysterious Deity.

And yet, with all the unconscious constraints imposed by circumstances, the new classicists made some conscious choices and hammered out a style, encouraged no doubt by their recognition of themselves as a distinct group. The moment and place of the emergence of this sense of identity can be pinpointed with some precision, as the spring of 1817, at Marlow in the Thames valley.

March 1817 was a notable month in the fortunes of English radicalism. After the riots, the disorders and the inflammatory campaigning of the previous autumn and winter, the government at last that month put through repressive legislation, including the repeal of Habeas Corpus. Shelley, Peacock, Hunt and Hazlitt had all been writing on the radical side: the latter two as journalists, Shelley as the anonymous author of the pamphlet *A Proposal for Putting Reform to the Vote*, and Peacock in the longest and most political of his satires, *Melincourt*. For the next two or three years, the publication of such outspoken opinions as they had all of them uttered was unpopular and became hazardous, as the number of prosecutions for seditious libel mounted. The course of thinking of the liberal writers could be interpreted as a necessary retreat from the political battleground, and a search to find esoteric compensations for the blocking of more direct outlets to the public. Alternatively, the kind of concentration they achieved through direct contact with one another made it possible to write poetry of an altogether more intense and satisfying kind.

The leading spirits in forming the group were first Shelley and Peacock, who this spring both settled at Marlow within a few minutes' walk of one another, and Leigh Hunt, who took his family to stay with the Shelleys between April and July. Afterwards, back in London, Leigh Hunt was also seeing Keats and Hazlitt; a year later, in the spring of 1818, Shelley went to Italy and thereafter maintained contact with Byron. What happened at Marlow in 1817 was the counterpart to what happened at Alfoxden between Wordsworth and Coleridge in 1797.

At first sight the activities of the group look almost determinedly a-political, the 'tea, Greek and pedestrianism' which is rather unsympathetically associated with Peacock in particular. He and Shelley became immersed in the Cupid and Psyche myth, which occurs in *The Golden Ass* of Apuleius; later, in the autumn, Mary Shelley translated about half of it. Shelley also became absorbed in the Homeric hymns and in some of Plato's dialogues, many of which he was to translate over the next few years. Neither he nor the others read for the sake of the language, nor inclusively; indeed, they were highly selective. Shelley for example picked out Homer's hymns, rather than the more obvious epics. The kind of quality he found in them may be guessed at from a phrase in his enthusiastic review of Peacock's poem *Rhododaphne* (1818): 'It is a Greek and pagan poem . . . . There is here, as in the songs of ancient times, music and dancing and the luxury of voluptuous delight.'

It is plain that the group always interpreted their shared taste for what they thought was characteristically Greek – comic, elegant and harmonious – as a deliberate rejection of the taste for the German, which Coleridge was advocating in 1817 in *Biographia Literaria*. The various members of the circle are explicit about the two polarities. T. J. Hogg teased Shelley in September 1817 for his unregenerate past, 'when you did not esteem the Classics . . . there was a time when you preferred the ghost seers of Germany to the philosophers of Greece.' In the same year, 1817, Peacock was accompanying Shelley to the theatre, and trying to persuade him out of a taste for pastiche Jacobean tragedy, and into a taste for comedy. He failed altogether with Sheridan and Beaumont and Fletcher, but did succeed in getting Shelley to enjoy one of the greatest of comic artists, Mozart. In 1818 Peacock commemorated the victory with a satire that is itself elegantly Mozartian: *Nightmare Abbey*, a send-up of Coleridge's recent criticism (*Biographia Literaria*), Byron's recent poetry (*Childe Harold* III), and Godwin's recent novel (*Mandeville*), all of which are fashionably gloomy and Germanic. *Nightmare Abbey* is in fact a complete statement on the subject, a dramatization of the intellectual battle between north and south with all the political implications made explicit. Though Peacock, like Hogg, teases Shelley for his past weakness for Gothic effects, there is evidence that by now the classicists had done their work, and that Shelley was a wholehearted convert to the urbane, harmonious, even comic spirit of the south. Perhaps the finest of all

Shelley's translations is the Homeric Hymn 'To Mercury', in which Mercury is a prankish comic spirit. He wrote it in Italy in July 1820, borrowing the metre of *Don Juan* – 'ottava rima, which is', Shelley noted with satisfaction, 'infinitely comical.' He used the same metre and the same light vein of comedy a month later for 'The Witch of Atlas', one of the most definitively classical of his poems.

The Marlow group were serious about their cult of Greek laughter. Though Peacock and Shelley in particular might enthuse about the aesthetic qualities of Greek poetry, its polish or its grace, they preferred it ultimately as the formal expression of an intellectual system. The intellectuality of Shelley's approach is illustrated by his absorption in certain philosophical questions. In 1817 he translated one of Plato's dialogues, the *Symposium*, in which the central topic is the nature of love; some time later, in an essay 'On the manners of the Greeks relating to love', he considered the strengths and weaknesses of Greek sexual mores, dealing with homosexual as well as heterosexual love. But why love? Why did he single out this issue among all others as central to the Greek message?

To some extent the answer must be speculative, but in the absence of clearer evidence it is worth recalling the theoretical grounding which Shelley and Peacock already had from their reading in comparative religion. At least one of the sceptical mythologists in whom they were interested, Drummond, had followed Dupuis in interpreting primitive religions as cults relating to the cycles of the year. But there were a number of others (like Erasmus Darwin and a scholar particularly intriguing to Peacock, Richard Payne Knight) who believed that the key lay in a universal sexual myth. Critics of Christianity's claim to unique revelation had picked out the host of rituals and fables from all cultures which appeared to imitate the action of the sun impregnating matter – and thus implied that early man worshipped the driving force in nature, the principle of life itself.

Darwin in *The Botanic Garden* (1791) both popularized the biologist's understanding of the propagation of species, and wedded it to ancient mythology. He not only fancifully invented his own 'myths', using nymphs and sylphs with a recklessness which it is now easy to mistake and ridicule; he produced parallels from classical and oriental stories which he declared were mythopoeic representations of the natural processes he was analysing. Though Darwin subordinated his mythology to his biology, each were plainly up to date. Any careful reader of *The Botanic Garden* should have grasped what was for the general public in the 1790s an unfamiliar concept – that the well-known classical tales of the loves of gods and goddesses were anthropomorphic representations of general truths about nature. Pagan mythology seemed preoccupied by love (a demerit, to admirers of the Bible like Coleridge, who is quoted above on p.82) because primitive man perceived that the natural world was driven by sex.

Among the immediate sources of Darwin's acquaintance with fertility cults and rites with obvious sexual meaning were a number of scholarly works which drew on the excavations at Herculaneum and Pompeii. England's wealthy ambassador to Naples, Sir William Hamilton, was both a collector of ancient objects and a Voltairean critic of unenlightened Catholicism. Hamilton became a key figure in an iconoclastic vein of French and English scholarship. His 'Account of the Remains of the Worship of Priapus' was largely given over to the demonstration that phallic items and ceremonies survived in the practices of eighteenth-century Italian Catholicism. This essay was distributed privately in 1786 to the Society of Dilettanti by a wealthy connoisseur, Richard Payne Knight, together with Knight's own 'Discourse on the Worship of Priapus, and its Connection with the mystic theology of the ancients'. Knight argues that the frequent traces of phallic worship which recur in all religions, including Christianity, indicate that the phallus is 'a very rational symbol of a very natural and philosophical system of religion', which he goes on to typify as a generally accurate and enlightened Nature-worship. He is enthusiastic about Greek religion, with its festive celebration of the generative principle, and unfavourable to Judaism, the precursor of Christianity: 'the Jews ... being governed by a Hierarchy, endeavoured to make it aweful and venerable to the people, by an appearance of rigour and austerity' (pp.182–3). He clearly implies that throughout the ages organized religion has been an instrument of political oppression as well as a malign influence on personal happiness.

When in 1818 Knight issued a modified version of his theory for the general public – *An Inquiry into the Symbolic Language of Ancient Art and Mythology* – he worded some of his descriptions more judiciously, and tempered his political insinuations, without in any way recanting from his system. Indeed his discussion this time includes an expanded survey of the symbols used in Greek and Egyptian mythology, which is of considerable interest to a reader of Shelley in particular. Knight's summary of the ritual accompaniments of the gods of fertility – their births as offspring of the Sun-god, or miraculous births, their boats or chariots (representing the sun's journey across the heavens), their attendant water-nymphs (water being necessary to fertility), their fountains, caves and symbolic animals – altogether might serve as a description of the furniture of Shelley's mythopoeic poetry.

There is no proof that Shelley read either book by Knight, though it is hard to believe that Peacock did not. Peacock not only knew and admired Knight's writings of old; in 1818–19 he was caught up, like Byron, Hunt, Keats, and other poets of their acquaintance, in a raging literary fashion for Pan-worship and 'nympholepsy'. The timely appearance of Knight's book in 1818 is perhaps most interesting as evidence that the ideas of the infidel anthropologists continued to circulate in England after the war, and, along with other pre-war radical books, enjoyed something of a revival among the heterodox. Paine's revolutionary classics were reissued between 1817 and 1819 by the bookseller Richard Carlile, who spent six years in prison for his intransigence. In the circumstances the interest in paganism of sophisticates like Peacock and Shelley looks far more serious than dilettantism. The anthropologists had provided a naturalistic 'explanation' for religion, as man's imaginative re-enactment of under-lying truths in the natural world. Such an explanation was far less reductive than earlier accounts of mythology as poetic corruptions of originally monotheistic religions. But it also conveniently fortified the post-war liberal's wish to challenge a resurgent, institutional, politically reactionary Christianity. The crucial fact about the classicism of Shelley and Peacock is that it does evolve into paganism – not so much an aesthetic as an ideological cult, an interpretation of man's oldest beliefs which stresses first that they are inventions, and second that they belong to a natural rather than a supernatural order. What is more – a significant advantage in a propaganda war – the cult of sexuality is celebratory and joyous; it shows up in its most unfavourable light the authoritarian, ascetic and life-denying tendencies of Hebraic Christianity.

Shelley's best poetry is intellectually so subtle that his use of the sexual myth could be adequately illustrated only by sustained analysis. Two major poems suggest the extent of the debt. In *Prometheus Unbound* he counters the anthropomorphic One God of Hebraic tradition (for the characterization of Jupiter derives from that of Milton's God) with a more naturalistic alternative cosmology. Prometheus the Sun God and fire-bearer couples with Asia, one of the Oceanides; the act which releases him from the mountain to which Jupiter has chained him is the revocation of his curse upon his enemy – that is, an act of love. Thus an action which begins with Jehovah in a familiar Old Testament posture, the authoritarian father exacting retribution, is resolved in terms of pagan mythology, with its allegorical and characteristically sexual fable. The mythopoeic lovers enter a kind of alliance with Demogorgon – an ancient enough figure in his chariot, and yet also suggestive of such modern conceptions as the impersonal laws of Nature and processes of history. Shelley, like Erasmus Darwin, insists that the pagan conceptions contain more abstract truth as well as more humanity than the Christian.

Two years later, in his enchanting 'Witch of Atlas', Shelley appears to give his most direct account of myth. The Witch is the child of a union of the Sun with the Ocean – one of the Atlantides – although her birth occurs marvellously and spontaneously in a cave: so ancients expressed the centrality of the sexual process, so they described the birth of their gods. Knight in his earlier book mentions the recurrence in myth of androgynous beings, apparently symbolic of organized matter in its first stage, immediately after its release from Chaos (pp.70ff): when the Witch makes a hermaphrodite, she too is re-enacting the Creation cycle. She has all the attributes and accompaniments of pagan divinity, including the animals, the attendant nymphs, fountain, cave, and boat as chariot. She is both myth herself, and the sophisticated modern poet's meditation upon myth, and, perhaps beyond that again, a projected *alter ego* to convey his anxieties about his own creativity. As the creative idea, she personifies art as well as religion, since the two kinds of myth expressing truth and beauty cannot be separated. But she may not interfere in human affairs, nor command the survival of the individual soul, however ethically deserving. She is an 'emanation', an idea of the good originating in men's minds, and thus a part rather than a master of the natural world; a pagan god, and not the God of the Christians.

A commoner motif in the work of the whole group is the myth first taken up with such enthusiasm at Marlow in 1817, the story of Cupid and Psyche. As the story is related by Apuleius, Cupid falls in love with Psyche, a mortal. He builds an enchanted palace in which to celebrate their love, and comes to her there at night, since she is forbidden to know him. Spurred on by her envious sisters, she lights a lamp one night, but it drips oil on him and wakes him. He and the palace vanish, and it is only after much suffering that Psyche finds him again, and is rewarded with immortality. Though the possibilities are 'poetic' enough, in all conscience, the Psyche story had been attracting attention since the late eighteenth century precisely because it lent itself so very obviously to allegorical interpretation. Quite what it was supposed to signify was by no means agreed. The interpretation best known to the twentieth century is the one by Thomas Taylor, who published a translation of Apuleius's version in 1795, and explained it in his introduction as an allegory of a very transcendental kind. Psyche, the Soul, descends from a lofty mountain into a beautiful valley. This signifies the descent of the soul into a mundane condition, without wholly abandoning the Heavens: for the palace Psyche finds is divine, its gems symbolize the stars, and its mysterious voices are otherworldly. Psyche's marriage to an invisible being suggests the uniting of the soul with Love itself, pure Desire, uninfluenced by outward forms. But the intervention of her more mundane sisters, whom Taylor interprets as Imagination and Nature, induces her to explore the form of her husband. So the rational part becomes tainted with impure, terrene desire; for vision symbolizes union between the perceiver and the thing perceived. Cupid flies away, and Psyche is precipitated to earth. She wanders with stumbling gait in search of Love, suffering and descending to Hades, until Cupid retrieves her and she is taken to heaven to live the life of an immortal. Read thus, the myth portrays the soul's suffering in the body, its search for a lost original condition of purity.

However, Erasmus Darwin refers to Psyche in *The Economy of Vegetation* (iv.47–62) as the embodiment of fulfilled sexual love, a proof that there is sexual happiness in Heaven. Darwin is always as unsympathetic as Volney and Knight to the ascetism of the Christianized later Platonists whom Taylor and Coleridge so much admired; he would no doubt have been equally inclined to ridicule their procedures as fantastic literalism, or wholly misplaced ingenuity. Similar in tone to Darwin's treatment is Knight's own allusion to Psyche in the 'Discourse on the Worship of Priapus': from the context it is evident that like Darwin he sees the story as above all an example of the centrality in ancient myth of the sexual act. When William Godwin, using the pen-name Edward Baldwin, retells the story in his collection of Greek myths for children, *The Pantheon* (1806), he too turns it into an example of the temporary loss and eventual restoration of fulfilled (sexual) love. Briefly then, Taylor reads Psyche's physical love as an allegory of material life in conflict with the spiritual; classically minded progressives may alternatively propose that the carnal love in itself represents a universal natural process.

It would be a rash critic who claimed to be certain that one kind of reading regularly excludes the other in the complex, esoteric effects of early nineteenth-century poetry. What will be conceded is that the part of the story which interests the poets is not Psyche's arduous quest to re-enter Heaven (for Taylor the central point of her story), but rather the first episode, her beautiful but sad experience of love as a mortal. Certainly the issue raised by Taylor, the ascetic suspicion of sexuality, could be said to inform the poets' treatment; but equally certainly they appear to be describing a natural sexual act, and defending it precisely as such. One theme of Peacock's poem *Rhododaphne* (1818) would for example seem to be that an essentially innocent physical love is first opposed and then destroyed by conventional morality. Love's enemies include the pious, respectable elder; but they can also be the young, who have learnt taboos that make them fearful and frigid. In Peacock's version of the Psyche myth the sexual roles are reversed – his shepherd boy Anthemion is seduced by the enchantress Rhododaphne – but the catastrophe is similar. Rhododaphne's idyllic palace is dissolved and the enchantress slain by a malevolent spirit called Heavenly Love, brought to life only, it seems, by the boy's active conscience. Peacock's Thessaly is a pagan world of immanent magic, conjured up by men themselves. Love there would be beautiful and free, provided that men thought it so. It becomes guilty and deadly when they introduce an arbitrary asceticism, and make the fulfilment of desire a subject for shame.

The year after *Rhododaphne* was published, in 1819, Keats wrote two poems on related themes, the 'Ode to Psyche' and *Lamia*. Whether Peacock's poem was the immediate source for Keats hardly matters; their common friendship with Leigh Hunt means that Keats had access anyway to the complex of ideas initiated at Marlow. Keats's letters show that he was aware that Psyche was the word for soul, and his reflection in the same context that life is a vale of soul-making has been taken as an allusion to Thomas Taylor's ascetic reading of the story. The 'Ode' however is more in keeping with the interpretation of the pagan anthropologists (though it is no part of Keats's intention to work out his argument with Peacock's intellectual precision). Keats contrasts Psyche, born a mortal, with the remote and faded deities of Olympus. He will worship her in her physical reality, which is warmly contiguous with that of the natural world of wood, mountain and stream. For what she finally comes to represent, like Peacock's enchantress in *Rhododaphne*, and unlike the Olympians (by implication, unlike Christian supernaturalism too) is an alternative credo, human-centred, fulfilled, undivided, a Psyche-soul whose final act is 'to let the warm love in'.

Keats's *Lamia* has strong parallels with the Psyche myth and with Peacock's reworking of it. Lamia is like Cupid in Apuleius or like Rhododaphne. She could be seen as a monster, a wicked enchantress, and the ill-disposed, the prudish, the old and envious, or the guardians of conventional morality (in this case, the sage Apollonius) do see her that way. But to Lycius she is beautiful and loving. Serpents may be evil in Christian iconography, in which they are associated with man's fall from perfection through his own sexual frailty, and through woman; but there is nothing in nature or in other mythologies to sanctify this reading. Keats's description of Lamia's change from serpent to woman allows for both possibilities – the ominousness of her serpenthood, the beauty and naturalness of it. Leigh Hunt, when reviewing the poem, believed that the latter point was being stressed – Keats 'would see fair play to the serpent, and makes the power of the philosopher an ill-natured and disturbing thing'. Lycius is happy in the enchanted house she makes for them until he feels the impulse to introduce her into the conventional world, whereupon his suspicions and guilt are aroused. As in Peacock's version, it would seem to be knowledge, conscience, false consciousness in the mortal man which kills her, and causes her beautiful sensuous world to vanish.

Keats took his story from Burton's *Anatomy of Melancholy*, and it is hard to say whether features he found in the source should be given symbolic significance. The Lady's origin as a serpent surely reminded him of Christian sex-taboos: how far did he develop the hint? Burton sets the story at Corinth: is it then an accident that when Lycius makes his passionate appeal to save Lamia, he twice, emphatically, addresses his hearers as 'Corinthians'? It was in the First Epistle to the Corinthians that Paul made his famous strictures against fornication and the claims of the flesh: this, for the modern layman, is perhaps the text above all others which expresses the Christian's rejection of the body. By Apollonius's 'cold philosophy' Keats may have had the Pauline dogma principally in mind. Lycius's speech may be a call on behalf of the pagan and against the Christian approach to the life of the senses:

> Shut, shut those juggling eyes, thou ruthless man!
> Turn them aside, wretch! or the righteous ban
> Of all the Gods, whose dreadful images
> Here represent their shadowy presences,
> May pierce them on the sudden with the thorn
> Of painful blindness; leaving thee forlorn,
> In trembling dotage to the feeblest fright
> Of conscience, for their long offended might,
> For all thine impious proud-heart sophistries,
> Unlawful magic, and enticing lies.
> Corinthians! look upon that grey-beard wretch!
> Mark how, possess'd, his lashless eyelids stretch
> Around his demon eyes! Corinthians, see!
> My sweet bride withers at their potency.

(ii.277–90)

This sounds very like the challenge to Christian asceticism implicit in the intellectual paganism of the post-war era. There are times when propositions can be held so naturally among a group of people that they do not need to be spelt out. They shape ways of saying: they are carelessly alluded to in conversation. The cult of naturalism, paganism or innocent sexuality was such a proposition. Its currency can be illustrated by two anecdotes, quite familiar in the appropriate literary biographies, but treated in later times as odd and inexplicable, precisely because no contemporary thought it necessary to supply a footnote on paganism.

One story concerns the meeting in December 1817 in London between Wordsworth, the acknowledged greatest poet of the day, and the nearly unknown Keats. Haydon long afterwards wrote down his recollection of the meeting:

Wordsworth received him kindly, & after a few minutes, Wordsworth asked him what he had been lately doing. I said he has just finished an exquisite ode to Pan [in *Endymion*] – and as he had not a copy I begged Keats to repeat it – which he did in his usual half chant, (most touching) walking up and down the room – when he had done I felt really, as if I had heard a young Apollo – Wordsworth drily said
    'a Very pretty piece of Paganism' –
This was unfeeling, & unworthy of his high Genius to a young Worshipper like Keats – & Keats felt it *deeply*.

Haydon found Wordsworth's response not merely brutal but un-accountable. Yet to proclaim the cult of Pan at that time to Wordsworth's face was surely itself a kind of affront; a Wordsworth who, as Haydon admitted, was smarting from Coleridge's censures of the *Lyrical Ballads* in the *Biographia Literaria*, with their hint that even he had not always lived up to his destiny as a Christian poet. Wordsworth had gone out of his way in his Greek-inspired 'Laodamia' (1815) to reprove unlicensed sexuality in a woman. Laodamia is struck down, apparently by the gods, for her carnality; Wordsworth must have been pleased with so puritanical a pagan story. Is the cult of Pan in general, like *Lamia* in particular, a kind of rejoinder? If we doubt that the issue was specially meaningful to contemporaries, what of an otherwise strangely obscure attack (or counter-attack) Hazlitt levelled at Wordsworth a month or so after the snub to Keats in one of the 'Lectures on the English Poets', delivered at the Surrey Institute, which Keats attended? 'From the *Lyrical Ballads*', Hazlitt remarked, 'it does not appear that men eat or drink, marry or are given in marriage.' If Keats is extraordinarily different in respect of the physical appetites, it is not solely a matter of personal temperament, but of the worked-out credo of his literary generation.

In Shelley and in Peacock, the original Marlow intellectuals, the cult of sexuality appears at its most abstruse and intellectually ambitious. It stands for a whole ideal of harmony, a challenge to arbitrary divisions between mind and body, man and his environment, man and God; and a challenge also to an institutionalized Christianity that was part of the apparatus of State. The younger poets proclaimed their rejection of the political ideology of the older poets primarily via their challenge to religious orthodoxy. From 1818 a more popular treatment of the subject was available in the most sensational new poem of the day, *Don Juan*. In its formal qualities *Don Juan* matched ideally the concept of the literature of the South – liberal, Mediterranean, extrovert, comic. It spoke for the same cause in its substance. *Don Juan* is, as the title indicates, a poem in praise of sexuality, its beauty and its naturalness; it is a poem written against the sexual taboos enjoined by official religion. Its most attractive character, Haidee, inhabits a kind of Eden, but sexuality already exists there, and is natural and good. She is, of course – like Rhododaphne, Lamia and Psyche – a beautiful girl, and a Greek. It is common to read Byron's masterpiece as eccentric, irresponsible and wholly personal, but all such impressions are qualified when the poem is read in the intellectual context of 1817 and 1818. The glorification of sexual love has become an accepted challenge to orthodoxy over its whole range of influence, cultural, moral and political. Behind *Don Juan* is the unwritten manifesto of Marlow.

6 The War of the Intellectuals: from Wordsworth to Keats

The years 1815 to 1819 produced unrest during which England probably came nearer to serious violence than at any other time during the French revolutionary period; but they were not years when radicalism as an intellectual cause found much support among the educated reading public. A working-class radical movement developed, as in the early 1790s. It circulated the radical literary classics of the earlier period, among them Paine and Volney, and also pirated Shelley's youthful *Queen Mab*. Among the book-buying middle classes, and hence in the great majority of journals and reviews, there was little or no real impulse towards political change. Yet thanks to the existence of these same journals and reviews, with their techniques of popularization, ideas could be disseminated and issues isolated with remarkable sharpness and intensity. With the restoration of peace, the stage was set for literary war, and it was no less ferocious for the unequalness of the struggle in real political terms. But the vested interest of any probable reader in the existing order of society, and his consequent fear of violence, extremism or reckless idealism, provided the decisive condition, the ineluctable terrain over which the war had to be fought.

Between 1814 and 1819 the major poets and novelists virtually all made some kind of appearance on the public stage, often to comment on the political implications of the work of other writers. Well before the gathering of the Marlow poets in 1817, the Lake poets were publicly identified as the bards of orthodoxy. Even Jane Austen, retired, genteel and dying, promised with *Sanditon* (begun in 1817) a direct satiric commentary on the public scene. With *Ivanhoe* (1820) the relatively bi-partisan Scott edged further into the public arena. The political nuances of Scott's career illustrate how the manner in which writers took up the cudgels altered as the political crisis changed its form. Three more or less chronological phases emerge, of which the third is from the literary point of view the richest. First, the era of the peace, and the writers' response to peace, from 1814 to mid-1816; it is an era in which English literature is dominated by Wordsworth's great commemoration of victory, *The Excursion*, though no doubt a more popular work concerned with national reconciliation, Scott's *Waverley*, found more readers. Second, the acute social and political crisis of 1816–17, when the writers tended to put aside their singing robes and to present themselves in the midst of public events as journalists, pamphleteers and commentators. Third, following the alarm of the propertied classes and the government, which was expressed in 1817 and again in 1819 by repressive legislation, overt literary radicalism had to take subtler forms. Younger writers like Hunt, Keats, Shelley and Peacock became on the face of it preoccupied with alternative imaginative worlds, ancient Greece, the Italian Renaissance, faery lands forlorn, while Scott looked back to the Middle Ages. It is a question for further analysis how complete that withdrawal was; how far the third phase of literature, from 1817 to about 1822, should be seen as a counter-attack on a more specialized cultural plane.

The peace of 1814 was celebrated by the Poet Laureate, Southey, in for example his *Odes to his Royal Highness the Prince Regent, his Imperial Majesty the Emperor of Russia and his Majesty the King of Prussia*; and much more grandly by Wordsworth in *The Excursion*, which he claimed was the culmination of his whole career. Wordsworth's Preface impresses upon the reader the largeness of the enterprise. What he holds in his hand is a long blank verse philosophical poem in nine books, but it is still only a part of the whole. *The Recluse* – the name of the larger incomplete poem – incorporates an autobiographical prefatory section, already written and as long again (which we now know as *The Prelude*). But more than this, the shorter poems Wordsworth has published at different times – presumably the *Lyrical Ballads* and the *Poems in Two Volumes* of 1807 – are also to be seen as in some way associated with and indeed dependent on this culmination. Wordsworth converts his own œuvre into a whole which is both organic and dedicated. *The Recluse*, claims the Preface, is a great Gothic Church, to which the lesser works are the 'little cells, oratories, or sepulchral recesses'.

The modern reader, who tends to skip *The Excursion*, does not see Wordsworth as he was seen by the three younger poets, who knew him as the dominant poet of the age and consciously measured themselves against him – Byron, Shelley and Keats. In *The Excursion* they found a poem appropriate to Wordsworth's image for it – a poem which aspires to permanence in a traditional, institutional, orthodox Christian vein. Wordsworth celebrates the victory against innovatory, Voltairean France, but he claims that it will be final only if England holds to her inner strength – if Englishmen are pious, dutiful and inwardly secure. (In the same year of the peace, another Christian and conservative writer, Jane Austen, makes a similar point in *Mansfield Park*.) The stress on inward resource and moral victory is conveyed by the poem's structure. *The Excursion* is a series of lives, all in a sense spiritual autobiographies. They are generally lives of poverty and of suffering and loss; yet the poem's admirable men and women – especially its central figure, the Pedlar – have found in the mountains and in solitude a fulfilment that schemes to change society could not give. Although *The Prelude* remained unpublished, its personal and religious import is expressed in *The Excursion*, that ultimate truths are to be found within, and by man on his own. However, we do not generally think of *The Prelude*, written and rewritten over many years, and finally published only in 1850, as a topical poem. *The Excursion* is designedly topical: it is pointedly polemical and controversial. Its failed revolutionary, the Solitary, was not only derived by Wordsworth from real-life French sympathizers he had known in the 1790s, such as Joseph Fawcett and John Thelwall; the figure was bound to remind knowledgeable contemporaries of such men. More generally, Wordsworth advocated that restored society should revert to traditional ways, after a period when Europe has seen 'Long-reverenced titles cast away as weeds/Laws overturned' (ix.338–9). The injunction upon the individual to be pious, dutiful and reverent is not primarily a matter of personal salvation. The English state had rested during its hour of trial and would continue to rest upon its churches and its cohesive village communities.

In the long run the classic riposte to *The Excursion* was Byron's *Don Juan*, which gaily substituted a sexual ethic for Wordsworth's solemn asceticism. More immediately the need to answer Wordsworth acted as a spur to Shelley, who was as yet barely known, the author of *Queen Mab* and of a trio of radical pamphlets. In September 1814 Shelley returned from France, whither he had eloped with Mary Wollstonecraft Godwin. *The Excursion* was one of the first books he read on his return, and the feelings about Wordsworth which the poem induced were recorded by Mary in her journal – 'Much disappointed. He is a slave.'

It was a full year before Shelley's disapproval yielded fruit in a major poem. In September 1815 he began *Alastor*, which renders the quest of a young poet led on by abstract idealism and indifferent, until it is too late, to 'the spirit of sweet human love'. Most critics seem to have fancied that Shelley has primarily himself in mind as the protagonist of *Alastor*. But his Preface to the poem suggests that on the contrary he is projecting the fate of an imaginary idealist who, in good faith but in the end unhappily, follows the moral prescription issued by Wordsworth in *The Excursion*:

The Poet's self-centred seclusion was avenged by the furies of an irresistible passion pursuing him to speedy ruin . . . . . . Among those who attempt to exist without human sympathy, the pure and tender-hearted perish through the intensity and passion of their search after its communities, when the vacancy of their spirit suddenly makes itself felt. All else, selfish, blind, and torpid, are those unforeseeing multitudes who constitute, together with their own, the lasting misery and loneliness of the world. Those who love not their fellow-beings, live unfruitful lives, and prepare for their old age a miserable grave.

Those last two sentences are a reference, unusually personal and sharp for Shelley, to Wordsworth and perhaps Southey and Coleridge, living on after their youthful genius and their belief in the brotherhood of man had died. One of the main planks in the platform of the younger writers in opposition is to be the rejection of the way of solitude for the poet, which Wordsworth sees as spiritual and contemplative, and they invariably represent as self-indulgent, narcissistic, cowardly or immoral. The Victorians, thoroughly imbued with introverted religious feeling, found the hostility of the 'young Romantics' to the concept of solitary idealism hard to credit, and they initiated the misreading of *Alastor* which continues to be common in the present day. The point is that *The Excursion* caused a controversy which precluded a series of self-examinations or monologues by Wordsworth's younger rivals; he had to be answered by some kind of public discussion, in what would pass for a detached spirit, of the poet's proper role in society. Was it enough for the writer to offer moral and spiritual leadership with his 'visions of recluse genius', as Coleridge proposed in the *Lay Sermons*? Since such visions are essentially religious, the leadership they afford in current circumstances can be in only one political direction. Shelley disapproved of the political intention and hence of the poetic posture, and in 1816 assailed both directly in anti-Wordsworthian poems composed on a second Swiss visit – 'Ode on Receiving a Celandine' and 'Mont Blanc'. The latter poem contemplates a mountain, now the archetypal Wordsworthian subject, but finds there deist or atheistic truths. The contemplation of Mont Blanc does not convey to Shelley what Wordsworth's Pedlar finds in the Lakes, or Coleridge found in his 'Hymn before Sunrise in the Vale of Chamouni,' the evidence of a benign Deity mindful of human affairs:

> Power dwells apart in its tranquillity
> Remote, serene and inaccessible:
> And *this*, the naked countenance of earth
> On which I gaze, even these primaeval mountains
> Teach the adverting mind.

Shelley's wife Mary, the daughter of Mary Wollstonecraft and Godwin, invented during that same Swiss visit a fable which conveyed the same point. *Frankenstein* is the story of a man who goes off alone on what he represents to himself as an idealistic quest. In fact everything

Frankenstein does is evil, because it is egotistical. He makes his Monster as an act of self-glorification, while neglecting his family; even so, all need not have turned out so appallingly badly had he not failed, characteristically, to love his creation. The Monster is evil only because it is rejected and unsocialized. Mary's book too associates the Wordsworthian mountains of Frankenstein's Swiss homeland with solipsism and sterility.

The motif is picked up by Peacock in his satire *Melincourt* (March 1817), where the criticism is brought home specifically to Wordsworth and his group of literary friends:

MR FORESTER

The names of Hampden and Milton are associated with the level plains and flat pastures of Buckinghamshire; but I cannot now remember what names of true greatness and unshaken devotion to general liberty are associated with these heathy rocks and cloud-capped mountains of Cumberland. We have seen a little horde of poets, who brought hither from the vales of the south, the harps which they had consecrated to Truth and Liberty, to acquire new energy in the mountain winds: and now those harps are attuned to the praise of luxurious power, to the strains of courtly sycophancy, and to the hymns of exploded superstition.

(ch.xxxvii)

Melincourt has proved too explicit for Post-Romantic literary taste, but it belongs with a cluster of works not generally dismissed as crudely didactic. The topic is the writer, but the viewpoint is strictly external: what should his demeanour be in relation to society, engaged or withdrawn? Peacock, who saw this as one of the leading issues dividing the classic from the romantic, or (since he did not use the word 'romantic') the ancients from the moderns, made it a leading theme of his work throughout his long writing life. But the same might be said of Shelley, from *Alastor* on. In *Prometheus Unbound* (1818–19) another solitary hero frees himself from sterility and self-inflicted punishment among mountains. *Julian and Maddalo* (1818) is, *Excursion*-like, a study of a series of intellectual lives, framed by a debate between two kinds of writer, Shelley's type and Byron's. In *Adonais* (1821), Keats's career is generalized and analysed and Southey's very different orthodox apologetics alluded to. *The Triumph of Life* (1822) finds in Dante's *Divine Comedy* the framework for yet another pageant of would-be moral leaders, failed heroes, of whom Rousseau is the leader and prototype.

It is easy to see why Shelley's fondness for a poet or intellectual as a leading figure encouraged the typically Victorian biographical reading, that he was writing in a narcissistic manner about himself. The pattern he shares with his two closest intimates between 1815 and 1817 suggests strongly that his intention was to *dramatize* the intellectual, exploring the hazards of his life, like sterility, loneliness, ineffectiveness and self-pity, and the temptations, such as Byron's cynicism and Rousseau's worldliness. If Shelley identifies himself emotionally with his poet-protagonists to a degree avoided by Mary and by Peacock, it is far from clear that this is in literary terms a shortcoming. Shelley's response to the emergence of the writer as a distinct type is much richer than that of the other two; however inconvenient in the contemporary political disagreement, a new self-consciousness has entered literary discourse, and Shelley instinctively uses it. Nevertheless it remains true that for Shelley as for Peacock that leading topic, the portrait of the artist, is to an important degree abstracted and generalized. In their reluctance to countenance the poet's withdrawal into privacy, these two anticipate the commoner position of writers in the first half of the nineteenth century. The concept of a duty to society, a duty if possible to achieve action, recurs in the writing of Tennyson, Browning, Arnold and George Eliot. On the whole they are uneasy with the openly 'Romantic', that is otherworldly, argument; and so, of course, were Wordsworth and Coleridge. Even the case they made in 1814–17 for the contemplative life had a social connotation, and was frankly and positively committed to politics. It is one of the peculiarities of polemic, that both sides lay claim to the same virtues and the same ground; and one of the ironies of literary history, that even writers of the more 'Romantic' position in the second decade of the century should have accepted what we now feel to be a classical or utilitarian premise, that the poet is bound by society's claim on him.

In 1816 and 1817 riots, machine-breaking and civil disorders occurred in many parts of the country, while the campaign for parliamentary reform commanded huge crowds and masses of signatures, if minute representation in the legislature. What alarmed the middle classes was that virtually for the first time agitation was taken to the lower orders by journalists – most notably by Cobbett, but also afterwards by William Hone (1780–1842) and Richard Carlile (1790–1843). A natural populist, Cobbett had moved from a sturdy wartime patriotism to a thunderous radicalism on behalf of the small farmers and yeomen of the southern counties. As an orator on the page he had gifts similar to Paine's, and was as much feared. Newspapers were taxed as a matter of public policy: it was thought safer to make them expensive. By reprinting the leader-column only of his *Political Register* as a broadsheet, Cobbett could legally charge only two pence – the famous 'Twopenny Trash', which was believed by government supporters to be playing so incendiary a part in the radical winter of 1816–17. Cobbett's favourite topics included

campaigns against paper money and against parliamentary representation, but his real effectiveness, like Paine's, lay in the brilliant simplicity
with which he presented lesser grievances as a single large one – the
oppression of the many by the few, through a corrupt and omnipresent
System.

At such a time and with such an example, the theoretical issue of how
an intellectual ought to behave had to be translated into action. Southey
took to writing on general topics, notably in a vitriolic article in the
Quarterly Review of October 1816 which recommended that strict
censorship ought to be introduced to curb the activities of his brother-
journalists. Less popularly, indeed very obscurely, Coleridge in the *Lay
Sermons* advocated élitism, restraint, piety and duty. He too thought that
press censorship should be introduced; only Wordsworth among the
conservative poets did not canvass this suggestion. Meanwhile the radical
cause was supported in a vein half literary but wholly political by the
brothers John and Leigh Hunt in their weekly the *Examiner*, and by a
rising journalist, William Hazlitt.

Hazlitt, born 1778, worked not only for the *Examiner* but (since 1814)
prestigiously for the middle-of-the-road and Whiggish *Edinburgh Review*, which preserved a cautious silence on the present discontents.
Hazlitt certainly considered himself a liberal, and as an admirer of
Napoleon refused to rejoice at the restoration of the Bourbons. But he
generally avoided committing himself in print on domestic affairs, the
sensitive issues where radical views were likely to give offence to readers
– and, to do Hazlitt justice, to cause dissension among the reformers
themselves. His favourite topics were the restored European despotisms,
for which most Englishmen felt more or less distaste, and the older, more
conservative poets. Quite often he managed to work both targets
together, as in January 1818, when he attacked French moves against the
freedom of the press, and sardonically demanded to know where
England's own senior writers stood on the issue. A 'sort of shuffling on
the side of principle, and tenaciousness on the side of power, seems to be
the peculiar privilege of the race of modern poets'.

On the Tory side, Coleridge prided himself that he tried to go back to
principles, rather than to stick with personalities. Among the rather more
liberal, Jeffrey could claim with reasonable justice to do the same.
Hazlitt's best friend could not say that as a journalist he either studied
principles or tried to avoid personalities. He was annoyed, on one
representative occasion, by an article in the Tory *Courier* defending
Southey, which he guessed must have been written by Coleridge:

Whoever this Defender of Mr. Southey may be, he is evidently sore on the
subject, from an alarmed fellow-feeling and a wounded vanity . . . This hack writer

of the *Courier* has a spell upon him, which denies him the happy power of invisibility. From the forced and quaint images, the vile puns, the uncouth and floundering attempts at humour, the bloatedness of the eloquence, and the slang of the blackguardisms, we cannot be mistaken in the writer of this effusion of disinterested generosity. This sympathy is natural. The author of the *Conciones ad Populum*, and the author of THE *Wat Tyler*, are sworn brothers in the same cause of righteous apostasy.

(*Examiner*, 5 April 1817)

After more in this vein, Hazlitt charitably draws on his own acquaintance with Coleridge, by recalling a scene in a library at Bristol when Coleridge, behind Southey's back, ridiculed him as a poet.

It is not surprising that the older poets came to detest Hazlitt as the prime personal enemy among their opponents. For liberals Southey occupied the same role. As Poet Laureate he offered an obvious target, and his prompt loyal effusions provided tempting material for satire. To fellow-writers and journalists his 1816 *Quarterly* piece on the freedom of the press was an even more serious offence, a kind of *trahison des clercs*. Nevertheless, it is surely one of the injustices of literary history that Hazlitt has on the whole got away with his trivializing and his nastiness – which are not replied to in lasting literature – while the less malicious Southey attracts such very devastating and memorable literary fire: from Peacock intermittently in *Melincourt*, *Nightmare Abbey* and *Maid Marian*; from Shelley in *Adonais*; from Byron, most hilariously, in *A Vision of Judgment*.

All these assaults, like other literary relationships and transactions of the time, are politically inspired. Southey is not attacked for such literary matters as his style or his quality as a poet, though once the political offence is established both come in for incidental aspersions. The relationships between English writers are peculiarly political, and never more than in this period of semi-journalistic effort from 1816 to 1819, when there is virtually no disinterested reviewing. It is hard to understand the reception of an apparently unpolitical poet like Keats, unless we first accept that no such animal existed in his lifetime. The sneers against Keats in the *Quarterly* and Lockhart's savage and snobbish assault in *Blackwood's* are alike the moves of Tories who associate Keats with the opposition camp. Leigh Hunt's favourable reviews in the *Examiner* and *Indicator* are, similarly, politically motivated. Even Jeffrey's silence on Keats's first volume in the *Edinburgh* could well be political. Editors have always mislaid or otherwise neglected worthy books, but in these dangerous times it was also in the interest of the *Edinburgh Review* to avoid controversial subjects, in order neither to support the Government nor to bring aid and comfort to the disaffected.

What, then, of the poetry? After the government had in the spring of 1817 repealed Habeas Corpus – that safeguard against arbitrary arrest and imprisionment, and most resonant of statutes – how did the major writers react?

To some extent they had no choice but to conform. Late in 1817 Shelley was obliged by his publisher to trim *Laon and Cythna*, which came out in a modified form as *The Revolt of Islam*. In 1819 he planned a volume of political poems for a popular audience, including *The Masque of Anarchy*, 'The Song to the Men of England', and the burlesque play dealing with George IV's unpopular attempt to divorce Queen Caroline, *Swellfoot the Tyrant*. His publisher, who would take a reasonably guarded text designed for an educated audience, would not take one for the masses. Effective censorship was, then, one factor determining the style of liberal poetry after 1817. But another was a kind of self-censorship. The writers were themselves subject to the fears and pressures felt by the propertied classes. Their attitude to popular disaffection was at a certain level ambivalent. It may have been caution which led the Marlow circle to mythologize their disagreements with Church and State, in the richly allusive and inaccessible way they did. It may have been doubt, and a possibly unconscious fear of what they might unleash.

Take, for example, one of the sharper and more clearcut statements against Toryism and Tory cultural influence in 1818, Peacock's *Nightmare Abbey*. This most amusing and elegant satire lampoons Germanism, as practised by Coleridge, on the grounds that the forces of reaction have a way of using obscure systems of belief for their own ends. Peacock's Coleridgean figure, the transcendental Mr Flosky, is a political reactionary who knows he has a vested interest in not being understood: the last thing he wants to shed is light. This is a specific and appropriate riposte to Coleridge's two recent works of Christian apologetics, the *Lay Sermons* and the *Biographia Literaria*.

Peacock is not the sitter-on-the-fence he has been represented as being. He is as surely the prose satirist of the younger generation as Byron is its satiric spokesman in verse. The main burden of *Nightmare Abbey* is that if a young poet means to be liberal he had better not take up with the style of Coleridge. Peacock's hero, Scythrop Glowry, alludes to Shelley, who had been fond of Gothic excess, obscurity and gloom in the past. His Byron-figure, Mr Cypress, has been so carried away by morbidity and introspection that he seems temporarily lost to liberalism. 'Sir, I have quarrelled with my wife; and a man who has quarrelled with his wife is absolved from duty to his country.' So the main drive of Peacock's book is towards an Enlightenment clarity and a Greek sense of social commitment. He does not tell but shows that the best literary vehicle will be comedy.

And yet just a hint of political ambivalence emerges in Peacock's presentation of Scythrop. For what precisely is Scythrop ridiculous? For writing so obscurely that he found only seven readers? Or for actually having 'a passion for reforming the world'? This phrase which Peacock attaches to Scythrop derives from a discussion of political extremism in a book by a little-known Scottish philosopher called Robert Forsyth. Unquestionably Forsyth, like Peacock, inclined to liberalism, and a large part of his strictures on unbridled revolutionary fervour are liberal precautions: if we overdo things and become fanatical our attempt at rational reform will fail. Nevertheless, implicit in Forsyth and perhaps in Peacock is an overmastering fear of this breakdown of control: the memory of the Terror arises afresh at intervals to haunt the imagination even of the reformer. There are thus two ways of summing up the message conveyed by Peacock in *Nightmare Abbey*. The overt thrust of what he is saying is surely that he wants a commitment to liberalism; yet a reforming zeal that is sensible, rational and cool is the only sure way to get things done. Alternatively, or additionally, for a second meaning accompanies the first meaning, the men of moderation are those who get things *safely* done. There comes in Peacock's career about this time a parallel to that tendency in Hazlitt to choose topics which are not too divisive. It may be no accident that his really political and national satire, *Melincourt*, 1817, is followed in 1818 by the more confined *Nightmare Abbey*; and that in the summer of 1818, with *Maid Marian*, he too turned to ridiculing the reactionary crowned heads of Europe and the mystique of feudalism. Though *Maid Marian* was not completed until 1822, it was begun in the fraught period of political controversy, and its topic was significantly less sensitive than Peacock's concerns of the previous two years.

The modern radical observer, looking back, might feel inclined to accuse the radical poets, all of whom were upper or middle class, of intellectual and moral cowardice. This would be at best a simplification and probably as a whole quite inappropriate. It was after all a common-sense political strategy to concentrate on those causes where opposition might find middle-of-the-road support; it would conversely have been suicidal to harp on themes which frightened moderate opinion off, as the question of reform at home now did. One can reasonably represent Hazlitt, Byron and Peacock as politically adroit in turning their satiric attention on to Castlereagh, whose foreign policy – an alliance with backward-looking foreign despotisms – was infinitely less attractive to educated British opinion than was the government's firm domestic policy.

Shelley, safely abroad in Italy in 1819, saw fit in *The Masque of Anarchy* to address the masses, and to urge upon them the most effective political action they could undertake – combination, and passive resistance:

> And these words shall then become
> Like Oppression's thundered doom
> Ringing through each heart and brain
> Heard again – again – again –
>
> Rise like Lions after slumber
> In unvanquishable number –
> Shake your chains to earth like dew
> Which in sleep had fallen on you –
> Ye are many – they are few.

There were a number of reasons, and cowardice was surely not the first, why few of his group in England hit the same note. There was indeed vigorous satire from polemicists like William Hone and caricaturists like George Cruikshank (1792–1878), crude enough for the most popular taste, and bold as Gillray's two decades earlier, though it was not equally skilful. Keats late in 1819 began 'The Cap and Bells', a skit in the manner of *Don Juan* on the royal marital scandal and on the Lake poets' asceticism. The best work was of another kind. Caught in the very strong pressure of middle-class fear of revolution, liberal writers whether abroad or at home continued to tackle public issues, but in terms which stressed their problematic quality, the damaging face of change.

The great literature of the years immediately after 1817 – what is normally designated the era of the younger Romantics – discovers a great nineteenth-century preoccupation: the necessity of historical change, but also and more particularly the damage done to individuals by that process. If this is the poetry of revolution, it is revolution explored from the perspective of its potential victims, the middle classes. Most of the writers tackling the theme in England are liberals; there is at least one great exception in the Tory Scott; political opponents can sound alike when the subject is the imprinting of remorseless events upon the lives of vulnerable individuals. Shelley's greatest poetry rises above the simplification entailed in his call to the masses. It holds in a striking dual perspective the natural cosmos, fluid, destructive, impassive, and the fragile, delicate bloom of individual consciousness. The dualism underlies many of Shelley's greatest poems, from 'Ode to the West Wind' to *Adonais* and perhaps *The Triumph of Life*. As a literary response to revolution, it takes a long step beyond the generalized single perspective of *Queen Mab* or even *The Masque of Anarchy*. But nothing so well illustrates the omnipresence and gravity of the awareness of revolution as its appearance in writers not normally thought of as political, Scott and Keats.

Just as an alteration comes over Byron's style around 1818 in favour of a rhetoric more clearly associated with liberalism, so a change of a less drastic kind comes over Scott. Paradoxically *Ivanhoe* (1820), his first novel to take up a medieval theme, is thematically his most contemporaneous novel to date. Its plot turns on class warfare, the hostility between a ruling caste, the Normans, and the common people – who are no mere rabble, but have an egalitarian tradition which goes back into their Saxon past. In taking up this theme Scott must have been deliberately drawing on a live controversy. Nothing short of consciousness explains why he deserted the setting of all his novels to date, his native Scotland, for an English story, or why he undertook the difficult task of writing a realistic novel about so remote a society. The explanation usually given is Scott's nostalgia for feudal times; but, though he happily confessed at times to such a sentiment, this is not what is primarily conveyed by his text. Instead, *Ivanhoe* draws on a favourite topic of radicals, revivified since Burke had claimed that England's past was an organic, seamless whole. Whig and radical historians of the 1780s and 1790s, the age of Burke – John Millar, Tom Paine and Joseph Ritson, who as a ballad-collector could claim to be retrieving the viewpoint of the populace – had variously gone out of their way to show that aristocratic government was not necessarily validated by historic tradition. The real England, that is Anglo-Saxon England, had been a freer, more popular society; the Normans who overran it in 1066 brought in the Continental concept of hereditary kings and peers, and imposed upon the people legal and clerical systems designed cynically to perpetuate their own power. The republication after the end of the war both of Ritson's popular *Robin Hood* and of all Paine's works no doubt assisted the return to currency of the old radical battle-cry against the Norman Yoke. Most inviting of all was the comparison between the Norman brigands and the various Continental despots who had just been restored to their thrones by force. In the spring of 1817 Hazlitt wrote for the *Examiner* a vigorous 'history' of the French monarchy, from Hugh Capet to modern times, in which the Bourbon line is represented as a series of robber-barons rather than as the sacred legitimists of right-wing propaganda.

Against this background, it is surely significant that with *Ivanhoe* Scott both takes up the 'radical' theme and avoids recourse to the most obvious conservative tactic – the romanticizing of his Plantagenets and Normans. His hero and heroine are Saxons (though unusually aristocratic ones).

One of his Norman barons is the thug Front de Boeuf. Another, Bois-guilbert, belongs to the Templars, a knightly and religious order, so that he represents the Norman hierarchical concept both in secular and spiritual life; Bois-guilbert's principal aspiration during much of the action is to rape Rebecca. He oppresses both the Saxon lower orders and the vulnerable minority, the Jews.

Scott therefore allows much of the criticism which had been directed against feudal institutions by radicals, incorporating it within his fable. But he also preaches compromise and reconciliation. Ivanhoe has taken on the characteristics of a Norman knight, and clearly believes in reforming the system from within rather than in attacking it from without. Scott makes the head of his Norman hierarchy, Richard, enough of a true knight to suggest that the nation can and will rally behind him. That conclusion is foreseeable in a Tory writer. What could not have been anticipated is the amount of human suffering Scott depicts within a medieval and legitimist society. His representation could be seen as almost cynical – a world bonded neither by religious ardour nor by chivalric dedication, but by guile and brute force.

Scott was indeed never a single-minded polemicist, nor over-sanguine. A few months before *Ivanhoe* he wrote a novel set at the time of the union of Scotland and England, *The Bride of Lammermoor*, in which he killed off both his hero and his heroine. The message conveyed by this, his first tragic dénouement, is that some historical reconciliations have been very shoddy ones, and achieved at a great cost to individuals. Most critics have concluded that Scott's performance declined after *The Heart of Mid-lothian* (1818), which seems to round off his series of realistic, near-contemporary Scottish novels. His later work appears more fantastic, deploying as it does ghosts, magic, and other Gothic accoutrements suitable to the remoter past. It is indeed true that the loss of the realism and richness of the earlier vein seems a high price to pay. Yet at the same time there is development in Scott's work after 1819, for the central characters are conceived more emotionally: the frustrations of a Roland Graeme, a Nigel Olifaunt or a Darsie Latimer convey a new kind of truth about the human condition, to which the reader's access is sensitive and profound. As comments upon society and upon politics, *St. Ronan's Well* (1823) and *Redgauntlet* (1824) are more pessimistic and perhaps even intellectually more complex than the great early series, with their resolute optimism. *The Monastery* (1820) and *The Abbot* (1820), elegiac and yet also necessitarian studies of the end of monasticism, tacitly refute the sentimentalizing of so much conservative contemporary writing about the Middle Ages. Along with his refusal to idealize the past, Scott conveys his doubts about the stability of the present social synthesis, and his growing anxieties about the future.

Keats's 'Hyperion', and the revised version 'The Fall of Hyperion', as well as 'The Ode to Autumn', are not now read as political or public poems. Yet 'Hyperion' does after all describe a revolution, the overthrow of the Titans by the Olympian gods. Its main literary source, *Paradise Lost*, is about the father of all rebellions, Satan's. There is evidence in the letters that Keats, a great reader of Hazlitt's journalism, had become interested in the French Revolution and in the greater revolution that was still accomplishing:

All civil[iz]ed countries become gradually more enlighten'd and there should be a continual change for the better. Look at this Country at present and remember it when it was even though[t] impious to doubt the justice of a trial by combat ... Three great changes have been in progress – First for the better, next for the worse, and a third time for the better once more. The first was the annihilation of the tyranny of the nobles ... The change for the worse in Europe was again this. The obligation of Kings to the multitude began to be forgotten ..: ... The example of England, and the liberal writers of france and england sowed the seed of opposition to this Tyranny – and it was swelling in the ground till it burst out in the french revolution. That has had an unlucky termination. It put a stop to the rapid progress of free sentiments in England; and gave our Court hopes of turning back to the despotism of the 16 century. They have made a handle of this event in every way to undermine our freedom. They spread a horrid superstition against all in[n]ovation and improvement. The present struggle in England of the people is to destroy this superstition. What has rous'd them to do it is their distresses – Perhaps on this account the present distresses of this nation are a fortunate thing – tho so horrid in their experience. You will see I mean that the French Revolution [p]ut a tempor[a]ry stop to this third change, the change for the better. Now it is in progress again, and I think i[t] an effectual one. This is no contest between whig and tory – but between right and wrong.   ([18] Sept. 1819)

The cyclical action of 'Hyperion' expresses the necessitarian truth, that life is change and must embrace change in all its forms, including defeat and death. Small wonder that Shelley admired the poem and hailed it as Keats's greatest achievement yet; he died with it open in his pocket. But Keats's emphasis no more commits him to welcoming revolution like a nineteenth-century progressive, than to justifying the divine order like a seventeenth-century Christian. He begins with the experience of the fallen, suffering Titans. This only seems like an echo of Milton, who also begins with the fallen angels: the sensibility, the bewilderment of loss, the essential innocence of Keats's fallen gods capture a modern pity for the helpless individual victims of the historical process.

Keats's revised version, 'The Fall of Hyperion', gives the poem a further dimension, and makes it more sharply contemporary. By relocating the action in the consciousness of a modern poet, Keats takes up a topic more familiar in the work of Shelley and Peacock – contemplation of the role of the writer, especially in the light of the religious, vatic stance urged by the living older poets. 'Fanatics have their dreams': 'The Fall of Hyperion' begins with some observations unsympathetic to privacy, spirituality, primitive or fundamentalist insights, the various strands which go to make up the seer-poet recently sketched by the Lakists. The 'fanatics' here are Christian believers in general but also, more particularly, Wordsworth's simple and pious Wanderer, as he is described in the first and fourth Books of *The Excursion*. Keats's narrator learns from his goddess or Muse, Moneta, a conception of the true poet that is as consciously social in its orientation, as much a rejection of the inwardness and solipsism of *The Excursion*, as are *Alastor*, *Melincourt* and *Frankenstein*. Not surprisingly, considering who she is, Moneta's aesthetic values are those of a classicist. Meanwhile the narrator, more familiar with modern times, feels free to apply her observations to his contemporaries. Keats meant to cancel these topical and pointedly personal lines, but it seems clear that he was thinking of Tom Moore, Wordsworth, and Byron in his earlier and more self-indulgent phase:

> Apollo! faded! O far flown Apollo!
> Where is thy misty pestilence to creep
> Into the dwellings, through the door crannies.
> Of all mock lyrists, large self worshippers
> And careless hectorers in proud bad verse?
>
> (I.204–8)

But more than any of his other contemporaries, Keats was surely thinking of Coleridge. On the face of it, the shift from 'Hyperion' to 'The Fall of Hyperion' involves the substitution merely of one model for another, Dante for Milton. But Keats could not make the transition to Dante in 'The Fall of Hyperion' without also invoking Coleridge, who in his 1818 series of lectures had done more than anyone, more perhaps than the translator Cary and certainly more than Sismondi, to make Dante fashionable in England. Moreover, in the second of his *Lay Sermons* Coleridge used Dante in a way that may have done as much as Keats's own reading of the *Divine Comedy* to stimulate him to 'The Fall of Hyperion'.

It is in the second *Lay Sermon* that Coleridge launches an attack of several pages on contemporary radical intellectuals, including Keats's friends Hunt and Hazlitt, though he withholds the names of the individuals, much as Keats does in 'The Fall of Hyperion'. But before

Coleridge descends to personalities he opens the second *Lay Sermon* with an allegorical dream-vision in the Dantesque manner which is meant for a generalized portrait of the current intellectual scene. Coleridge's Dreamer encounters the false idol of the present day, whose real name is Superstition, though he is worshipped by modern man as science or materialism. He also meets alone (for she is much neglected) a statuesque goddess, who turns out to be Religion. Keats certainly knew of the existence of the *Lay Sermons*, since he refers to them in a letter of October 1817: could the key to the re-ordering of his poem lie here? In 'The Fall of Hyperion' the protagonist also in a dream meets a goddess, impressive and forbidding, who does not represent supernatural religion, as in Coleridge's version, but Coleridge's false deity, humanism. Keats's debate in the shrine re-enacts the classic contemporary literary controversy, between the poet as activist or physician, and the poet as visionary or dreamer. He would appear to be invoking the Coleridge location in order to refute Coleridge's conclusion. For Keats and his Muse 'the poet and the dreamer are distinct', and it is the classical role of activist that he prefers to the 'romantic' one of Recluse.

Keats's larger intention in both 'Hyperions', though they are even more obscure and allusive than most work of the period, is broadly to represent historical change as the liberal habitually sees it: continuous, inevitable, and on the most universal level grand, for it is Progress – the survival of the fittest, the best, the most beautiful and the quintessentially human. Like Shelley in *Prometheus Unbound*, he revises *Paradise Lost*, replacing Milton's Christian cosmology with an evolutionary one, substituting a natural order for a divine order. Yet Keats, writing at least a year earlier, 1818–19, does not sound by any means as resolutely optimistic as Shelley. In the first 'Hyperion', the reader enters sympathetically into the experience of the fallen gods: for them the historical process has entailed loss, doubt, anguish and sacrifice, and the possibility that they could discover any kind of renewal or resurrection on earth is sternly avoided. When in 'The Fall of Hyperion' Keats adds the narrator-figure, that of an individual modern poet, the reader encounters another surrogate for personal suffering, compounded of the poet's struggle to establish his artistic identity and every man's need to confront the certainty of death. What it means to be a poet can be established only by overthrowing the misconceptions and outmoded systems of other writers – Wordsworth, Coleridge, Milton – as Dante supplanted Virgil and Apollo Hyperion, but the poet-narrator's victory in his struggle with previous poets seems far from assured. Moneta is the most abrasive of Muses. Though classical all right, she conveys anything but the calm tranquillity of the commonest classical stereotype. She gives the poet no reason to believe that *his* art will perform a healing function: indeed, the very principle that it should is disquietingly touched by time. In the new version of Keats's poem, Moneta's wan visage is the reader's first intimation of the sufferings of the doomed Titans. Her shrine is part of a ruined world which recalls 'the superannuations of sunk realms'. She is so old that in the present day of the poem even the god who is to be shown triumphing over her order has himself been superseded – 'Apollo! faded! O far flown Apollo!' And so her precepts, though clearly preferable to those of the modern self-worshippers, are, for Keats's poet-persona, anything but a simple or idealized vision of art. In the truly evolutionary world, even the verities are not eternal.

This is why it would be misleading to represent the best poetry of 1817–20 as in any important sense evasive. The more simply committed work of the younger Shelley and Peacock and on the other side Scott may give way to a complex, often pessimistic portrayal of change, one that reflects the doubts of the literate classes for which all the writers catered and to which they belonged. It is not the business of literature in the last resort to do the work of the political propagandist; both Shelley and Keats became conscious of having moved beyond didacticism. When abstract concepts are taken up in literature, in good literature at least, they undergo the transformations that the single subjective consciousness imposes. In these years of public issues and growing private awareness, a unique opportunity existed for an idiosyncratic yet also concerted exploration of great themes. The writers of the day made a literary movement which represented revolution, but one could not call it revolutionary literature. It is in fact more interesting than that. Just as political disillusionment and the sudden contraction to a personal focus produced the literary efflorescence of 1798, so once again it was the conflict between revolutionary expansion and energy and the self-doubt induced by social isolation that drew from the writers work no ideologue would have countenanced. Formalistic and experiential, traditionalist and progressive, the poetic mode of the years from 1817 to 1822 probably produces more great works than any comparably short time in our literature. Its paradoxes reflect the considerations that made it – a commitment to the public cause, but no ascertainable public to address; sometimes a willed optimism about the political future, but more often an involuntary fear of what living through change entails.

7 Romantic Novel, Romantic Prose

What is a Romantic novel? German critics like the Schlegels were not interested in a fictional tradition that smacked of empiricism and materialism. Friedrich Schlegel approved of works that created fanciful worlds rather than mirrored this one: he also sought the controlling hand of irony, which ensured the author's objectivity. He liked Aristophanes, Shakespeare, Cervantes, Swift, Jean Paul, and grouped Shakespeare with Cervantes, two authors of works which are full of 'artfully arranged confusion, charming symmetry of contrasts, eternal alternation of enthusiasm and irony'. In his lifetime, ironic and fantastic novels which matched his description were emerging in Germany. Even Goethe, who thought Romanticism a disease, seems to English readers to have caught an unfamiliar mannered dreamlike tone in *Wilhelm Meister* and in *Elective Affinities*. Judged by these German standards, the English novel remains aloof from Romanticism.

Yet 'the Romantic period' is a great one for the English novel, even if the significant trend is unquestionably in the direction of realism. Reviewer after reviewer in the journals, considering the novels of Maria Edgeworth, Walter Scott, Jane Austen and a host of lesser figures, stresses that a revolution is occurring in fiction, which Croker, reviewing *Waverley* in the *Quarterly* in 1814, defines by an analogy with painting. After the exaltation of Raphael, Correggio and Murillo – the equivalents for the novel's older classics, *Gil Blas* and *Tom Jones* – the form is now 'minute and Dutch'. Its characters are not merely '*men*, but Irish, Scotch and French'. Scott himself admired the domestic fidelity of Edgeworth and Austen. The English nineteenth-century novel is by consensus entering a new phase of engagement with observable facts in the real external world.

Critics in journals of all shades of opinion notice and welcome this development. They utilize the critical criteria appropriate to a naturalistic movement, so that increasingly verisimilitude becomes the test of truth. They also sense in the new realistic interest in delineating society what is, effectively, a political or ideological commitment to society as it is. 'Vraisemblance', the 'vigorous and at the same time refined and delicate delineation of character' and 'unexaggerated truth of manners in all walks of society' are linked in the Edgeworth tales with 'excellent moral lessons, touching the conduct of everyday life'. But not only in the Edgeworth tales. Despite the real ideological differences between Edgeworth, Austen and Scott, all three end by teaching their central characters to put society (however far from ideal) before self. Realism in the aesthetic field is the corollary of empiricism in scientific enquiry, and not necessarily of conservatism, but certainly of gradualism in approaching the political and social order. In terms of its underlying aesthetic procedures, the English novel is equipped to resist the contemporary ferment of ideas, or at least abstractions and extremes. In the revolutionary period its Dutch minuteness easily conveys an antipathy to theory (generally thought of about 1800 as radical) and its social ethic rebukes individualism, which also temporarily has a libertarian connotation. In the third decade of the century, the same qualities may be inhospitable to the ardour and the inward interest of the religious revival.

This strong movement in the direction of realism clearly receives an impetus, in the 1790s particularly, from the rejection of certain fictional modes that emerged in the second half of the eighteenth century. Three significant modes appeared between 1760 and 1790 in England, France and Germany; all attracted major talent; all came to be associated with subversion during the 1790s, which meant that in England especially they fell at once into disrepute. An awareness of this aesthetic revolution, and the reasons for it, is necessary to an understanding of the English novel in the period, first because the rejected styles helped to determine the tone and quality of the countervailing movement – a blend of documentary realism with civic morality – and second because the 'radical' alternatives lurked on in the period out of the middlebrow mainstream, in popular pulp fiction and in experiments by the highbrow liberal poets. The three literary traditions in retreat were the Gothic, the sentimental and the intellectual-ironic, the point at which the Enlightenment most clearly impinged on fiction in the philosophic tales of Voltaire and Marmontel.

Of these, it is the Gothic which we most frequently associate with the idea of a Romantic novel. In fact, the Gothic is a product of the three decades of quickening pulse, the revolutionary era from about 1760 to about 1797, reaching a culmination in England with the mature work of Ann Radcliffe, *The Romance of the Forest* (1791), *The Mysteries of Udolpho* (1794) and *The Italian* (1797). The feverish mid-1790s made a vogue of *Udolpho* and of a host of German translations, though nothing competed in notoriety with Matthew Gregory Lewis's spectacular part-plagiarism, *The Monk* (1795). Excitement quickly became alarm; after

1797 not only the respectable Ann Radcliffe but any novelist who cared for reputation tended for about two decades to keep clear of Gothic. Its images project an evil or disturbing environment, and though no specific moral need be pointed concerning the corruption of the present order or the desirability of rejecting authority, the subliminal frame of reference is felt to be a breakdown of control, both in the psyche and in the state.

At the same time and for the same reasons, sentimental fiction came under the edict. Since the age of Locke the representation of character in the drama and in fiction had been strongly influenced by a prevailing optimism about human nature, a rejection of original sin in favour of the innate goodness of natural man. After the middle of the century, and aided by the example of Rousseau's *Nouvelle Héloïse* (1761) and *Émile* (1762), a strongly subjective fictional kind had emerged which regularly put the feelings of the heart above parental authority, law and inherited morality. Like the Gothic, sentimentalism enjoyed a last, feverish flowering at the end of the 1790s, fed also by translations from the German, especially the plays of the second-rate Kotzebue; and, also like the Gothic, it quickly fell out of favour with reputable authors. Both modes were satirized in public in *The Anti-Jacobin* and by James Gillray, and in private by the apprentice novelist Jane Austen. As for witty didactic tales in the style of Voltaire, these exerted some influence on liberal writing in the eighties and nineties, most obviously on the satiric novels of Robert Bage, but also, more discreetly, on the tales of the rational Maria Edgeworth. Her evolution after the turn of the century into the novelist of sober working life is symptomatic of the loss of prestige of fiction too overtly directed to the discussion of ideas.

Like so much else that was openly liberal, then, the Gothic, the sentimental and the Voltairean ceased to be in vogue during the wartime years, after the crisis point of 1798. Up till then, ambitious young writers were still taking up these genres, precisely because they had both imaginative and intellectual potential. In 1798–9 the young Scott translated German ballads and Goethe's play *Goetz von Berlichingen*, and wrote a drama of his own, *The House of Aspen*, which features a spectacular secret tribunal. In 1798 Charles Lamb wrote a tale, *Rosamund Gray*, which is, like other good fiction of those years – Elizabeth Inchbald's *Nature and Art* (1796), or Maria Edgeworth's *Simple Susan* (1798) – a marrying of the strong lines of the didactic tale with the warmth and simplicity of sentiment. In pulp fiction and in the London theatres, which catered for a more popular audience than the middle-class novel, sentimental motifs and, more obviously, the sensational paraphernalia of the Gothic lived on to feed the melodrama of the next century; as far as the novel proper went, the loss of prestige that turns away serious writers was sudden and decisive. When all three suspect modes enjoyed a revival in the middle of the second decade of the new century, it was, like so much else in liberal writing then, a deliberate revival of the practices of the Enlightenment.

It is surely most interesting and significant that none of the younger first-class poets – Byron, Shelley or Keats – was attracted to the realistic novel, even though fiction of this kind was put by reviewers so high above Gothic 'romance'. Shelley had always hankered after the Gothic, and as a schoolboy wrote two novels in this genre. His *Zastrozzi* and *St. Irvyne* are strongly influenced by three particularly intellectual and implicitly radical Gothicists of the 1780s and 1790s – the German Schiller, the Englishman Godwin, and the American Brockden Brown. It was his wife Mary who became the novelist of the Marlow group. Her work is touched by all the liberal kinds: the Gothic or science-fiction plot, the sentimental or subjective placing of character, and the strongly philosophic or didactic outline of the tale as opposed to the seemingly casual development of the naturalistic novel. The most attractive aspects of the Voltairean model, the satire, the wit, the urbanity and the iconoclasm, were meanwhile revived most successfully in the satires of Peacock.

Through the war years some vestige of the liberal tradition was in fact kept alive by William Godwin, who, though not a major novelist, is a minor one of real stature. Godwin's novels of the 1790s, *Caleb Williams* and *St. Leon*, are moral and political fables which employ a strong element of Gothic. *Fleetwood* (1805) is a fictionalized confessional autobiography which reminds the reader now of Rousseau's *Confessions*, now of Wordsworth. *Mandeville* (1817) has all the ingredients, as a didactic tale with a Gothic backdrop and a strongly subjective viewpoint. Though in *Nightmare Abbey* Peacock ridiculed *Mandeville* for its modish gloom, and Shelley had similar reservations, it is interesting to notice how thoroughly Mary Shelley's work combines the same elements as her father's.

What is always remembered about *Frankenstein* (1818) is its splendid central image, the inventor hunted down by a Monster of his own creation. Writers of mystery and imagination in the nineteenth century are fond of the idea of an evil familiar spirit, or *doppelgänger*: it recurs in for example Hogg's *Confessions of a Justified Sinner* (1824), Emily Brontë's *Wuthering Heights* (1848), Melville's *Moby Dick* (1851) and Stevenson's *Jekyll and Hyde* (1866). This is a motif which has readily lent itself in the twentieth century to a psychic, that is primarily introspective, interpretation:

To say flatly that the Monster is Frankenstein's id on the rampage and that he subconsciously desires his family's extermination would be pretentious and anachronistic ... It is quite different to argue that Frankenstein and his Monster have much in common, that they are objectified parts of a single sensibility, and that they represent the intimate good and bad struggle in the human personality. Evil is within, in one's own works and creations.

So says an American critic, Lowry Nelson. But the presence in *Frankenstein* of a sustained critique of Wordsworth (see above, p.142) also suggests that it is a controlled and explicit didactic fable or allegory. The serious intellectual impulse underlying Ann Radcliffe's kind of Gothic in the 1790s is naturalistic or behaviourist: she is interested in how the mind reacts under pressure. The early Wordsworth has the same scientific interest in psychology, which is typical of the Enlightenment. In Mary Shelley this study of the personality has been replaced by a non-realistic, non-behavioural general intellectual argument.

It is of course open to any of us to claim that Mary Shelley's story is *really* about the unconscious, and ultimately about her own. This sort of assertion cannot easily be disproved; nor, using rigorous standards, can it be proved; and meanwhile it has to be set against an explicit allegory in favour of humanistic social idealism, and against the conservative religious idealism of the recluse. Frankenstein, like the novel's other solitary protagonist, Walton, claims through his scientific explorations to be serving his fellow-men. In mind he is apparently as beautiful as in person. But he is solipsistic, and always motivated by selfish considerations. His initial failure to love the Monster is a failure to love something unlike himself: for Frankenstein, love is narcissism. The Monster has already killed Frankenstein's brother, father and friend, yet when he threatens, 'I will be with you on your wedding night', Frankenstein assumes that he rather than his bride is in danger. However the story may have rooted itself in the popular consciousness, as a study in the frightfulness of what may be within, it seems clearly designed to convey a social message, which indeed argues against the very kind of inward interest it is usually taken to illustrate.

Mary Shelley's novel is part of a general revival of the Gothic as a form with serious literary potential. Its elements included the post-war European fashion for things Germanic, and the excitement generated by powerful, gloomy heroes such as Byron's. Tragedy, especially Shakespeare's, was the prestigious stage form. In England the tragic spirit was interpreted by a new actor with an intense, melodramatic style, Edmund Kean, and by a new drama critic, William Hazlitt. The eclectic nature of these conjunctions in taste is important. Hazlitt's interest in the expressive, the passionate and the extreme is, like his concern above all for character, an aspect of his individualistic liberalism; and yet it flowers in the very years when many liberals associate morbid literary introversion with the continental brand of conservatism which Hazlitt the political journalist excoriates. There is clearly a paradox in the fact that one of the most notable post-war Gothicists, C. R. Maturin, was felt by conservatives to be subversive. Coleridge denounced Maturin's play, *Bertram* (1816) in the *Biographia Literaria* for much the same reasons as he had objected to *The Monk* two decades earlier. His fine novel *Melmoth the Wanderer* (1820) met with similar complaints: one Tory reviewer spotted 'the cloven hoof of infidelity'.

No form is confined to a single political message. Everything turns on how it is used, and on how the public at a given time is ready to read it. The Gothic, with its motifs of isolation and suffering, has a diverse potential. For Schiller's or Godwin's generation it provided a setting for the embattled consciousness of the individual; for a new post-war generation of German writers, like E. T. A. Hoffmann, its introspection, emotional colouring and otherworldliness opened the way to religious treatment of a semi-mystical Catholic kind. The point about Maturin, as Coleridge rightly detected in the case of *Bertram*, is that, like Mary Shelley, he is nearer to the early Godwin than to Hoffmann.

To first appearances, *Melmoth* is a shocker in the full Romantic manner. Maturin's central figure is a blend of Satan, Cain and the Wandering Jew, doomed to eternal life unless he can find someone to take the burden from him, at the price of damnation. Like so many of the best Gothic stories this one is structurally complex, a series of discrete first-person narratives rather than an easily grasped plot. Melmoth appears to a series of sufferers in their darkest hour, and tempts them to escape from their troubles in this world at the price of damnation in the next. Maturin is much more interested than Mary Shelley in human psychology and behaviour, in rendering suffering, and in analysing cruelty: the latter is lavishly presented in his sadistic parricide, a remarkably sophisticated study in believable abnormality. And yet, no less than Mary Shelley, Maturin also has a topical and didactic purpose. As a clergyman of the Protestant Church of Ireland, he detests and fears the Catholic Church. At home, Catholic Emancipation has emerged as a liberal cause, and Maturin is bent on separating liberals and Catholics by dwelling on the most notorious of current tyrannies, those of Catholic Spain.

The restoration of the *anciens régimes* had led to particularly unsavoury results in Spain. Ferdinand, heir of a line which at best lacked distinction, was being kept in power by the Catholic Church, along with its Inquisition, and by his brother European monarchs of the Holy Alliance. The terrifying figure of Melmoth is very compelling in Maturin's novel, just as the Monster is in Mary Shelley's, but the terror each may arouse is equally off-centre to the theme. In a way our sympathies are properly with Melmoth, as with the Monster: both, for all their power, are perceived as victims within their respective fictional worlds. Maturin is concerned to portray a series of suffering individuals, in themselves sympathetic and innocent, who are horribly oppressed by the vast elaborate interlocking mechanisms of Church and State. Most of the episodes are set in Spain, an unmistakably topical reference to the link between the Catholic Church and despotism. Though Maturin's position may seem innocuously in line with Protestantism's individualistic traditions, in the political context of 1820, when there was a Spanish rising of liberals, and a move by the Catholic Holy Alliance to quell it, his general political tendency is oppositional. A few years later, when Catholic Emancipation was a leading domestic issue, a tale similar to *Melmoth* might have served as a text in favour of the *status quo*.

Since *Frankenstein* and *Melmoth* are intended as attacks on the current alliance between conservative politics and High Church or Catholic religion, they revive the conscious liberalism of Gothic in the 1790s, and run counter to the strongest trend in immediately contemporary Romantic writing from the Continent. As novels they contain some of the most powerful and emotive images of English Gothic fiction, and to that extent evoke the irrational, but they are pleas for the claims of the external world and for the autonomy of the rational mind, and some of their devices go straight back to the intellectualist age of Voltaire. The contradictions plainly arose in the divided minds of the authors, who responded to the Gothic and exploited its imagery of violence, evil and disturbance, but within parables which would associate their opponents rather than themselves with the dark side of human experience.

Developments to the realistic novel in the 1820s seem equally complex and paradoxical. In the second decade of the century the form appeared to contemporaries to be dominated by Scott, writing novels that were at once studies of society and myths about social reconciliation. After 1820 Scott turned increasingly to more disturbing themes and to supernatural devices, and in thus internalizing his approach he was joined by a number of able compatriots. Galt, Hogg and Lockhart all in their different styles preferred to represent the Scottish scene through a more subjective focus. As early as 1816, Scott's *Old Mortality*, which presented the seventeenth-century Covenanters through the eyes of an emotionally detached upper-class hero, provoked James Hogg to *The Brownie of Bodsbeck* (1818), in which the same movement was evoked subjectively and impressionistically, in the words of the Covenanting folk themselves – for, as Hogg breaks off impatiently, in a passage of formal narration, 'such scenes, and such adventures, are not worth a farthing, unless described and related in the language of the country to which they are peculiar' (chapter xv). Hogg is not only more sympathetic than Scott to this essentially popular movement; he also seems to imply that there can be no external, generalized judgement passed upon the people, nothing that deals adequately with their experience, save the effort to recover its impact upon their consciousness and memory. *The Brownie of Bodsbeck* will not stand aesthetic comparison with *Old Mortality*, but its technical newness is a striking reminder of the entire introverted perspective that the English novel had recently preferred not to indulge; and Hogg's masterpiece, *The Confessions of a Justified Sinner* (1824) does challenge Scott on his own ground, for its confident use of first-person narrative brings alien peasant habits of thought to life with extraordinary intensity.

And yet it would also be true to say that the Scottish novelists of the 1820s were committed to a fuller documentation than Scott had been, to detailing the manners of the people as an objective in itself. The chronology of the period shows it sharply inclined to swings of the pendulum (see below, pp.180–3). Scott, who began his writing career as something of an antiquarian, in retreat from the ideological bias of the polemical 1790s, now at the end of the polemical second decade of the nineteenth century himself seemed a little too concerned with public affairs and with principles. Those who reacted against him did so in the interests of more detail about the inner and outer lives of ordinary people, at the expense of an Enlightenment concern with issues. The line between Scott and the Scottish school marks the end of an era, not only for fiction but for intellectual life.

If the novel in England seemed rational rather than irrational, more concerned with moral and political choices than with inward experience during the counter-revolutionary period of 1796–1820, its vehicle, the common medium of prose discourse, on the whole matched its concerns. The dominant prose style in England remained what Coleridge called, disparagingly, Anglo-Gallican. Any departure from that style (like Coleridge's own) was likely to draw down on the author's head the charge of obscurity or pretentiousness or plain incompetence. The Anglo-Gallican style is terse and epigrammatic, and aims, like Augustan verse modes, at wit, clarity and perspicuity. It often resembles the couplet in its favourite devices, such as symmetry, antithesis, and, for satiric effect, bathos or incongruity. All these are features of the two masterly anglo-Gallican stylists among the fiction-writers, Jane Austen and

Peacock. In occasional writing the same manner, or a toned-down version of it, remains the medium for acknowledged stylists like the best reviewers for the *Edinburgh*, who include the editor, Francis Jeffrey, and also regular contributors like the cleric Sydney Smith and the lawyer James Mackintosh. Jeffrey, for example, has a model reviewer's style, clear, natural and forceful. His notorious opening to his review of *The Excursion* could from a professional point of view hardly be bettered – 'This will never do.' Informally, in conversation, in letters, in journals, it is a period of wit, and wit depends upon precision in the choice of words and upon the elegant arrangement of the sentence. Sydney Smith on Macaulay displays both: 'More agreeable than I have ever seen him. There were some gorgeous flashes of silence.' So does Byron's jotting in his *Journal* after his first meeting with Southey: 'The handsomest bard I have seen for some time. To have his bust, I would almost have written his Sapphics.'

Such precision evokes the couplet, and yet as a poetic style the couplet and its neat cerebration had been under fire since the age of Johnson. In Germany in 1798 Wordsworth spoke of it dismissively to Klopstock: a mode which turned upon brevity, and upon making a point every second line, could hardly co-exist with the poetry of nature and the human heart. It is not easy to determine what Wordsworth thought the prose equivalent of the couplet's chop-chop might be, although his own prose avoids the pointed short sentence and the play of antithesis. Other members of his circle have more positive ideas of the prose style they want. Just as the poets of the 'elder age', pre-couplet, are favoured as models, so for Coleridge, Lamb and De Quincey are the prose writers of the early seventeenth century, especially Burton, Sir Thomas Browne and Jeremy Taylor. Coleridge and De Quincey favoured a complex, florid style, using an elaborate sentence-structure, or the mannerisms and sudden exclamations of that highly conscious period. Enlightenment primitivism here transformed itself weirdly into a new sophistication. De Quincey is the artist of the revival of pre-Augustan prose, its theoretical rhetorician. He achieves marvellous effects with his medium when, as in the climax to *Confessions of an English Opium-Eater* (1821), an elaborate archaic manner is suitable to the matter in hand:

The waters now changed their character, – from translucent lakes, shining like mirrors, they now became seas and oceans. And now came a tremendous change, which, unfolding itself slowly like a scroll, through many months, promised an abiding torment; and, in fact, it never left me until the winding up of my case. Hitherto the human face had mixed often in my dreams, but not despotically, nor with any special power of tormenting. But now that which I have called the tyranny of the human face began to unfold itself. Perhaps some part of my London life might be answerable for this. Be that as it may, now it was that upon the rocking waters of the ocean the human face began to appear: the sea appeared paved with innumerable faces, upturned to the heavens: faces, imploring, wrathful, despairing, surged upwards by thousands, by myriads, by generations, by centuries: – my agitation was infinite, – my mind tossed – and surged with the ocean.   (pp.107–8)

It is a less happy tool for every day. Neither De Quincey nor Coleridge shows at his best in expository prose. But then they are extremists, just as Peacock and Sydney Smith are extremists on the Anglo-Gallican side. Charles Lamb is an archaist with more flexibility, who manages to echo seventeenth-century masters and yet sound perfectly himself. Hazlitt likewise picks up the short periods, the balances and antitheses of the Anglo-Gallican manner while putting all such devices to a distinctive use. The habits of a judicious, impersonal medium are over-emphasized in his essays until they serve to draw attention solely on to the speaker; the hammering insistence of tone conveys not an urbane, agreed certainty, but the thwarted energy of an isolated consciousness. But Lamb's and Hazlitt's best writing, with its acute sense of personality, is the achievement of a new era after 1820; and it is significant that De Quincey's success with the *Confessions*, written in a poetic vein that belongs to the nineteenth rather than to the eighteenth century, should have been achieved at just the same time.

Fiction apart, 'prose' for many modern students is primarily a vehicle for the discussion of literature. Criticism acquired a new role in the post-Enlightenment period, as a central and significant aspect of the ideological struggle. Before the revolution the debate about society was cast on a very large historical scale. Its typical schema might be the contrast between primitive and advanced society, as in Rousseau's *Discours sur les sciences et les arts* (1750): though clearly the arts did figure in such a discussion, it was as a function of society in a particular stage of development. Enlightenment philosophic abstraction and historicism had a tendency to belittle the significance of the individual writer and the individual work of art (a fact which no doubt contributed to the unpopularity of the eighteenth century among the aesthetes of the later nineteenth century, and has maintained it since). Conversely, intellectuals of the reaction of the mid-1790s came to value literature very greatly.

Unlike their contemporaries the German counter-revolutionaries, Wordsworth and Coleridge do not often use the grand historical perspectives of the Enlightenment. At the end of the 1790s, not only in the subject-matter of the *Lyrical Ballads* but in the scale of discussion in the Preface they achieve a startling contraction, a domestication of their subject to the scale of a single individual and his experience. Where the range is so rigorously localized, one man may be of immense moment; if he is a poet who can tell his thoughts, he may be seen to encompass everything. Wordsworth and Coleridge support the validity of this drastically altered perspective by exalting the meditative life above the active, and by claiming that the patterns available to the eye of inward perception take primacy over factual or material realities. The poet's Imagination becomes the key concept: it is the aggregative or transforming power by which the individual can be said to master the universe. Wordsworth and Coleridge confront a difficult problem in deciding how much conscious, voluntary activity can safely be left to the individual. The Imagination cannot be merely passive, for that would imply the subjection of the individual to the material world. But nor is it a function of the rational, conscious mind, for reason and initiatives by individual thinkers remain deeply suspect. Although preached by many of the cleverest men of the age, including in England the much-admired Coleridge, the counter-revolution is committed to certain positions which are virtually anti-intellectual. It subordinates the individual, together with his thoughts and arguments, to superior forces: to a divine ordering, to a traditional wisdom, to a national organic identity. A desire to stabilize and to preserve existing society prompted the movement in which Coleridge participated, a fact which did not prevent him from achieving a larger, subtler, more inspiriting concept of art and creativity than what had gone before.

In the polemic period after the close of the war, the concern of counter-revolutionary critics with irrationalism, the emotions and the Imagination on the whole gave place to a new topic, the role of the artist in society. Coleridge, Southey and Wordsworth accorded with Burke in interpreting the intellectual as a learned man, priest, preserver of a society's past and keeper of its conscience, the champion of the old order but in an ideal form. Their opponents of the Marlow group or Cockney school maintained that the artist should be independent of the established hierarchy, though still fulfilling a social function as a critic and satirist. In arguing for their interpretation of the concept that the artist has social obligations, they magnified their disagreement with the older literary generation, and in particular exaggerated the extent to which the Lakists actually now stood for the way of the hermit. The direct problems of contemporary society, as well as the artist's contribution to it, were the leading topics of Coleridge's literary writing of this period – which includes his critical *magnum opus*, the *Biographia Literaria* (1817) –

just as they are the leading topics of the liberal *Round Table* (1817), by Hazlitt and Hunt, and of Shelley's *Defence of Poetry* (1821).

At the same time the *Biographia Literaria*, though it *is* nominally addressed to the topic of what makes a virtuous, engaged intellectual, is also suffused with Coleridge's twenty-five-year long absorption in the inner life, spiritual and creative. It is the masterpiece of the counter-revolutionary phase, updated to meet the needs of a time when a more active conservatism was called for. Conversely, Shelley's *Defence of Poetry* (written 1821), the masterpiece of the post-war phase when liberal writers pursued classicism and commitment, nevertheless draws freely and ingeniously upon the case for the Imagination. This is a paradox which does not wholly obscure the significant shift in the terms of literary discussion which occurred between the period when Coleridge's literary ideas were formulating, and Shelley's intellectual coming-of-age after the war.

The actual attack which called for Shelley's *Defence* came from Peacock. The latter cast his argument in a characteristically whimsical form, by adapting a serious Neoclassical proposition which appeared in the work of Winckelmann as early as 1755: namely, that poetry plays a less significant role in advanced society than in primitive society. Peacock's essay *The Four Ages* (1820) brings the Enlightenment cliché up to date and gives it a new point and wit. Peacock is fully aware that Winckelmann's evolutionary generalization has been succeeded by new kinds of claims about art – the one which bestows semi-religious and prophetic status upon the artist, and the one which exalts the imaginative or irrational functions of the mind above the reason. He ridicules the notion of the poet-seer by insinuating that from first to last the bard has been no better than he should be. The primitive king needs a publicist,

and this organ he finds in a bard, who is always ready to celebrate the strength of his arm, being first duly inspired by that of his liquor. This is the origin of poetry, which, like all other trades, takes its rise in the demand for the commodity, and flourishes in proportion to the extent of the market.   (p.4)

In other contexts Peacock queried the pretensions to wisdom of such modern sages as scientists and political economists. Here, where the subject requires him to challenge the complacency of poets, he argues that the rational and empirical sciences have made more contribution than the arts to modern life. The rationale underlying Peacock's resentment of the modern poet, at least in his fashionable current self-projection, is perhaps best elucidated by comparing his tone with that of another politically liberal critic, Hazlitt, writing on Shakespeare's *Coriolanus* in July 1816:

The cause of the people is indeed but little calculated as a subject for poetry. . . . The imagination is an exaggerating and exclusive faculty: it takes from one thing to add to another: it accumulates circumstances together to give the greatest possible effect to a favourite object. The understanding is a dividing and measuring faculty. . . . The one is a monopolising faculty, which seeks the greatest quantity of present excitement by inequality and disproportion; the other is a distributive faculty, which seeks the greatest quantity of ultimate good, by justice and proportion. The one is an aristocratical, the other a republican faculty. The principle of poetry is a very anti-levelling principle . . . . . . it has its altars and its victims, sacrifices, human sacrifices. . . . 'Carnage is its daughter'. Poetry is right-royal. It puts the individual for the species, the one above the infinite many, might before right. (iv.214–15)

Hazlitt, who had still thought of Wordsworth's as a 'levelling muse' when he reviewed *The Excursion* (1814), now explicitly associated Wordsworthian poetic theory and practice with ruthless élitism. The intervening two years had of course been remarkable for their sense of political crisis, for Coleridge's deployment of theories of the imagination and of literary exclusivity to support a conservative ideology, and for Wordsworth's notorious address to the Deity in his *Ode, 1816* – 'Yea, Carnage is thy Daughter'. As for Peacock's censure of modern literature as trivial, a similar case would be more formally developed a few years later, when in 1824 James Mill assailed the *Edinburgh Review* and the Whiggish culture for which it stood, on the grounds that the prime intention was to maintain an oligarchy in power by amusing rather than challenging the reading public. In short, Peacock's case against most modern literature, in which he clearly includes Wordsworth, Coleridge, Southey, Scott and the leading journals, revives familiarly the historical perspective of the Enlightenment. His criticism takes a form at first less obscure than it has become since, for it has much in common with the arguments of other liberals, especially perhaps the utilitarians or philosophic radicals. Implicitly, literary value must (for these progressive critics) be related to social utility; a mature art would tend to be intellectual and critical, as satire is. The personal cult of the poet, with its emotional appeal, is alien to this approach.

Shelley's *Defence* is a sustained response to Peacock's liberal critique of the Coleridgean elevation of poetry and the poet. By contemporary standards *A Defence* is not excessively allusive; actually Shelley is more willing than Coleridge or Hazlitt habitually are to meet an implicitly rational case rationally. Shelley accepts the historical Enlightenment premises upon which Peacock grounds his discussion. He accepts the diagnosis, that art-forms are the product of a period and a culture, but he denies the direct and literal dependence of the artist upon his culture. He stresses the unconscious element in art, and the transforming imaginative process, which together make poetry as distinct from the sciences as from propaganda. He concludes with one of those direct surveys of contemporary writing which are so typical of these polemical years, but the Shelley version is either more generous than Peacock's to their conservative opponents, or even more subtly ironic. In a sense, Peacock has been indulging in an unhistorical personality-cult when he makes the individual characters and opinions of writers so important, for, Shelley points out, neither side believes that these determine poetry:

Poetry, as has been said, differs in this respect from logic, that it is not subject to the control of the active powers of the mind, and that its birth and recurrence have no necessary connexion with the consciousness or will. ... the literature of England, an energetic development of which has ever preceded or accompanied a great and free development of the national will, has arisen as it were from a new birth. ... we live among such philosophers and poets as surpass beyond comparison any who have appeared since the last national struggle for civil and religious liberty. The most unfailing herald, companion, and follower of the awakening of a great people to work a beneficial change in opinion or institution, is poetry. ... The persons in whom this power resides, may often, as far as regards many portions of their nature, have little apparent correspondence with that spirit of good of which they are the ministers. But even whilst they deny and abjure, they are yet compelled to serve, the power which is seated on the throne of their own soul.   (pp.57–9)

Shelley has ingeniously used the conservative poets' irrationalist terms, the Imagination and Inspiration, to support his historical and broadly utilitarian argument. Because poetry 'is not a power to be exerted according to the determination of the will' (p.53), its effects cannot be confined to the individual poet's own favoured causes, such as the upholding of order. Unlike Peacock, he welcomes the new doctrine that poetry is generated in the unconscious, because he sees that this can be made to serve his own agnostic historicism, his belief in the impersonal, irresistible momentum of change. The flowering of poetry in a period is a symptom of general mental activity, and thus in principle serves the cause of enlightenment. Wordsworth and Coleridge, though by conscious intention reactionary, serve by a historical process beyond their control the *Zeitgeist* of a revolutionary period. If Shelley had lived, or even if his *Defence* had been published intelligibly, as the adroit, reasonable reply to a utilitarian attack, English culture would have had what it sorely needed in the next generation, a major writer capable of a constructive dialogue with utilitarianism.

But Shelley was drowned in 1822, *A Defence* was not published until 1840 (and then without its essential provocation and context, *The Four*

Ages), Bentham and many of his disciples took a philistine line on the arts, and the role of leading critic on the liberal side fell indisputably to William Hazlitt. This fact was of incalculable importance in determining the tone of English cultural life in the second quarter of the century, and in bestowing retrospectively a kind of character on the literature of the first quarter.

In 1820, when Peacock issued the challenge to Shelley by writing *The Four Ages*, Hazlitt was already forty-two years old. Among English intellectuals, he surely suffered the hardest of all courses through the French revolutionary turbulence. Like Priestley, Paine, Godwin and Blake, he came from the classic stock of the English left, the Dissenters: his father was a unitarian minister, and a vigorous defender of the Bible, the sects and the individual conscience, rather in Priestley's mould. At fifteen, in the year of revolutionary ferment 1793, William Hazlitt the younger went to the celebrated Dissenting academy at Hackney to train for the ministry. Like Coleridge, whom he met in 1796, he absorbed together religious and political controversy. But because Hazlitt was so much more deeply entrenched than Coleridge by his family tradition and his upbringing in Dissent, the general retreat of Dissenters from radicalism was much more painful to him. Hazlitt retained the demeanour and many of the intellectual habits of the sectarian, including the staunch individualism, but long after Coleridge had snapped his 'squeaking baby-trumpet of sedition', Hazlitt also retained the political hopes of the early 1790s. In consequence he became and acutely felt himself a 'loner', a man cut off by his mental cast not only from the orthodox and conservative majority, but from what survived of intellectual Dissent and radicalism too.

The irony – a bitter irony for both Hazlitt and Coleridge over the years – was that it was the poets of the *Lyrical Ballads* who gave Hazlitt one of his greatest and longest-lasting insights. In 1797–8, those years when overt political radicalism was so beleaguered and a generalized faith in man so difficult, the poets seemed to propose a way out to youthful idealists through literature. It is possible to glimpse how for Hazlitt Godwin's credo of inward liberty, his aspiration that man might evolve into a rational individual capable of free choice, might blend with Coleridge's introversion and passionate intensity and emerge as a distinct cult of the self. It was no doubt largely because of Coleridge that the arts became so central in Hazlitt's thinking, as the opportunity and product of the individual imagination. For Hazlitt literature was above all expressive, and self-expressive, a function of the personality of the individual writer and thence of his sympathetic *alter ego* the reader. In drama and the novel, *character* is of immense significance, since here again the individual writer and reader can achieve by empathy a kind of consciousness, a further imaginative life. Stylistically the most admirable of qualities is energy or gusto, through which the author again conveys a sense of his presence and uniqueness. Hazlitt felt that he had this insight from Coleridge; he never forgave his mentor for not sharing it. Looking back we can see how far Hazlitt's position and the imperatives acting upon him really were from those of Coleridge. Hazlitt is always so much more the old-style Dissenter; thus, to the end, an individualist, a thinker who believes in an egocentric naturalist philosophy, and in the capacity of the mind of man.

A certain obstinacy in sticking to radical ideals marks Hazlitt out after the crisis of 1797–8. He had evidently been shaken in his boyhood optimism about the progress of mankind, as who had not, but believed that France under Napoleon would salvage something of the liberty and equality the 1790s had dreamt of. The great public art collection he saw in 1802 in the Louvre, where kings held sway before, pointed to some kind of social advance, and perhaps revealed the internalized means – mental life, and above all the arts – by which progress would yet be made. Though the war was resumed in 1803, Hazlitt battled on with a work of philosophy in the Enlightenment manner, *An Essay on the Principles of Human Action* (1805), a difficult project in the anti-intellectual atmosphere of that epoch. After the failure of this book his work became more impressionistic and personal. From 1813 he became a journalist and theatre critic, and with France's defeat criticism became a more appropriate and serious vehicle for him than direct commentary on affairs, though he wrote both.

Even as a critic, Hazlitt suffers from having caught, about a decade later than Coleridge, the counter-revolutionary aversion to generalization, system and even rational connected argument that became so strong a fashion after the late 1790s. His assertive, exclamatory style – 'Poetry is the high-wrought enthusiasm of fancy and feeling' – makes it sound as though his precepts are based on no case that was ever reasoned by himself or others, but on a sudden intuition. He told one of his editors that his opinions were not really as arbitrary as they seemed; he merely saw a tactical advantage in letting his audience supply the connecting tissue of inductive reasoning:

I confess I am apt to be paradoxical in stating an extreme opinion when I think the prevailing one not quite correct. I believe however this way of writing answers with most readers better than the logical. I tried for some years to express the truth and nothing but the truth, till I found it would not do. The opinions themselves I believe to be true, but like all abstract principles, they require deductions, which it is often best to leave the public to find out.   (*Letters*, p.158)

Hazlitt's method had a number of advantages, of which readability was one; another, that a personal and non-ideological style prevented him from being identified too closely with an unpopular political minority. The fact is that during the highly polemical years of 1816–19, when Hazlitt wrote most of his literary criticism, very similar opinions to his were held and defended more systematically by fellow-liberals. For example, his case against Wordsworth in his lecture of 1818 (published as *Lectures on the English Poets*) is characteristic of the Marlow group in that the issues turn on the claims of art against nature and sociability against egotism (see above, pp.128ff.) Though notable himself for his fiery and emotional response to tragedy and tragic acting, Hazlitt in his *Lectures on the English Comic Writers* in 1819 proclaims – Marlow-like once more – that comedy is an equally great literary form. Those who feel that they know Hazlitt's personal preferences are often surprised to find the assertion here that the warm comedy of character, epitomized in Shakespeare's portrait of Falstaff, is intrinsically less mature than Restoration comedy, with its satiric social function. Practically in his own satires as well as intermittently in his criticism, Peacock made out this case more clearly. He and Shelley also wrote on a number of occasions in favour of a natural, spontaneous sexuality (see above, pp. 130ff.), a subject to which Hazlitt alludes only opaquely when he discusses Restoration comedy, and to which he returns so strangely and privately in his semi-autobiographical fiction, the *Liber Amoris* (1823).

A similar absence of the type of theory which may be over-committing is evident in Hazlitt's political writing of the immediate post-war period. On the whole, as we have seen, he steered clear of the specific domestic campaigns for which the radicals were now unpopular, and concentrated on ridiculing foreign monarchs or on abusing literary individuals like Wordsworth, Coleridge and Southey. It is possible that this tactic was not Hazlitt's but the idea of John Hunt, brother of Leigh Hunt and now the proprietor of the new radical journal *The Yellow Dwarf*. If so the fact is suggestive, for it may be that Hazlitt's apparently bewildering shifts of tone, his quirkiness and gift for emotive self-dramatization, rather than sustained thought, are all the characteristics of his new professional type, the star journalist.

For Hazlitt's career in the second decade of the century seems to evolve under the auspices of the series of editors who employed him – notably Francis Jeffrey of the *Edinburgh*, whose requirement was the review-essay, and the Hunt brothers, who might want more lively political polemic, or the cosy conversation-pieces of *The Round Table*. In 1820 a new journal, John Scott's *London Magazine*, arose to challenge the journalistic domination of Scotland, which had been strengthened since

1817 with the arrival of *Blackwood's Edinburgh Magazine*. Scott's prospectus promised a new metropolitan openness and lightness of touch. He would replace the long, sober articles of the *Edinburgh* and *Quarterly* with a miscellany, enquiring, independent, irreverent, reflecting the manner in which issues momentarily rise to the surface in the busy life of the capital:

> Opinion now busies itself with more adventurous themes than of yore; discussion must start fleeter and subtler game; excitements must be stronger; the stakes of all sorts higher; the game more complicated and hazardous. The spirit of things generally, and, above all, of the present time, it will be our business, or at least our endeavour, to catch, condense and delineate.   (*London Magazine*, i, 1820, p.v)

Hazlitt's great period was to be 1820–3, when he wrote over half of his best work, the discrete pragmatic essays that read like fragments of one man's consciousness. Much of this first appeared in the *London*, and the brief was the *London*'s: was the initiative too? The mood of introspection, pessimism and bitterness which suffuses these essays is generally traced to biographical events, to the failure of Hazlitt's marriage, to his disappointment in his love affair with Sarah Walker, and to his sensitivity to the attacks made on him by his political opponents, especially in *Blackwood's*. But the forty-three-year-old Hazlitt's ability to exploit such experience, to appropriate it for his arbitrary individual essays, was what made him, because it was exceedingly well timed. Faith in man had hardly been a hallmark of liberals since the 1790s; it had nevertheless been succeeded during the post-war period, for example in the work of Shelley, by a willed, rather theoretical and remote conception of eventual progress – to be followed around 1820–2 by writing which, whatever its formal commitment to comedy, seems distinctly devoid of hope. At such a moment Hazlitt adopted his persona, that of the unhappy man, the good hater. Essays like 'The Indian Jugglers' and 'On Going a Journey' read like trains of thought; their reminiscences of men and books are introduced as aspects of Hazlitt's own personality and part of the indivisible fabric of his experience. Such subjectivism at once makes the Neoclassicists' formality seem like a throwback to the Enlightenment, and startlingly out of date. It is of course a literary irony that Hazlitt now subscribed to an introversion which the liberals of 1817 had seen as a conservative or counter-revolutionary posture, and equally odd that in his last, most productive decade he was adopting so solipsistic a vein, just when his great conservative opponent, Coleridge, was exploring ideas of communal responsibility.

In spite of such paradoxes, Hazlitt remains recognizably a man of the left. His criticism proper belongs to the liberal new wave of 1816–19;

even the restless, sceptical, self-tormenting and doubting essays are rooted in an individualism which goes back to Dissent and always retains its idiosyncratic critical posture, its rational and activist potential. Because Hazlitt matured so late, when the English liberal-intellectual renaissance of the post-war years was effectively in retreat, his œuvre is that of an isolated no-sayer driven by unpropitious circumstances into himself, and into wholly notional opposition. It makes him still, to the end, a very English figure: for England, with its social stability and conservatism, has not bred the powerful intellectual radical movements of the Continent. The appeal of Hazlitt's best work seems private, not directly political at all. It speaks to the educated, displaced urban reader, who no longer has anything to hope for from social goals, but retains a kind of imaginative approximation to them, a concept of revolution in his mind and memory.

It is curious how once again the point around 1820, when Hazlitt came into his own, seems to mark a decisive change. Politically, it was the last of the fraught post-war years in England. After the noisy demonstration accompanying Queen Caroline's divorce had subsided, a curious period of relative stasis followed. Literature, which up to about 1820 had so angular a political content, blurred and became ideologically apathetic or confused. Though Byron, Shelley and Keats were still alive, a new wave of blander, less divisive poets succeeded them, led by 'Barry Cornwall' and George Darley. An antiquarian type of closet-drama, Greek or Elizabethan in inspiration, opposed good to evil in unexceptionable, stylized terms, after the shock-tactics of *Prometheus Unbound* and *Don Juan*. Meanwhile, young men at the two universities began the process of soul-searching and religious discussion that helped to transform the Church. Within a few years, German studies and German mysticism were fashionable. Medievalism became an irresistible vogue, in literature, painting and architecture, and as a social model. Not only the erstwhile right-wing Coleridge and Southey but the radicals Cobbett and Robert Owen began to hanker after monasticism as the social experiment representing a link between the spiritual and the temporal, the rich and the poor.

So emotionalism and medievalism eventually prevailed: in Scott's later novels; in the Jacobean tragedies of the young Thomas Lovell Beddoes (who was, so incongruously, Maria Edgeworth's nephew); in the discovery of Blake by a religious group of young artists; in the retreat at last of the Neoclassical taste before the Gothic. Ten years after Shelley and his friends at Marlow put up statues to the pagan gods, Tennyson's friends at Cambridge were calling themselves the Apostles. By the early 1830s, the new literary genius was the Germanist Thomas Carlyle. So the 1820s are transitional, a decade of compromise and synthesis. English culture partakes in a European movement, which is partly a powerful religious revival, often High Church or Catholic in tendency, and partly a search for kinds of idealism which are not individualistic but organicist. France, the land of Neoclassicism, takes up Romanticism. Such a period is fertile ground for the cult of the isolated, introverted literary personality.

It seems appropriate to this age of 'opinion' that it is a journal, the *London Magazine*, that brings in the new wave. Hazlitt's *Table-Talk*, published there in 1820–1, is the first of his series of essays, experiments at self-dramatization or self-projection which seem to shun the appearance of formal art. Lamb's equally personal and discursive *Essays of Elia* begin to appear in the same years. So does Thomas De Quincey's imaginatively written and extravagant memoir, *The Confessions of an English Opium Eater*. All three are classics in a new kind of literary autobiography, more quirky than anything of the kind before. The idiosyncrasy becomes the more marked because all three authors are middle-aged men of not quite first-rate achievement themselves, but mediators between the public and the literary genius, for their experience goes back to the heyday of the Lake Poets. There is a kind of wistfulness about all three, a hint of failure even, but there is also a compensatory sense that unlike the writer-prophets, the Miltons who should have been living at this hour (and perhaps mercifully were not), these men would offer not vatic solutions but a painful knowledge of daily urban living. As John Scott's Prospectus to the *London Magazine* intimates, heavy theorizing is inappropriate to 'the spirit of things generally', and best left to foreigners. 'We are not, on the whole, sorry, that our authors have rather suggested systems than engaged in them' (p.v).

De Quincey presents his highly ambivalent work partly as a true account of his own life, partly as an apology for his opium addiction, but even more than most such narratives it is an exercise in self-vindication. It ends not so much apologizing for as glorifying the world of the imagination, the literary alternative world which De Quincey equates with the opium dream. The displaced middle-class artist had a motive for promoting his dream-world morally and aesthetically above the world of everyday. Perhaps the task was peculiarly hard in England, where the Protestant middle classes had inherited a suspicion of fiction as lying, and a strong materialistic stake in the present social order of things. To offset this disadvantage De Quincey shows a rhetorician's cunning. As a political conservative, he is careful to begin by disassociating his *Confessions* from those of Rousseau, the archetypal apologist for himself, who moreover made self-realization and fulfilment a potentially liberal cause. Yet De Quincey is more essentially egotistical than Rousseau, or than that other autobiographer Wordsworth. Both Rousseau and Wordsworth pursue an earnest, Enlightenment aim not to write the censored, official, external kind of autobiography, but something more complete, more objective, and hence finally more true and representative. De Quincey's narrative, on the other hand, avoids objectivity and deliberately selects its material in order to maximize the interest and intensity of the writer's sufferings.

It is often said that De Quincey is a great autobiographer, a great projector of the self. The claim is justified if we mean that the most effective self-betrayals are those that look like accidents. His *Confessions* are a clever medley of the facts of his life with fables, inconsistencies and probable lies – like the story of his writing love-letters for girls in Wales, which is surely borrowed from Anna Letitia Barbauld's *Life of Richardson* (1810), or his obviously self-deluding fantasies about his role as protector of two female waifs in London. His so-called opium dreams read like an amalgam of the Oriental poems of Southey and of Beckford's fantasy *Vathek*. Even if modern medical opinion has queried whether dreams of this kind are typical of opium addiction, De Quincey does not encourage such scepticism, for he seems yearningly anxious that we should admire him for his dreams; his credit with us is pinned to their exclusive, distinguishing excellence. 'A man whose talk is of oxen will dream of oxen.' Nevertheless, it seems that we must admire him today not for telling us painful truths about opium addiction – that sort of verisimilitude, though valued by Victorians, was not his goal – but for his vulnerable tissue of forgeries. De Quincey's concocted 'fantasies' tell another kind of truth, about the addictive, neurotically self-doubting man who needs both narcotics and the world's esteem. Provided we are totally sceptical as to the relationship with fact, it is the raw material of a fascinating case-study, and its success in 1821 is revealing too. The Opium-Eater appealed at once to the public, who found in his exotic narrative either a meaningful comment on the relationship of art and life or, what seems more likely, a vulnerable 'character' who offered an absorbing compound of richness and self-abasement. De Quincey gave the middle-class English public its first memorable portrait of the modern artist, simultaneously drop-out and saint.

So the *Confessions* are a clever man's book, and wonderfully gripping on one level as self-revelation, though on another oppressively narrow and insubstantial, like most of the creative work that belonged to the German Romantic movement in its strictest definition. In the long run English nineteenth-century readers were more at home with a very different portrait of the artist of 1821–3 – the equally literary but more controlled and perhaps more comfortable figure of 'Elia' created by Charles Lamb.

In life, Lamb experienced the same desolating alienation as the others, and indeed as the new type of artist in general. 'Life itself, my waking life, has much of the confusion and perplexity of an ill dream. In the day time I stumble upon dark mountains.' His mother was killed by his much-loved sister Mary in a fit of insanity; he disliked his work as a London clerk chained to a desk. Old books and the theatre made refuges which Lamb valued for their unlikeness to his real urban surroundings. He also made an enclosed world of his circle of friends, of conviviality, food, and especially drink. Lamb too had traits of the addictive personality, and his life was a struggle against tobacco and alcohol. His descriptions of succumbing to the latter are as memorable in their comic vein as the descanting of Coleridge and De Quincey upon opium.

Lamb took as long as Hazlitt to find the right form. His early tale *Rosamund Gray* (1798) and his play *John Woodvil* (1802) are pleasant but undistinguished, typical products of the fag-end of Sentiment in the late 1790s. Even in these early days his true gift begins to emerge in his letters, written in a style which is as bare as liberal fashion in dress and in ballads in the 1790s, though he allows it to be touched for humorous effect by echoes of his favourites Burton, Browne and Sterne. The measure of Lamb's quality is his control of these echoes: a brief touch of quaintness, carrying a suggestion of the pose he wants to strike, as the heir to seventeenth-century antiquarians or to Walter Shandy. Incessant quotation, usually not more than half relevant, is a disease of prose at the time, which Coleridge does not keep enough in check, and Hazlitt indulges to the point of mannerism. Lamb's style, though continually allusive, is also homogeneous, for his literariness is inseparable from his personality. His mildly eccentric inconsequential flow carries an infinitude of anecdotes and character-sketches, from chance encounters with Quakers, to portraits of Mrs Battle and Cousin Bridget, to deliberately provoking unfashionable views on books. He likes old fairy-stories for children, not the new, educational, progressive children's reading matter (though his own *Tales from Shakespeare*, 1807, were commissioned by William Godwin, who had set himself up as a publisher for children in the utilitarian tradition). Lamb avoids criticizing contemporary poetry, but brings out an enthusiastically annotated edition of old plays, and commends poets like Quarles and Wither. He prefers as a historian (to the systematic and philosophical Hume and Gibbon) the gossipy seventeenth-century Bishop Burnet – 'quite the prattle of age, and outlived importance' (1 March 1800).

Lamb, born in 1775, the schoolfellow and friend of Coleridge, comes to stand equally with Coleridge as the enemy of system. His letters

vividly evoke his opposing positives, daily domestic life, private affections, small pleasurable intensities. He is unbeatable on food – 'Welsh
mutton, collars of brawn, sturgeon fresh or pickled, your potted char'.
He likes describing familiar interiors and the people he knows, though no
portrait in the *Essays of Elia* rivals the portrait of the writer himself.

Lamb is less, not more 'natural' in his autobiographical enterprise than
De Quincey. He creates a Shandean humorist, a composite conveyed to
us through his tastes, and a man (as the flexible style conveys) acutely
sensitive to every momentary impression, whether of laughter or tears.
The making of such a mask is a lifelong enterprise, which begins in the
letters over twenty years before Elia is thought of. The stereotype is not
quite that of a Dickensian Mr Cheeryble, nor the irritating St Charles of
Thackeray's imagination. Lamb is not a Victorian. An early letter is
phrased robustly – 'Coleridge is settled with his wife (with a child in her
guts)' (9 August 1800). In a late one he hilariously defends himself to his
host and hostess of the previous night for having had to be carried home
on the back of their footman, dead drunk (?April 1830). Whether meant
for the general public or not, Lamb's many sketches of his own life are
consistent, intimate and believable. He makes no claims that could not
have been tested within the scope of one man's experience. He excludes
both the old Neoclassical posture of addressing the world in generalities
in order to change it, and the modern Coleridgean posture of the literary
man as a sage, as extraordinary. Lamb's ordinariness made him in the
1820s, for, as Hazlitt discerned, his variant of the man of letters was the
figure with which the middle-class readership could empathize. Carlyle,
it is true, hated him for his debunking wit and scepticism, his anti-
heroics. He does not sentimentalize himself, as Leigh Hunt does, nor
favour himself, as Coleridge and De Quincey do. Daily life is present,
and often grim, in his work. His brand of escapism, his reading, is
presented in a uniquely 'characterized' way, as the recourse of his own
personality rather than as a universal panacea. Such precision, and such a
strictly limited claim, is one symptom of Lamb's eighteenth-century
origins. Another is the degree to which he suggests (more than Hazlitt
and De Quincey) the controlling hand of the craftsman. He is a reminder
that an emerging tradition of literary self-portraiture, of consciousness of
the writer–reader relationship, was a long-term process already apparent
in his natural precursors Goldsmith and Sterne. Such writers are too
polished, or too comic, or have too much 'manner' for the emotional
post-Romantic, which accounts for the precipitous decline in Lamb's
reputation in the twentieth century. Yet he played a significant part in
that process of isolating, defining and coming to know the writer which
marked the artistic endeavour between 1790 and 1830.

8 Conclusion: the Question of Romanticism in England

Around the year 1830, as pressure for political reform built up, the minds of Englishmen returned to the topic of the French Revolution. A number of the brightest young intellectuals, including Carlyle, Macaulay and John Stuart Mill, began to write histories of that cataclysmic event, or contemplated doing so. Peacock broke a silence of some years with a satire, *The Misfortunes of Elphin* (1829) which allegorically compared the last revolution in France with the present threat to stability in England. On the conservative side, Southey and Coleridge each published a book – *The Colloquies* (1829), and *On the Constitution of the Church and State* (1830) – which conveyed an idealized half-nostalgic portrait of how a paternalistic old system worked, at least in theory. Thus intellectuals at the time tended to see the period 1789–1830 as a unity: the period in which England's *ancien régime* faced radical social change and the threat of revolution. A process which for France at the beginning of the era had been a débâcle was at the end of that era coming gradually and peacefully in England. For, however dubious the status of the new compromise, however far off the sovereignty of the people, it did seem clear that the old system was ending, or that it had ended, even before the passing of Catholic Emancipation in 1829 and the Reform Bill in 1832 changed some of its constitutional principles.

Awareness of society as an organism was relatively new. Within the short history of social consciousness there was an even more recent perception, that like other organisms societies developed and declined in a perpetual evolutionary process. Awareness of change might find its way into general reflections by the new breed of intellectuals, men like John Stuart Mill (1806–73). It is of even more interest in the most expressive outlet for man's perception of his world and his own place in it, the arts.

In England at any rate the political and constitutional reforms arrived at in 1832 were hardly of an order to account for the sense in clever contemporaries of a change that amounted to a social revolution. Looking back from the twentieth century but admitting the opinion of the nineteenth in evidence, we may feel that two general circumstances did have special significance for culture. The first was that the period from the 1780s to the 1830s was for England an era of continuing aristocratic government. In this, its last unchallenged phase, the upper-class ascendancy was more aggressive and financially better endowed than ever before. The wealth of the English landed classes was aug-mented by new speculations into agricultural experiments, industrial ventures, overseas trade and colonial development. The example of radical political change, in America in the 1770s and in France in the 1780s and 1790s, could and did make the English gentry more self-conscious, more bent on self-definition and self-justification, but did not for the time being threaten their effective control. The tone of this class was the major determinant in the tone of the arts so long as it remained culture's paymaster.

But a second general historical trend to some extent runs counter to the first. The rapid economic expansion of the second half of the eighteenth century, and the pressures that partly caused and partly accompanied it, were beginning to change the English social structure from within. Rising population made the agrarian revolution necessary, and in turn created both the market and the work-force for the Industrial Revolu-tion. Increasingly from the later eighteenth century people in the upper, middle and lower middle social orders had the opportunity to purchase possessions, the new artefacts like Isabella Thorpe's muslin and John Thorpe's curricle in *Northanger Abbey*; and among the possessions they could borrow and buy were books. The number of books in circulation rose steeply towards the end of the eighteenth century. Their prices remained relatively high throughout the Napoleonic Wars – at six to ten shillings a volume, a three-volume novel remained a rare luxury – but with new techniques of mass-production in the 1820s a process truly revolutionary in cultural terms could be seen to be finally under way. Already in the eighteenth century the literary artist, like the painter, the etcher and the composer, came to address himself not to a patron but to a public. At first, in pre-revolutionary times, that 'public' seemed made up of gentlemen and ladies like the 'society' which strolled freely and easily about at Vauxhall or at Bath. Under the conditions of the 1820s the very notion of visualizing society – of an educated class sufficiently small and homogeneous to mingle in gathering-places with more or less open access – had become out of date. These successive revolutions in the marketing of the arts, which are symptomatic of larger economic changes, surely make up the second large factor affecting their tone and quality. There is one probable link between the first expansion in production of books and other artefacts and the Neoclassical habit of optimism, humanism, universality. There is another link between the uncertainty and impersonality inherent in the new situation, and the Romantic habit of alienation, frustration and solipsism.

Social pressures are complex, and the literary movements which reflect them may not succeed each other, but continue to coexist. In an effort to summarize the cultural crosscurrents of the revolutionary period one might point to some sort of division into successive phases, but these would be rough and the dates unreliable. It would seem that from about 1760 to the mid- or late 1790s a style prevailed which modern art critics have designated Neoclassicism. Its characteristics include a radical simplicity of manner, subject matter and setting; conversely, a rejection of elaboration, which is now associated with earlier eighteenth-century modes such as in painting the rococo, and in versification the heroic couplet; an interest in motifs and forms associated with primitive or simple people, like the ballad; a liking for the elemental; a willingness to allow a single human figure to dominate a painting or a narrative; and so on. One way of typifying this movement would be to point to its content, that is to its primitivism or historicism; another would be to stress its affinity with individualism, philosophical and economic. Baudelaire in 1855 could still see the emergence of this style as the parallel in the arts to the political revolution. Neoclassicism is clearly designed for an upper-class market, but this may not be the paradox it seems: the eventual violent outbreaks of the time, the American and perhaps the French revolutions, can also be linked with upper-class optimism and expansion. The human figure – serene and heroic, or suffering and affective – predominates in the paintings of David as of Blake, in the poems of Burns as of the youthful Wordsworth. It is only after the Revolution that individualism is widely perceived as a threat to ordered society.

The second powerful cultural movement of the age is under way well before the first is over, and holds sway from about 1790 to about 1818. Like Neoclassicism, the style engendered by the counter-revolution is European-wide. Burke's *Reflections* (1790) were the classic denunciation of the Revolution in England; similar arguments were circulated on the Continent by the French royalist Joseph de Maistre and the German Friedrich von Gentz. The Burkean positives are family affections and loyalties, hearth and home; hence, by extension, the greater family made by the nation, a hierarchy with the king at its head; and continuity with the past, especially with the inherited creed which it is the Church's business to preserve. Against this imaginative concept of an organic nation, Burke is able to depict as puny and unwholesome the intellectuals, French and English, who want to change the fabric or body of the state: he is in effect anti-individualist and anti-rationalist.

The counter-revolution is also a native English phenomenon, complicated for English intellectuals by the tension between traditional English radicalism, which had been strongly Dissenting in flavour, and a contemporaneous French theory based on natural rights. Among English creative writers, Coleridge is the most profoundly touched by the tone of the counter-revolution, by its emotionalism and organicism, by its reverence for the domestic and its suspicion of the rational. Jane Austen and the middle and later Wordsworth are other classic exponents of conservatism, although in their attitudes to individualism they can be ambivalent. In the commonest of counter-revolutionary plot patterns, an over-confident individual is led astray by too much reliance on his or her reasoning: Wordsworth's Marmaduke and Oswald in *The Borderers* are examples of the type, as are a host of Austen leading characters from Marianne to Emma. Yet both Wordsworth and Jane Austen remain intensely conscious of individual experience in the world of every day; they rely upon the conscience, which is the analytic and moral aspect of consciousness, to lead their protagonists to self-knowledge. In the importance they give to a rational mental process, as in their central placing of their human figures, these two English conservative and religious writers are very different from their German contemporaries the *Frühromantiker*, who include Friedrich Schlegel, Tieck and Novalis. Though they might be said to have as their moral goal the maintenance of old-established society, Wordsworth and Austen also retain the tastes and some of the upper-class individualism of the Enlightenment.

A revival of Neoclassicism began with Byron's *Childe Harold* (1812), and was already fading when it lost its leading intellectual with the death of Shelley in 1822. Just as English counter-revolutionary writing had many characteristics of the Enlightenment, so this later liberal movement, though progressive in intention, is coloured by the personal doubts and uncertainties of tone which generally affected the arts from just before 1800. Pre-revolutionary Neoclassicism had drawn confidence and clarity from its simpler conception of an accessible, socially homogeneous public. These virtues now looked like generalities or systemizations. Partly, perhaps, because the post-war readership was potentially larger but actually more obviously divided along class lines into very different types of people, the difficulty of making a statement which would be universally meaningful was much more apparent. For the liberal artist, the perception that the audience for literature belonged to the leisured ruling orders of society constituted a problem that hardly admitted of a satisfactory solution. Both Peacock and Shelley strongly deplored the idea of a merely élitist culture, of the kind Peacock bestows on his 'dilettanti' or represents in his typical drawing-room reader, Mr Listless of *Nightmare Abbey*. Both tried to live up to the Enlightenment principle, which was also the Greek principle, that art functioned within and for the community. In practice both were so allusive as to preclude their being understood except by those as well educated or (in Peacock's case) as socially and intellectually in the know as themselves.

The subtly pessimistic flavour of the kind of revived or extended Neoclassicism practised by writers like the liberal Shelley and Peacock (as well as the conservative Scott) ought not to be crudely misrepresented. The tension in their work, between its willed public optimism and its private doubt, reads like a symptom of sensitivity and of intellectual honesty, and it gives their art its stature. Nevertheless it is important to notice what a potentially crippling situation the liberals at least were put in by the period's heightened sociological awareness, its sense both of class and of public opinion. In *Nightmare Abbey* and in private letters to Shelley, Peacock urged on his friend the necessity of considering his audience, but realistic consideration of the public's probable attitudes did not actually promote simplicity (as Peacock seemed to think) so much as the opposite. Allusiveness and indirection became a necessary strategy. Indeed, the more popular and hence politically unpalatable the theme, the more refined, often, the treatment. The aristocratic demeanour of Shelley and Peacock – their esoteric learning, their eccentric fancy, their rejection of materialism in favour of a 'religion' which was certainly far more exclusive than Christianity – all these were devices enjoined on them by the intellectual's growing knowledge of the social and intellectual composition of the reading public.

Only such a consciousness on the part of artists, editors and others who catered for the literary market can account for some of the features of the final phase of culture within the period. Around 1820 the Enlightenment attempt to reach Everyman (that is, every reader) through universally accessible modes dwindled into the private, introverted communications of the autobiographers and essayists, for whom the arts were not so much the objective mirroring of man and his culture as the subjective expression of men in private rooms. The new era of introversion in the early 1820s differed from the counter-revolutionary movement of the late 1790s in being far more fully withdrawn from the public issues of religion and politics. In fact, this stage marks the end of what had been a most exceptional and grandiose phase for the arts as a theatre for public opinion and for intellectual war. It also marks the final emergence of the artist as a recognized public phenomenon – lonely, introverted, unhappy, but marked out from the commonalty by his genius.

Because the arts became fundamentally politicized in this period, the dialectical pattern into which they fell has clear ideological significance, though this does not of course mean that any writer need be mistaken for a mere polemicist. Enlightenment art, with its humanity, its individualism, its universalism, is potentially a revolutionary art, reacting against what is perceived as the more frivolous, decorative manner appropriate to an unrepentant aristocracy. The humble, modest, quietist tone of the counter-revolution functions as an appropriate answer to the self-assertion of Neoclassicism. Coleridge in the *Biographia Literaria* needs a text to preach against, and picks the *Lyrical Ballads* of his own friend Wordsworth in unregenerate days. The Neoclassical revival led by the Marlow group preaches humanism, not religion, and social commitment, not introspection, with Wordsworth's *Excursion* as its main target. Even the last movement of the 1820s seems to begin in a mood of rejection of what has gone before – a rejection either of the importance or the possibility of making a change in public life; though once this drastic step is taken, the dialectical chain of the immediate revolutionary period is inevitably broken.

We began with the received view that at some time at the end of the eighteenth century a Romantic Revolution occurred, which worked a permanent change in literature and in the other arts, and scored a decisive victory over the classicism which was there before. In reality there would seem to have been no one battle and no complete victory. It is not even clear that there were defeats. Our own cynical age is likely to be well aware that what has happened since the Fall of the Bastille falls far, far short of the more sanguine hopes of the Enlightenment. Mass education has made technically elaborate and learned literary forms even more obviously élitist than they were before, so that hindsight is a harsh light in which to view the effort of Shelley. But in general there are no victories and no defeats because the external problems do not admit an end. The role in which the artist found himself in Hazlitt's day is in all essentials his role in the twentieth century. What solutions he finds for his solitariness, what modes he uses in his effort to reach his uncongenial or unknowable public, what issues he takes up, whether private or public, aesthetic or moral – these artistic strategies are responses to problems set in the last resort by history. It was not personal idiosyncrasy that made the writers of 1789–1820 actors in public affairs, while most after 1820 played the part of private men.

As for other received notions about English Romanticism, some of these too are hard to reconcile with the conclusions just summarized. There is René Wellek's influential and representative generalization (quoted above, p.7) that all Romantic poets 'see the implication of imagination, symbol, myth and organic nature . . . It is a closely coherent body of feeling.' Nothing in the present book directly challenges Professor Wellek's formulation, since the aesthetic theories of the poets in question have not been the subject principally under review. And yet the preceding chapters have tended to highlight differences rather than common ground between the writers. The impression left is hardly of a closely coherent body of feeling.

'Romanticism' is inchoate because it is not a single intellectual movement but a complex of responses to certain conditions which Western society has experienced and continues to experience since the middle of the eighteenth century. There seems small chance of understanding how social pressures worked upon the artistic process except by making careful discriminations between the atmosphere of different cultures, notably England, France and Germany, and different times (England in 1789, for example, differentiated from England in 1798 or in 1817). 'It belongs to a philosophical critic', as Shelley observed in *A Defence of Poetry*, 'to distinguish rather than confound.' In some cultures rather more clearly than others, intellectuals began to emerge as a distinct sub-group of the middle class, and here especially it may be possible to discern the developing psychopathology of the modern artist. On the one hand the marketing of the arts became organized on lines typical of late eighteenth-century business, and the relationship of the artist with his public became more distant; on the other, intellectuals, like most educated men, became more aware of themselves, in relation to a historic past, in relation to present-day society, and as isolated and alienated consciousnesses.

From these circumstances it becomes possible to list a set of preoccupations which apparently set the 'Romantic' or modern artist apart from his predecessor, the 'classical' artist; but the list which can be agreed may not be long, since the response of individuals to the newly-perceived situation is not uniform but various. Blake the engraver is made more sharply aware than any literary man of commercial circumstance. Though all in this historicist, primitivist era feel the burden of the art of the past, he as a visual artist is pressured more sharply than the poets, for the art world's Neoclassical revival at once promises universality and imposes authority. There are social reasons as well as theological ones why Blake among all the English Romantics seems especially at odds with 'the world', society, the cultivated public; why, indeed, the sense of alienation between his mental world and the humane or natural world external to him becomes extreme. Wordsworth is touched by some of the same problems but not by all. Though he experiences a growing preoccupation with Mind and with Imagination, his inner world remains more continuous than Blake's with the external world of Nature.

For Harold Bloom in his influential study *The Visionary Company*, these two are the greatest of the six major poets, and in some sense they determine the preoccupations of the four others. I have suggested that, on the contrary, Shelley's generation responded afresh to new circumstances in post-war England and Europe; Shelley could no more ignore the problems posed by the alienated consciousness than any post-Enlightenment writer has been able to do, but they appeared to him in a different light, and his Mind is not at all the same quality as Wordsworthian Imagination. For Bloom and for critics like him, poets *as poets* exist primarily in their internalized imaginative worlds, and in relation to one another, which is why the two great writers who most favour Imagination are allowed to set the pattern for the rest. The historian-critic is inevitably more sceptical than this of theories which exalt the autonomy of art and the magus-role of the artist. Like many other latter-day pronouncements on Romanticism, Bloom's work seems itself ultra-Romantic. Its imaginative roots unmistakably go down to thinkers of a later period than the early nineteenth century, like Nietzsche and Freud, and seem more American than English: the transcendentalist Emerson is more of an inspiration than the cultural critic Coleridge.

Wellek's concern with Romanticism is less heady and intuitive than Bloom's. His is essentially the approach of the philosopher, who is trained to consider his subjects' arguments ahistorically, as a series of propositions disinterestedly reaching after truth. The object of the intellectual historian is, again, more particular and more contextual. It is less concerned with evaluation than with making a record of the opinions held by people in actual historical situations. The non-philosophical literary scholar notes a number of critical peculiarities to which philosophical critics are liable (which could, needless to say, be matched by comparable solecisms in critics of other persuasions). One of these is a tendency to read the writer's mind as more logical, coherent and academic than the human mind naturally is, to give a privileged part to the cerebral as opposed to the irrational element in literature, and to presuppose that the entire work is under the control of the conscious mind. (It is surely the fault of those trained in philosophy and not in history, if so-called 'historical criticism' has tended to drift into these assumptions.) Another is an inclination to take the most coherent expositor of an intellectual position – who for the Romantics might be Hartley, say, or Rousseau, Godwin, Kant or Coleridge – and use his formulation to interpret the work of an entire group of writers. The very existence of a coherent 'Romantic movement' arises perhaps from some such intellectual manœuvre. Yet if we take Coleridge as our example the dangers of the proceeding seem evident. Modern philosophy's academicism leaves out of account an important dimension of what Coleridge the historical man appeared to his contemporaries to be doing. That is, the training of the modern philosopher predisposes him to accept at face value (the historian might say naïvely) Coleridge's claims on behalf of metaphysics. But this was a selection, a series of extrapolations from the fields of post-Kantian moral philosophy, aesthetics and Bible criticism, which struck hostile contemporaries as far from disinterested. The metaphysician lays claim to permanence; there are times when this claim in itself becomes a rhetorical tool supporting a particular ideological position. Unwarily, the philosophical critic favours unduly authors of Coleridge's type, in other words of a theoretical school, in a historical situation in which theory was temporarily pitted against anti-theory, the empirical, engaged or activist position.

There are historical reasons for the high prestige of Coleridgean inwardness and metaphysics in modern times, just as there are reasons why Bloom the scholar-poet should greatly admire Blake. In the position of post-Romantics ourselves, even of post-war post-Romantics, we are also sympathetic to approaches to literature like Hazlitt's. The arts become self-expression by figures with whom we can empathize. Theories which exalt the arts (and those who study them) have a still-current function. History, with its greater complexity and its patterns of personal defeat, disillusionment or unimportance, is a less emotionally rewarding study than the quest for culture-heroes. But it is not without its compensations. The wisdom of Shelley's generation was the observation that the concept of literature as irrational and introverted may be ideologically partisan; we cannot, at least, take it for granted that the new subjectivity is idealistic or disinterested. The social upheavals of the twentieth century, and the pessimistic temper of the aftermath of war and revolution, have to some extent duplicated the experiences of the early nineteenth century, so that some of the more extreme cultural reactions then have a renewed appeal now. If we still confront many of the same issues, there is all the more reason to approach the debate of the earlier period with due respect for its disagreements. Going out to look for 'Romanticism' means selecting in advance one kind of answer. No intellectual discipline, certainly not philosophy, condones such a procedure, while the historian has no foolproof protection against it. But he has some safeguards in his empiricism, and in a methodology which gives weight both to the collection of evidence and to analysis as opposed to synthesis.

For it is, when all is said, a splendid and a splendidly varied body of literature. The pressure of ideas upon the entire social fabric made it that: English literature is at its most glorious in two brief sequences of years, after the beginning and after the end of the war with revolutionary France, when controversy was at its most intense, and art became one of its outlets. Perhaps the best of all reasons for shedding preconceptions about Romanticism is not the point of principle – that they may be untrue – but the point of pragmatism – that they interfere with so much good reading. How many students have puzzled themselves into antipathy, trying to fathom what the *Lyrical Ballads* initiated; or what the common denominator may be in various writers' attitudes to the self, to God, or to Nature; or precisely why Shelley, Scott and Byron must be said to be Romantic? It would be fitting after all if it should be the historical perspective that released to us Shelley and Scott, those two historically-minded men of the Enlightenment, traditionalists and innovators, creators who in the end both took society and its culture to be their proper subject.

Chronology

1760   George II d. Wedgwood opens pottery at Etruria, Staffordshire. Beckford b. Sterne, *Tristram Shandy*, i–ii (conc.1767).

1761   Pitt (Earl of Chatham) resigns. S. Richardson d.

1762   Bowles b. Cobbett b. Rousseau, *Contrat Social, Émile*. Goldsmith, *Life of Nash; Citizen of the World*. Hurd, *Letters on Chivalry and Romance*. Macpherson, *Fingal*.

1763   Peace of Paris ends Seven Years War. J. Wilkes publishes no.45, *North Briton*; is arrested. Smart, *Song to David*.

1764   Wilkes expelled from Commons. Hargreaves invents spinning jenny. Ann Radcliffe b. Brooke, *Fool of Quality* (conc. 1770). Goldsmith, *Traveller*.

1765   Stamp Act to tax American colonies. Johnson edits Shakespeare. Percy, *Reliques of Ancient English Poetry*. Walpole, *Castle of Otranto*.

1766   Rousseau visits England. Goldsmith, *Vicar of Wakefield*. Smollett, *Travels through France and Italy*.

1767   Townshend introduces tax on tea in American colonies. Ferguson, *Essay on the History of Civil Society*.

1768   Wilkes sentenced for libel. Royal Academy founded. Sterne d. Maria Edgeworth b. Gray, *Poems*. Sterne, *Sentimental Journey*.

1769   Wilkes expelled from Commons, thrice re-elected. Watt patents steam-engine. Chatterton, 'Elinoure and Juga'. 'Junius' letters begin. Reynolds, *Discourses to the Royal Academy*, i (conc. 1790). Robertson, *History of Charles V*.

1770   Hogg b. Wordsworth b. Chatterton d. Goldsmith, *The Deserted Village*.

1771   Scott b. Gray d. Smart d. Smollett d. Beattie, *The Minstrel*. Cumberland, *The West Indian*. Mackenzie, *The Man of Feeling*. Smollett, *Humphry Clinker*. West, 'The Death of Wolfe'.

1772   Boston Assembly threatens secession. Coleridge b. William Jones, *Poems . . . Translations from the Asiatick Languages*.

1773   Boston tea party. Jeffrey b. James Mill b. Chesterfield d. Goldsmith, *She Stoops to Conquer*. Graves, *Spiritual Quixote*.

1774   First American Congress. Accession of Louis XVI of France. Southey b. Goldsmith d. Goethe, *Werther*. Chesterfield, *Letters to his Son*. Langhorne, *The Country Justice*. T. Warton, *History of English Poetry* i (conc. 1781).

1775   Battles of Lexington, Concord, Bunker Hill. Jane Austen b. Lamb b. Landor b. M. G. Lewis b. Johnson, *Journey to Western Isles*. Mason, *Life of Gray*. Sheridan, *The Rivals*.

1776   American Declaration of Independence. Necker finance minister in France. Hume d. Bentham, *Fragment on Government*. C. Burney, *History of Music*, i. Gibbon, *Decline and Fall of Roman Empire*, i (conc. 1788). Hawkins, *History of Music*. Smith, *Wealth of Nations*.

1777   Burgoyne capitulates at Saratoga. Chatterton, *Poems ... by Rowley*. Mackenzie, *Julia de Roubigné*. Morgann, *Essay on the Dramatic Character of Sir John Falstaff*. Reeve, *The Champion of Virtue* (*Old English Baron*, 1778). T. Warton, *Poems*.

1778   Pitt (Earl of Chatham) d. Franco-American alliance; Britain declares war on France. Hazlitt b. Rousseau d. Voltaire d. Herder, *Volkslieder*. Fanny Burney, *Evelina*.

1779   War with Spain. Crompton invents spinning mule. Moore b. Galt b. Garrick d. Cowper and Newton, *Olney Hymns*. Johnson, *Prefaces ... to English Poets*.

1780   Yorkshire petition for parliamentary reform. Gordon riots. Crabbe, *The Candidate*.

1781   Cornwallis capitulates at Yorktown. Kant, *Kritik der reinen Vernunft*. Rousseau, *Confessions*. Schiller, *Die Räuber*.

1782   North ministry falls. F. Burney, *Cecilia*. Cowper, *Poems*. Priestley, *History of the Corruptions of Christianity*. J. Warton, *Essay on the Genius and Writings of Pope*, ii.

1783   Fox–North coalition. Pitt the Younger's first ministry. Blair, *Lectures on Rhetoric and Belles-Lettres*. Blake, *Poetical Sketches*. Crabbe, *The Village*. Day, *Sandford and Merton* (conc. 1789).

1784   Pitt's India Act. L. Hunt b. Johnson d. Diderot d. Beaumarchais, *Le Mariage de Figaro*. David, 'The Oath of the Horatii'. Herder, *Ideen zur Philosophie der Menschheit*.

1785   Warren Hastings returns from India. Cartwright invents power-loom. De Quincey b. Peacock b. Boswell, *Tour to the Hebrides*. Cowper, *Task*.

1786   Beckford, *Vathek*. Burns, *Poems, Chiefly in the Scottish Dialect*. Knight, *Essay on the Worship of Priapus*.

1787   U. S. Constitution signed. Millar, *Historical View of the English Government*. Wollstonecraft, *Thoughts on the Education of Daughters*.

1788   Trial of Warren Hastings begins. George III's first attack of 'madness'. Celebrations of centenary of 'Glorious Revolution'. French States-General summoned. Byron b. Charlotte Smith, *Emmeline*.

1789   George III recovers. Bastille falls. Declaration of Rights of Man. Bentham, *Principles of Morals and Legislation*. Blake, *Songs of Innocence; Book of Thel*. Bowles, *Sonnets*. E. Darwin, *The Loves of the Plants*. White, *The Natural History of Selborne*.

1790   Motion to modify Test and Corporation Acts to relieve Dissenters defeated. Franklin d. A. Smith d. T. Warton d. Blake, *Marriage of Heaven and Hell* begun. Burke, *Reflections on the Revolution in France*. Radcliffe, *Sicilian Romance*. Wollstonecraft, *Vindication of the Rights of Men*.

1791   Priestley's home wrecked by mob, Birmingham. Louis XVI's flight and capture at Varennes. Volney, *Les Ruines*. Boswell, *Life of Johnson*. Burns, *Tam o' Shanter*. Inchbald, *A Simple Story*. Paine, *Rights of Man*, i. Radcliffe, *The Romance of the Forest*. Ritson, *Ancient Popular Poetry*.

1792   Hastings acquitted. Continental allies invade France. Imprisonment of French royal family. September massacres. Wordsworth in France. Shelley b. Reynolds d. Bage, *Man As He Is*. Darwin, *Economy of Vegetation*. Holcroft, *Anna St. Ives*. Paine, *Rights of Man*, ii. Wollstonecraft, *Vindication of the Rights of Woman*.

1793   Trial and execution (21 Jan.) of Louis XVI. France declares war on Britain (1 Feb.). The Terror. Murder of Marat. Execution of Marie Antoinette, the Girondins (Oct.). Scottish treason trials. Clare b. Blake, *Vision of the Daughters of Albion; America*. Godwin, *Political Justice*. More, *Village Politics*. Smith, *The Old Manor House*. Wordsworth, *An Evening Walk, Descriptive Sketches*.

1794   Trial and acquittal of Horne Tooke, Holcroft and Thelwall. Danton executed (Apr.). Robespierre executed (July). End of Terror. The Directorate. Gibbon d. David, 'The Death of Marat'. Blake, *Songs of Experience; Europe; Book of Urizen*. Coleridge, *Monody on Chatterton*; (with Southey), *Fall of Robespierre*. Darwin, *Zoonomia*. Gifford, *Baviad*. Godwin, *Caleb Williams*. Holcroft, *Hugh Trevor*. Knight, *The Landscape*. Mathias, *Pursuits of Literature*. Paine, *Age of Reason*, i (conc. 1795). Paley, *Evidences of Christianity*. U. Price, *Essay on the Picturesque*. Radcliffe, *Mysteries of Udolpho*.

1795 Wet cold summer contributes to high food prices, scarcity. 'Two Acts': Seditious Meetings Act and Treasonable Practices Act. Boswell d. Carlyle b. Keats b. Blake, *Book of Los*; *Ahania*. Coleridge, *Conciones ad Populum*. Lewis, *Ambrosio or the Monk*. More, *Repository Tracts*.

1796 Napoleon Bonaparte's successful campaign in Italy. Burns d. Macpherson d. Bage, *Hermsprong*. Burke, *Letter to a Noble Lord*; *Letters on a Regicide Peace*, i–ii. Burney, *Camilla*. Coleridge, *Poems on Various Subjects*; *The Watchman*. Edgeworth, *Parent's Assistant*. Hays, *Memoirs of Emma Courtney*. Inchbald, *Nature and Art*. Roscoe, *Life of Lorenzo de' Medici*. Southey, *Joan of Arc*.

1797 Mutinies at Spithead and the Nore. Bank of England suspends payment. Battles of Cape St Vincent and Camperdown. Burke d. H. Walpole d. Wollstonecraft d. *The Anti-Jacobin*. Coleridge, *Poems*, 2nd ed., with adds. Lamb and Lloyd. Radcliffe, *Italian*. Southey, *Poems*.

1798 Irish Rebellion. Switzerland becomes Helvetian Republic, dominated by France. French in Syria and Egypt. Nelson in command in Mediterranean. *Athenaeum*, Berlin (to 1800). Baillie, *Plays on the Passions*, i. C. Brockden Brown, *Wieland*. Coleridge, *Fears in Solitude, France, an Ode, Frost at Midnight*. R. L. and M. Edgeworth, *Practical Education*. Godwin, *Memoirs of . . . [Mary Wollstonecraft]*. Lamb, *Rosamund Gray*. Landor, *Gebir*. Lloyd, *Edmund Oliver*. Malthus, *Principles of Population*. Wollstonecraft, *Maria, or the Wrongs of Woman*. Wordsworth and Coleridge, *Lyrical Ballads*.

1799 Corresponding Society and other radical groups suppressed. Combination Acts against formation of unions. In France Directorate falls. Bonaparte made First Consul. C. Brockden Brown, *Ormond*; *Arthur Mervyn*, i (conc. 1800); *Edgar Huntly*. Campbell, *Pleasures of Hope*. Godwin, *St. Leon*. Scott, trans. from Bürger, Goethe's *Goetz von Berlichingen*. Sheridan, *Pizarro* (trans. from Kotzebue).

1800 Act of Union with Ireland. Battles of Alexandria, Marengo. Blair d. Cowper d. J. Warton d. Bloomfield, *Farmer's Boy*. Coleridge, trans. from Schiller, *Piccolomini, Death of Wallenstein*. Edgeworth, *Castle Rackrent*. Wordsworth, *Preface* to *Lyrical Ballads*.

1801   Pitt resigns on refusal of George III to assent to Catholic Emancipation. Addington PM. Nelson seizes or sinks Danish fleet at Copenhagen. Bage d. Edgeworth, *Belinda*. Southey, *Thalaba*.

1802   Peace of Amiens with France (March). Bonaparte First Consul for life. Darwin d. *Edinburgh Review*. De Staël, *Delphine*. Lamb, *John Woodvil*. Scott, *Minstrelsy of the Scottish Border*.

1803   War resumed (May). Darwin, *Temple of Nature*.

1804   Addington resigns. Pitt PM. Napoleon becomes Emperor (May). Priestley d. Wilkes d. Kant d. Blake, *Jerusalem*, *Milton*. Edgeworth, *Popular Tales*. Opie, *Adeline Mowbray*.

1805   Battles of Trafalgar (Oct.), Ulm (Oct.), Austerlitz (Nov.). Schiller d. Cary trans. Dante's *Inferno*. Drummond, *Academical Questions*. Ellis edits *Early English Metrical Romances*. Godwin, *Fleetwood*. Hazlitt, *Principles of Human Action*. Horne Tooke, *Diversions of Purley*, ii. Roscoe, *Life of Leo X*. Scott, *The Lay of the Last Minstrel*. Southey, *Madoc*.

1806   Pitt d. (Jan). Ministry of All the Talents, Grenville PM. Fox d. (Sept.). Edgeworth, *Leonora*. Owenson (Morgan), *The Wild Irish Girl*.

1807   Abolition of Slave trade. Resignation of Grenville over Catholic question. Portland PM. French invasion of Spain and Portugal. De Staël, *Corinne*. Crabbe, *Poems*. C. and M. Lamb, *Tales from Shakespeare; Mrs. Leicester's School*. Malthus, *Letter . . . on Poor Laws*; Hazlitt, *Reply to Malthus*. Maturin, *The Fatal Revenge*. Moore, *Irish Melodies*. S. Smith, *Letters on . . . Catholics, by Peter Plymley*. Southey, *Letters from England by Don Espriella*. Wordsworth, *Poems in Two Volumes*.

1808   Spanish rising (May). J. Bonaparte enters Madrid as king (July). Convention of Cintra (Aug.). Sir J. Moore in command (Sept.), retreats (Dec.). Lamb, *Specimens of the English Dramatic Poets*. Scott, *Marmion*.

1809   Battle of Corunna; Sir J. Moore killed. Defence of Saragossa (Jan – Feb). Wellesley in command in Portugal (Apr.). Walcheren expedition fails (July). Portland resigns. Perceval PM (Oct.). Holcroft d. Paine d. A. Seward d. Tennyson b. *Quarterly Review*. Blake, *Descriptive Catalogue*. Byron, *English Bards and Scotch Reviewers*. Coleridge, *The Friend*. Edgeworth, *Tales of Fashionable Life,* i. More, *Coelebs*. Wordsworth, *Convention of Cintra*.

1810   Lines of Torres Vedras (Lisbon besieged). Coleridge lectures on Shakespeare. De Staël, *De l'Allemagne* (trans. English 1813).

Crabbe, *The Borough*. Scott, *Lady of the Lake*. Shelley, *Zastrozzi*. Southey, *Curse of Kehama*. Stewart, *Philosophical Essays*. Wordsworth, *Topographical Description of the Country of the Lakes*.

1811　The Regency. Organized machine-breakers (Luddites) in Nottinghamshire and Yorkshire. J. Austen, *Sense and Sensibility*. Drummond, *Oedipus Judaicus*. L. Hunt, *The Feast of the Poets*. Lamb, 'On the Tragedies of Shakespeare'. Scott, *Don Roderick*. Shelley, *On the Necessity of Atheism*.

1812　Perceval murdered. Liverpool PM. Capture of Ciudad Rodrigo (Jan.). Battle of Salamanca (July). War with America. Napoleon's invasion of Russia (June), retreat from Moscow (Oct.). Browning b. Dickens b. Byron, *Childe Harold*, i and ii. Cary trans. Dante's *Paradiso* and *Purgatorio*. Crabbe, *Tales in Verse*. Combe, *Tour of Dr. Syntax*. D'Israeli, *Calamities of Authors*. Edgeworth, *Tales of Fashionable Life*, ii (incl. *The Absentee*). Landor, *Count Julian*. Shelley, *Address to the Irish People*. H. and J. Smith, *Rejected Addresses*.

1813　Battle of Vittoria (June). Wellington in Pyrenees. Southey Poet Laureate. Austen, *Pride and Prejudice*. Barrett, *The Heroine*. Byron, *Bride of Abydos*; *The Giaour*. Coleridge, *Remorse*. Owen, *A New View of Society*. Scott, *Rokeby*. Shelley, *Queen Mab*. Southey, *Life of Nelson*.

1814　Fall of Paris (March). Abdication of Napoleon (Apr.). Treaty of Ghent ends American war. Austen, *Mansfield Park*. Brunton, *Discipline*. Burney, *The Wanderer*. Byron, *Ode to Napoleon*; *Corsair*; *Lara*. Cary trans. *Divine Comedy* complete. Edgeworth, *Patronage*. Malthus, *Observations on the Effects of the Corn Laws*. Morgan (*née* Owenson), *O'Donnel*. Scott, *Waverley*. Shelley, *Refutation of Deism*. Southey, *Roderick*. Wordsworth, *The Excursion*.

1815　Landlords carry Corn Bill. Napoleon leaves Elba: the Hundred Days (March – June). Waterloo. Napoleon's surrender (15 July) and exile. Restoration of Louis XVIII. 'Holy Alliance' of European crowned heads. Schlegel, *Lectures on Dramatic Art and Literature*, trans. J. Black. Byron, *Hebrew Melodies*; *Collected Poems*. Malthus, *Inquiry into Rent*. Ricardo, *On the Low Price of Corn*. Scott, *Lord of the Isles*; *Field of Waterloo*; *Guy Mannering*. Wordsworth, *White Doe of Rylstone*; *Poems*.

1816　Depression and discontent. Spa Fields riot (Dec.). Sheridan d. Byron leaves England. Austen, *Emma*. Bentham, *Chrestomathia*. Byron, *Siege of Corinth*; *Prisoner of Chillon*; *Childe Harold*, iii.

Coleridge, *Christabel, Kubla Khan, Pains of Sleep*; *Statesman's Manual* (*Lay Sermons*, i). Hazlitt, *Memoirs of Thomas Holcroft*. Hunt, *The Story of Rimini*; 'Young Poets' (*Examiner*). Lady C. Lamb, *Glenarvon*. Maturin, *Bertram*. Milman, *Fazio*. Peacock, *Headlong Hall*. Reynolds, *The Naiad*. Scott, *The Antiquary*; *Tales of my Landlord* (*The Black Dwarf* and *Old Mortality*); *Paul's Letters to his Kinsfolk*. Shelley, *Alastor*. Southey, *Poet's Pilgrimage to Waterloo*; *Lay of the Laureate*. J. Wilson (Christopher North), *City of the Plague*. Wordsworth, *Thanksgiving Ode*.

1817   Suspension of Habeas Corpus (March). Cobbett leaves for America. Seditious Meetings Bill drives democratic societies underground. Princess Charlotte (dau. of Prince Regent) d. *Blackwood's Edinburgh Magazine*. Jane Austen d. Germaine de Staël d. Byron, *Tasso*; *Manfred*. Coleridge, *Sibylline Leaves*; *Lay Sermons*, ii; *Biographia Literaria*; *Zapolya*. Edgeworth, *Harrington* and *Ormond*. Frere, *The Monks and the Giants*. Godwin, *Mandeville*. Hazlitt, *Characters of Shakespear's Plays*; *The Round Table*. Keats, *Poems*. James Mill, *History of British India*. Moore, *Lalla Rookh*. Nichols, *Illustrations of Literary History of the Eighteenth Century* (conc. 1858). Owen, *Report to Committee on Poor Law*. Peacock, *Melincourt*. Ricardo, *Principles of Political Economy and Taxation*. Shelley, *Proposal for Putting Reform to the Vote*.

1818   Congress of European Alliance at Aix-la-Chapelle, attended by Castlereagh. M. G. Lewis d. Austen, *Northanger Abbey* and *Persuasion*. Byron, *Childe Harold* iv; *Beppo*. Cobbett, *A Year's Residence in the U.S.A*; *A Grammar of the English Language*. Ferrier, *Marriage*. Hallam, *View of the State of Europe during the Middle Ages*. Hazlitt, *Lectures on the English Poets*. Hogg, *Brownie of Bodsbeck*. Hunt, *Foliage*. Keats, *Endymion*. Lamb, *Works*. Moore, *National Airs*, i (conc. 1827); *Fudge Family in Paris*. Morgan, *Florence Macarthy*. Peacock, *Rhododaphne*; *Nightmare Abbey*. Scott, *Rob Roy*; *Tales of my Landlord*, ii (*Heart of Midlothian*). M. Shelley, *Frankenstein*. P. B. Shelley, *The Revolt of Islam*. M. Sherwood, *History of the Fairchild Family* (conc. 1847). Sotheby, *Farewell to Italy*.

1819   Peterloo Massacre. 'Six Acts', restricting right to hold meetings and freedom of press. George Eliot b. Géricault, 'The Raft of the Medusa'. *Indicator* (conc. 1821). Byron, *Mazeppa*; *Don Juan*, i–ii. Crabbe, *Tales of the Hall*. Hazlitt, *Lectures on the English Comic Writers*; *Political Essays*; *Letter to Wm Gifford, Esq*. Hunt, *Hero and Leander*; *Poetical Works*. Hone, *Political House that Jack*

Built. Hope, *Anastasius*. Irving, *Sketch Book* (N.Y). Lockhart, *Peter's Letters to his Kinsfolk*. Polidori, *The Vampire*. Scott, *Tales of my Landlord*, iii (*Bride of Lammermoor* and *A Legend of Montrose*). Sheil, *Evadne*. Shelley, *Rosalind and Helen*. Wordsworth, *Peter Bell*; *The Waggoner*.

1820 George III d. George IV accedes. Trial of Q. Caroline. Cato St. Conspiracy. Revolution in Spain, Portugal and Naples. Hayley d. *London Magazine*. Barton, *Poems*. Clare, *Poems Descriptive of Rural Life and Scenery*. Edgeworth, *Mems. of R. L. Edgeworth*. Godwin, *Of Population*. Keats, *Lamia, Isabella, Eve of St. Agnes and Other Poems* (with *Hyperion*). Lamb, 'Essays of Elia', (*London Magazine*, to 1822). Malthus, *Principles of Political Economy*. Maturin, *Melmoth the Wanderer*. Milman, *Fall of Jerusalem*. Peacock, *Four Ages of Poetry*. Procter ('Barry Cornwall'), *Sicilian Story; Marcian Colonna*. Scott, *Ivanhoe; The Monastery; The Abbot*. Shelley, *The Cenci; Prometheus Unbound; Oedipus Tyrannus*. Southey, *Life of Wesley*. Wordsworth, *River Duddon; Memorials of a Tour on the Continent*.

1821 Napoleon d. Q. Caroline d. Greek War of liberation begins. Keats d. Hester Lynch Piozzi d. J. Scott killed in duel. Byron, *Marino Faliero; The Prophecy of Dante; Sardanapalus; Two Foscari; Cain; Don Juan*, iii–v; *Letter on W. Bowles's Strictures on Pope*. Clare, *Village Minstrel*. Cobbett, *American Gardener; Cottage Economy*. J. Fenimore Cooper, *The Spy*. De Quincey, *Confessions of an English Opium-Eater* (*London Magazine*). Egan, *Life in London*. Galt, *Ayrshire Legatees; Annals of the Parish*. Hazlitt, *Table Talk* (conc. 1822). Lockhart, *Valerius*. Procter ('Barry Cornwall'), *Mirandola*. Reynolds, *Garden of Florence*. Scott, *Kenilworth; Lives of Novelists* (Prefaces to Ballantyne's Novelists Library, conc. 1824). Shelley, *Epipsychidion; Adonais*. H. Smith, *Amarynthus the Nympholept*. Southey, *A Vision of Judgment*.

1822 Castlereagh commits suicide. Canning Foreign Secretary. Shelley d. Hoffmann d. *The Liberal*. Beddoes, *Bride's Tragedy*. Bentham, *Influence of Natural Religion upon Temporal Happiness*. Bloomfield, *May Day with the Muses*. Byron, *The Vision of Judgment* (in *The Liberal*). Cunningham, *Traditional Tales of the English and Scottish Peasantry*. Darley, *Errors of Ecstasie*. Galt, *Sir Andrew Wylie; The Provost; The Gathering of the West*. Hogg, *The Three Perils of Man*. Lockhart, *Adam Blair*. Peacock, *Maid Marian*. Procter, *Works*. Rogers, *Italy*, i. Scott, *The Pirate; Fortunes of Nigel; Peveril of the Peak*. Shelley, *Hellas*. Wilson

('Christopher North'), with Hogg, Lockhart and Maginn, *Noctes Ambrosianae* (in *Blackwood's*, conc. 1835). Wordsworth, *Ecclesiastical Sketches*.

1823   War between France and Spain. Ann Radcliffe d. Byron, *Age of Bronze; Werner; Don Juan*, vi–xiv. Galt, *Entail; Ringan Gilhaize; Spaewife*. Hazlitt, *Liber Amoris; Characteristics*. Hogg, *Three Perils of Woman*. Lockhart, *Reginald Dalton*. Moore, *Fables for the Holy Alliance*. Scott, *Quentin Durward*. M. Shelley, *Valperga*. Southey, *History of Peninsular War* (conc. 1832).

1824   Conference at St. Petersburg. Byron d. Opening National Gallery. London Mechanics Institution founded. *Westminster Review*. Bentham, *Book of Fallacies*. Byron, *Don Juan*, xv–xvi. Cobbett, *History of Protestant 'Reformation'* (conc. 1826). Ferrier, *The Inheritance*. Godwin, *History of Commonwealth of England*. Hogg, *Private Memoirs and Confessions of a Justified Sinner*. Landor, *Imaginary Conversations*, i–ii. Lockhart, *Matthew Wald*. Medwin, *Jnl. of Conversations of Lord Byron at Pisa*. M. R. Mitford, *Our Village* (conc. 1832). Morier, *Hajji Baba of Ispahan*. Scott, *St. Ronan's Well; Redgauntlet*. Shelley, *Posthumous Poems*.

1825   Industrial and financial crisis. A. L. Barbauld d. Fuseli d. Banim, *Tales by the O'Hara family*, i. Carlyle, *Life of Schiller*. Coleridge, *Aids to Reflection*. T. C. Croker, *Fairy Legends and Traditions of South of Ireland* (conc. 1828). Galt, *The Omen*. Hazlitt, *Table-talk; Spirit of the Age*. Macaulay, 'Milton' (in *Edinburgh Rev.*). James Mill, *Essays on Government*. Moore, *Memoirs of Sheridan*. Scott, *Tales of the Crusaders*. Plumer Ward, *Tremaine*.

1826   End of Liverpool's ministry. Gifford d. E. Barrett (Browning), *An Essay on Mind, with other poems*. Cooper, *Last of the Mohicans*. Disraeli, *Vivian Grey*, i–ii (conc. 1827). Galt, *Last of the Lairds*. Hazlitt, *Plain Speaker; Notes of a Journey through France and Italy*. Hood, *Whims and Oddities*, i. Lister, *Granby*. Scott, *Woodstock*. M. Shelley, *The Last Man*.

1827   Canning d. Battle of Navarino. University College London founded. Blake d. H. M. Williams d. Clare, *Shepherd's Calendar*. Cooper, *The Prairie*. De Quincey, 'On Murder Considered as one of the Fine Arts' (in *Blackwood's*). Hallam, *Constitutional History*. Keble, *The Christian Year*. Moore, *The Epicurean*. Scott, *Chronicles of the Canongate (Highland Widow, Two Drovers, Surgeon's Daughter); Life of Napoleon; Miscellaneous Prose Works*. Tennyson (with C. Tennyson), *Poems by Two Brothers*. Wordsworth, *Poetical Works*, 5 vols.

1828   Wellington PM. Repeal of Test and Corporation Acts. Dugald Steward d. Coleridge, *Poetical Works*, 3 vols. Hazlitt, *Life of Napoleon*, i–ii (conc. 1830). Hunt, *Lord Byron and some of his Contemporaries*. Landor, *Imaginary Conversations*, iii. Bulwer Lytton, *Pelham*. Napier, *History of War in the Peninsula* (conc. 1840). Scott, *Tales of a Grandfather*, i; *Chronicles of the Canongate*, ii (*Fair Maid of Perth*).

1829   Catholic Emancipation. Exclusion of O'Connell from Parliament. Huskisson killed by train. Carlyle, 'Signs of the Times' (in *Edinburgh Rev.*). Landor, *Imaginary Conversations*, iv–v. Peacock, *Misfortunes of Elphin*. Scott, *Anne of Geierstein*; *Tales of a Grandfather*, ii. Southey, *Sir Thomas More, or Colloquies on the progress and prospects of society*.

1830   George IV d. Accession of William IV. Wellington's ministry falls; Grey PM. Reform agitation. July Revolution in France: Louis Philippe recognized. Carleton, *Traits and Stories of the Irish Peasantry*, i. Cobbett, *Rural Rides*, i; *Advice to Young Men*. Coleridge, *On the Constitution of the Church and State*. Godwin, *Cloudesley*. Hazlitt, *Conversations of James Northcote*. Lyell, *Principles of Geology* (conc. 1833). Bulwer Lytton, *Paul Clifford*. Moore, *Life of Byron*, with Byron's *Letters and Journals*. Scott, *Letters on Demonology and Witchcraft*; *Tales of a Grandfather*, iii. M. Shelley, *Perkin Warbeck*. Tennyson, *Poems, chiefly Lyrical*.

Suggestions for further reading

The literature of the Romantic period is amply served by detailed bibliographies, from the inclusive *New Cambridge Bibliography of English Literature*, vols 2 and 3, to the numerous bibliographies of individual authors. There are a number of useful books which describe and try to evaluate work in particular areas, rather than merely listing titles, including *The English Romantic Poets and Essayists: a review of research and criticism*, rev. ed. by C. W. Houtchens and L. H. Houtchens (New York, 1966); *The English Romantic Poets: a review of research and criticism*, rev. ed. by Frank Jordan (New York, 1972); two *Select Bibliographical Guides*, ed. A. E. Dyson: *English Poetry* (Oxford, 1971) and *The English Novel* (Oxford, 1974); and F. W. Bateson's idiosyncratic *Guide to English Literature* (rev.ed., with H. T. Meserole, London, 1976). On the whole the suggestions for further reading below do not duplicate the literary information given more comprehensively in these bibliographies, but concentrate on titles which may be less familiar to the student of English, and which develop more fully the general issues raised in this book.

Introduction

The following are contributions to the literary debate about Romanticism – how far it is a single movement, and how its characteristics are to be defined: A. O. Lovejoy, 'On the Discrimination of Romanticisms' (1924: repr. in his *Essays on the History of Ideas*, Baltimore, 1948); M. H. Abrams, *The Mirror and the Lamp* (New York, 1953) and *Natural Supernaturalism* (New York, 1971); R. Wellek, 'The Concept of Romanticism in Literary History', *Comparative Literature* (1949), *History of Modern Criticism*, vol. iii (London, 1957), and 'Romanticism Reexamined', in *Concepts of Criticism*, ed. S. G. Nichols (New Haven, 1963); M. Peckham, 'Toward a Theory of Romanticism', *PMLA*, lxi (1951); H. Bloom, *The Visionary Company* (London, 1962), and elsewhere; N. Frye, 'The Drunken Boat', in his *Romanticism Reconsidered* (New York, 1963), repr. in his *Stubborn Structure* (Ithaca, 1970), and *A Study of English Romanticism* (New York, 1968); H. G. Schenk, *The*

Mind of the European Romantics (London, 1966); W. J. Bate, *The Burden of the Past and the English Poet* (London, 1971); G. Hartman, in his *Beyond Formalism* (New York, 1971) and in his *Fate of Reading* (Chicago, 1975).

For the visual arts, see Hugh Honour, *Romanticism* (London, 1979). Works primarily about Neoclassicism are cited below.

Chapter 1

For the economic and social background, see T. S. Ashton, *An Economic History of England: the Eighteenth Century* (London, 1955); *Johnson's England*, ed. A. S. Turberville (London, 1933); D. Marshall, *The English Poor in the Eighteenth Century* (London, 1926); M. Dorothy George, *London Life in the Eighteenth Century* (London, 1925). The first chapter of H. Perkin's *Origins of Modern English Society, 1780–1880* (London, 1969) gives a good sketch of gentry activity in the period. So in a more specialized vein does M. Girouard, *Life in the English Country House* (Yale, 1978).

The politics of the revolutionary period are discussed by Georges Lefebvre, whose work is translated as *The French Revolution from its Origins to 1793* (London, 1962) and *The French Revolution from 1793 to 1799* (London, 1964); and by R. R. Palmer, *Age of Democratic Revolution: A Political History of Europe and America, 1760–1800*, i: *The Challenge* (Princeton, 1959) and ii: *The Struggle* (Princeton, 1964). Palmer has also contributed a lucid chaper, 'Social and Psychological Foundations of the Revolutionary Era', to the *New Cambridge Modern History*, viii: *The American and French Revolutions, 1763–73*, ed. A. Goodwin (Cambridge, 1971).

For the intellectual and cultural background, see G. Bryson, *Man and Society: the Scottish Inquiry of the Eighteenth Century* (Princeton, 1945); S. Kliger, *The Goths in England* (Cambridge, Mass., 1952); R. E. Schofield, *The Lunar Society of Birmingham* (Oxford, 1963); P. Gay, *The Enlightenment*, i: *The Rise of Modern Paganism* (1966), and ii: *The Science of Freedom* (1969); J. W. Johnson, *The Formation of English Neoclassical Thought* (Princeton, 1967); L. Lipking, *The Ordering of the Arts* (Princeton, 1970); R. L. Meek, *Social Science and the Ignoble Savage* (Cambridge, 1976); R. Darnton, *The Business of the Enlightenment: a publishing history of the Encyclopédie, 1775–1800* (Cambridge, Mass., 1969). A number of Duncan Forbes's books, articles and introductions concerning the leading figures of the Scottish Enlightenment are of interest, notably 'Scientific Whiggism: Adam Smith and John Millar', *Cambridge Journal*, vii (1954), 643–70.

Works which in their different styles deal directly with the Gothic, including Kenneth Clark's *Gothic Revival* (London, 1928), S. H. Monk, *The Sublime: a study in critical theories in eighteenth-century England* (New York, 1935) and P. Frankl's *The Gothic* (Princeton, 1960), can be supplemented by Joseph A. Donohoe's *Dramatic Character in the Romantic Age* (Princeton, 1970), which discusses shifting emphases in the representation of character on the stage, and by Keith Thomas's *Religion and the Decline of Magic* (London, 1971), on popular superstition and its motivation. (See also under *Chapter 7*.)

For the visual arts, consult monographs on leading individuals such as Piranesi, Blake, Fuseli, Goya, David and Flaxman; and more general studies, e.g. E. K. Waterhouse, *Painting in Britain, 1530–1790* (Harmondsworth, 1953); B. Smith. *European Vision and the South Pacific, 1768–1850* (Oxford, 1960); R. Paulson, *Emblem and Expression: Meaning in English Art of the Eighteenth Century* (London, 1975); J. Burke, *English Art, 1714–1800* (Oxford, 1976). Joshua Reynolds's *Discourses on Art* have been edited by R. R. Wark (San Marino, California, 1957); see also F. W. Hilles, *The Literary Career of Sir Joshua Reynolds* (Cambridge, 1936). Architectural trends are outlined in John Summerson, *Architecture in Britain, 1530–1830* (Harmondsworth, rev.ed., 1963). The following are general studies of Neoclassicism, with relevance far beyond painting alone: Robert Rosenblum, *Transformations in Late Eighteenth-Century art* (Princeton, 1967); Hugh Honour, *Neoclassicism* (Harmondsworth, 1968) and general introduction to *The Age of Neoclassicism*, catalogue of the Council of Europe exhibition, Royal Academy and Victoria and Albert Museum (London, 1972); Lorenz Eitner, *Neoclassicism and Romanticism, 1750–1850: Sources and Documents*, 2 vols, (Englewood Cliffs, N.J. and London, 1971).

Chapter 2

For the background to radicalism, see A. Lincoln, *Some Political and Social Ideas of English Dissent* (Cambridge, 1938); R. N. Stromberg, *Religious Liberalism in Eighteenth-Century England* (Oxford, 1954); C. Robbins, *The Eighteenth-Century Commonwealthman* (Cambridge, Mass, 1959); E. P. Thompson, *The Making of the English Working Class* (London, 1963); and Albert Goodwin, *The Friends of Liberty* (London, 1979). Millenarian movements of the period are considered by J. F. C. Harrison, *The Second Coming* (London, 1979) and conspiratorial theories by J. M. Roberts, *The Mythology of the Secret Societies* (London, 1972). The reaction to Burke is treated specifically by James Boulton, *The Language of Politics in the Age of Paine and Burke* (London, 1963), and more generally by R. R. Palmer (for whom see under *Chapter 1*).

The fortunes of the Boydell Gallery are discussed in two articles in the

Journal of the Warburg and Courtauld Institute, T. R. Boase, 'Illustrations of Shakespeare's Plays in the Seventeenth and Eighteenth Centuries', x (1947), 83–108, and Winifred H. Friedman, 'Some Commercial Aspects of the Boydell Shakespeare Gallery', xxxvi (1973), 396–401. For the impact of revolutionary ideology on the arts, see J. A. Leith, *The Idea of Art as Propaganda in France, 1750–99* (Toronto, 1965). For Blake, both as artist and as poet, there is a large bibliography. He should be read in an annotated edition, such as that for Longman by W. H. Stevenson, *Blake: the Complete Poems*, London (1971). D. V. Erdman provided the text for this edition, and the most thorough study of Blake from a historical viewpoint, *Blake: Prophet Against Empire* (Princeton, 1954). For a pertinent discussion of one work in its context, see John Howard, 'An Audience for *The Marriage of Heaven and Hell*', *Blake Studies*, iii (1970), 19–52. A view by art historians rather than by literary scholars can be obtained from the catalogues of the recurring Blake exhibitions, such as that at the Tate Gallery, London, 1978, introduced by M. Butlin. See also D. Bindman's *Blake as an Artist* (London, 1978).

Gillray has been treated by Draper Hill, *Mr. Gillray the Caricaturist*, (London, 1965), *Fashionable Contrasts* (London, 1966) and *The Satirical Etchings of James Gillray* (New York, 1976). His French opposite numbers are discussed in an article by Hannah Mitchell, 'Art and the French Revolution', *History Workshop*, v (1978), 123–45. For the whole range of caricature in the period in England, M. Dorothy George, *English Political Caricature*, 2 vols (Oxford, 1959) remains indispensable.

Francis Jeffrey is best approached through the *Life* by Lord Cockburn, 2 vols (Edinburgh, 1852), John Clive, *Scotch Reviewers: the 'Edinburgh Review' 1802–1815* (London, 1956), and through his reviews: see D. H. Reiman (ed.), *The Romantics Reviewed*, 9 vols (New York, 1972).

The study of Wordsworth, as of Blake, needs a specialist bibliography. The following pursue apposite lines of inquiry on the *Lyrical Ballads* and its Preface: R. D. Mayo, 'The Contemporaneity of the *Lyrical Ballads*', *PMLA*, lxix (1954); C. Ryskamp, 'Wordsworth's *Lyrical Ballads* in their Time', in F. Hilles and H. Bloom (eds.), *From Sensibility to Romanticism* (New York, 1965); J. Scroggins, 'The Preface to the *Lyrical Ballads*', in H. Anderson and J. Shea (eds.), *Studies in Criticism and Aesthetics* (Minneapolis, 1967); and W. J. B. Owen, *Wordsworth as Critic* (Toronto, 1969). For *The Borderers*, see R. Sharrock in the *Durham University Journal*, lvi (1964), and D. V. Erdman, 'Wordsworth as Heartsworth' in D. H. Reiman, M. C. Jaye and B. T. Bennett (eds.), *The Evidence of the Imagination* (New York, 1978).

The fullest study of Wordsworth's politics is F. M. Todd, *Politics and the Poet* (London, 1957), but see also Mary Moorman's *Life of Words-worth*, 2 vols (Oxford, 1957 and 1965); E. P. Thompson, 'Disenchant-ment or Default? A Lay Sermon', in *Power and Consciousness*, ed. C. C. O'Brien and W. D. Vaneck (New York, 1969); and the appropriate chapter in Carl Woodring, *Politics in English Romantic Poetry* (Cam-bridge, Mass., 1970).

The editions used for quotation in the text are *Blake: the Complete Poems*, ed. W. H. Stevenson (see above); (for the *Lyrical Ballads*), W. J. B. Owen and J. W. Smyser, *Prose Works of William Wordsworth*, 3 vols (1974), i; Coleridge, *Biographia Literaria*, ed. J. Shawcross, 2 vols (Oxford, 1907).

Chapter 3

The issue of the early nineteenth-century writer and his reader has been treated variously in the following: M. H. Abrams, *The Mirror and the Lamp* (1953) and *Natural Supernaturalism* (1971); R. D. Altick, *The English Common Reader, 1800–1900* (Chicago, 1957); H Brunschwig, *Enlightenment and Romanticism in Eighteenth-Century Prussia* (Paris, 1947; Eng. trans. 1974); J. Gross, *The Rise and Fall of the Man of Letters* (London, 1969); J. Holloway, *The Victorian Sage* (London, 1953); R. Williams, *Culture and Society, 1780–1950* (London, 1958); R. and M. Wittkower, *Born under Saturn: the Character and Conduct of Artists* (New York, 1965) (primarily concerned with the Renaissance painter, but a wide range of psychoanalytic writing is discussed and listed in the Notes). The chapters on the arts in the *New Cambridge History*, viii and ix, are also worth consulting.

Modern writing about Coleridge, as about some other poets of the period, can take on a fervid tone, perhaps illustrating some of the arguments in the chapter above about the personal and emotional quality of his appeal. Exceptions include J. Colmer's useful *Coleridge: Critic of Society* (Oxford, 1959), E. Schneider, *Coleridge, Opium and Kubla Khan* (Chicago, 1953), and K. Everest, *Coleridge's Secret Ministry* (Hassocks, Sussex and New York, 1979).

The editions used for quotation are (for Coleridge) *Collected Letters*, ed. E. L. Griggs (Oxford 1956), i; *Notebooks*, ed. K. Coburn (London, 1957), i; *Lay Sermons*, ed. D. Coleridge, 3rd ed. (London, 1952). For other writers: *The Works of Charles and Mary Lamb*, ed. E. V. Lucas (London, 1903–5), T. Paine, *Age of Reason* (London, 1938) (Thinkers' Library).

Chapter 4

For Jane Austen's social context, see under *Chapter 1* above, especially H. Perkin, *Origins of English Society, 1780–1880*. A number of articles have tried to place Jane Austen accurately in her social background, including D. J. Greene, 'Jane Austen and the Peerage', *PMLA*, lxviii (1953), 1017–31; T. Lovell, 'Jane Austen and Gentry Society , *Literature, Society and the Sociology of Literature*, ed. F. Barker *et al.* (Univ. of Essex, 1977); B. C. Southam, 'Sanditon: the Seventh Novel', in *Jane Austen's Achievement*, ed. J. McMaster (London, 1976). See also D. Monaghan, *Jane Austen: Structure and Social Vision* (London, 1980). Jane Austen's intellectual and political links are discussed by A. M. Duckworth, *The Improvement of the Estate* (Baltimore, 1971), and M. Butler, *Jane Austen and the War of Ideas* (Oxford, 1975).

Editions used for quotation: *Mansfield Park*, ed. R. W. Chapman (Oxford, 1934); Coleridge, *Lay Sermons*, ed. D. Coleridge (London, 1852).

Chapters 5, 6 and 7.

For the political background, see E. Halévy, *History of the English People in the Nineteenth Century*, i: *England in 1815* and ii: *The Liberal Awakening, 1815–1830* (1st English paperback ed., London 1901); E. P. Thompson, *The Making of the English Working Class* (see under *Chapter 2*); R. J. White, *Waterloo to Peterloo* (London, 1957); C. Emsley, *British Society and the French Wars, 1793–1815* (London, 1979).

Some cultural fashions are described in C. P. Brand, *Italy and the English Romantics* (Cambridge, 1957), and H. Levin, *The Broken Column: a Study in Romantic Hellenism* (Cambridge, Mass., 1931). Christopher Hill's 'The Norman Yoke', in his *Puritanism and Revolution* (London, 1968) throws light on aspects of medievalism; see also A. Chandler, *A Dream of Order* (Nebraska, 1970). For the use of mythology in literature, see D. Bush, *Mythology and the Romantic Tradition* (New York, 1937); E. B. Hungerford, *The Shores of Darkness* (New York, 1941); A. J. Kuhn, 'English Deism and the Development of Romantic Mythological Syncretism', *PMLA*, lxxi (1956); F. Manuel, *The Eighteenth Century Confronts the Gods* (Cambridge, Mass., 1959); A. Zwerdling, 'The Mythographers and the Romantic Revival of Greek Myth', *PMLA*, lxxxiii (1964).

There has been no comprehensive study of the novel in the period since E. A. Baker, *History of the English Novel*, 12 vols (London, 1932). For the Gothic novelists, see A. Parreaux, *The Publication of 'The Monk'* (Paris, 1960); L. Nelson, Jr., 'Night Thoughts on the Gothic Novel', *Yale Review*, lii (1962); R. Kiely, *The Romantic Novel in England* (Cambridge, Mass., 1972); and, for an approach that is generic rather than historical or specific, T. Todorov, *The Fantastic*, trans. R. Howard (Ithaca, 1977).

Ian Jack's *Oxford History of English Literature, 1815–1832* (1963) is useful both for its discussions of minor writers and for its bibliography. But much of the best critical work on the period has been on individual major writers not treated as members of any group. First-rate biographies include L. Marchand, *Byron*, 3 vols (New York, 1958); N. I. White, 2 vols (New York, 1940) and R. Holmes (London, 1974) on Shelley; W. J. Bate (New York, 1963) and R. Gittings (London, 1968) on Keats. The effort to place Shelley in his context has however necessitated an approach via the history of ideas: see e.g. K. N. Cameron, *Young Shelley: Genesis of a Radical* (London, 1951) and *Shelley: the Golden Years* (Cambridge, Mass., 1974). Equally, writing on Hazlitt often necessarily enters the public domain: see the studies by H. Baker (London, 1962), R. M. Wardle (London, 1971) and J. Kinnaird, *Hazlitt: Critic of Power* (New York, 1978). Some of the conclusions arrived at above are supported more fully in my *Peacock Displayed: A Satirist in his Context* (London, 1979).

Editions used for quotations are Coleridge, *Essays on his Times*, ed. D. V. Erdman (Princeton, 1978); De Quincey, *Confessions of an English Opium Eater*, ed. A. Hayter (Harmondsworth, 1971); Peacock's *Four Ages* and Shelley's *Defence of Poetry*, ed. H. F. B. Brett-Smith (London, 1921); Hazlitt's *Complete Works*, ed. P. P. Howe, 21 vols (London, 1930–4).

Index

OXFORD

MORE OXFORD PAPERBACKS

Details of a selection of other Oxford Paperbacks follow. A complete list of Oxford Paperbacks, including The World's Classics, Twentieth-Century Classics, OPUS, Past Masters, Oxford Authors, Oxford Shakespeare, and Oxford Paperback Reference, is available in the UK from the General Publicity Department, Oxford University Press (RS), Walton Street, Oxford, OX2 6DP.

In the USA, complete lists are available from the Paperbacks Marketing Manager, Oxford University Press, 200 Madison Avenue, New York, NY 10016.

Oxford Paperbacks are available from all good bookshops. In case of difficulty, customers in the UK can order direct from Oxford University Press Bookshop, 116 High Street, Oxford, Freepost, OX1 4BR, enclosing full payment. Please add 10 per cent of the published price for postage and packing.

THE WORLD'S CLASSICS

The World's Classics Series makes available the greatest
works of world literature at reasonable prices.

'An addition to the library of anyone setting out either to
study or begin to read English literature.' *Times Educational
Supplement*

COLONEL JACK

Daniel Defoe

Edited by Samuel Holt Monk
With a new Introduction by David Roberts

'Born a gentleman, put 'Prentice to a Pick-Pocket, was Six and
Twenty Years a Thief, and then Kidnapp'd to Virginia. Came
back a Merchant, married four Wives, and five of them prov'd
Whores . . .'

Colonel Jack begins among the alleyways of London and ends
in crime, marital disaster, political adventurism, and penitent
prosperity. Its elusive hero has been compared to Oliver Twist,
Lucky Jim, and to modern criminals who have made their
fortune and escaped the law. Jack the occasional Jacobite
suceeds almost in spite of himself in making his world conform
to his highly individual ends. The result is a novel which subjects
a vast range of eighteenth-century life to the scrutiny of an
intriguingly unreliable narrator.

Samuel Holt Monk's Oxford English Novels text, the first to
use the rare first edition of 1722, is here re-issued with a new
introduction by David Roberts which shows why *Colonel Jack*
increasingly commands the attention of modern readers.

Also available in the World's Classics:

Peregrine Pickle   Tobias Smollett
Castle Rackrent   Maria Edgeworth
Joseph Andrews and Shamela   Henry Fielding
Camilla   Fanny Burney

OXFORD REFERENCE

Oxford is famous for its superb range of dictionaries and reference books. The Oxford Reference series offers the most up-to-date and comprehensive paperbacks at the most competitive prices, across a broad spectrum of subjects.

THE CONCISE OXFORD COMPANION TO ENGLISH LITERATURE

Edited by Margaret Drabble and Jenny Stringer

Based on the immensely popular fifth edition of the *Oxford Companion to English Literature* this is an indispensable, compact guide to the central matter of English literature.

There are more than 5,000 entries on the lives and works of authors, poets, playwrights, essayists, philosophers, and historians; plot summaries of novels and plays; literary movements; fictional characters; legends; theatres; periodicals; and much more.

The book's sharpened focus on the English literature of the British Isles makes it especially convenient to use, but there is still generous coverage of the literature of other countries and of other disciplines which have influenced or been influenced by English literature.

From reviews of *The Oxford Companion to English Literature Fifth Edition:*

'a book which one turns to with constant pleasure . . . a book with much style and little prejudice' Iain Gilchrist, *TLS*

'it is quite difficult to imagine, in this genre, a more useful publication' Frank Kermode, *London Review of Books*

'incarnates a living sense of tradition . . . sensitive not to fashion merely but to the spirit of the age' Christopher Ricks, *Sunday Times*

Also available in Oxford Reference:

The Concise Oxford Dictionary of Art and Artists
edited by Ian Chilvers
A Concise Oxford Dictionary of Mathematics
Christopher Clapham
The Oxford Spelling Dictionary   compiled by R. E. Allen
A Concise Dictionary of Law   edited by Elizabeth A. Martin

THE OXFORD AUTHORS

General Editor: Frank Kermode

The Oxford Authors is a series of authoritative editions of the major English writers for the student and the general reader. Drawing on the best texts available, each volume contains a generous selection from the writings—poetry and prose, including letters—to give the essence of a writer's work and thinking. Where appropriate, texts have been tactfully modernized and all are complemented by essential Notes, an Introduction, Chronology, and suggestions for Further Reading.

'The Oxford Authors series can always be relied upon to be splendid—with good plain texts and helpful notes.'
Robert Nye, *Scotsman*

OSCAR WILDE

Edited by Isobel Murray

The drama of Oscar Wilde's life has for years overshadowed his achievement in literature. This is the first large-scale edition of his work to provide unobtrusive guidance to the wealth of knowledge and allusion upon which his writing stands.

Wilde had studied Greek and Latin and was familiar with American literature, while he was as well read in French as he was in English, following Gautier and Flaubert as well as Pater and Ruskin. Through her Notes Isobel Murray enables the modern reader for the first time to read Wilde as such admiring contemporaries as Pater, Yeats, and Symons read him, in a rich, shared culture of literary and visual arts.

This edition underlines the range of his achievement in many genres, including *The Picture of Dorian Gray, Salome, The Importance of Being Earnest, The Decay of Lying*, and *The Ballad of Reading Gaol*. The text is that of the last printed edition overseen by Wilde.

Also in the Oxford Authors:

Sir Philip Sidney
Ben Jonson
Byron
Thomas Hardy